THE RICHNESS OF CONTRACT LAW

Law and Philosophy Library

VOLUME 28

The titles published in this series are listed at the end of this volume.

ROBERT A. HILLMAN
Associate Dean for Academic Affairs and Edwin H. Woodruff Professor of Law, Cornell Law School, New York, U.S.A.

THE RICHNESS OF CONTRACT LAW

An Analysis and Critique of Contemporary Theories of Contract Law

KLUWER ACADEMIC PUBLISHERS
DORDRECHT / BOSTON / LONDON

A C.I.P. Catalogue record for this book is available from the Library of Congress

ISBN 0-7923-4336-0

Published by Kluwer Academic Publishers,
P.O. Box 17, 3300 AA Dordrecht, The Netherlands.

Kluwer Academic Publishers incorporates
the publishing programmes of
D. Reidel, Martinus Nijhoff, Dr W. Junk and MTP Press.

Sold and distributed in the U.S.A. and Canada
by Kluwer Academic Publishers,
101 Philip Drive, Norwell, MA 02061, U.S.A.

In all other countries, sold and distributed
by Kluwer Academic Publishers Group,
P.O. Box 322, 3300 AH Dordrecht, The Netherlands.

Printed on acid-free paper

Printed in the Netherlands

For Betsy, Jessica, and Heather with love

TABLE OF CONTENTS

ACKNOWLEDGMENTS

I want to begin by thanking many people whose aid was essential in the writing of this book. Most important, several colleagues at Cornell Law School and elsewhere read and commented on various chapters of the book. I thank Gregory Alexander, Kevin Clermont, Stephen Garvey, George Hay, John Lee, Jonathan Macey, Dale Oesterle, Russell Osgood, Stewart Schwab, Katherine Stone, Robert Summers, and James J. White for their superb comments.

I presented Chapter 3 to the law faculties at Cornell and at William and Mary. Their comments and criticisms were invaluable.

The following students at Cornell Law School provided excellent research assistance: Stephen Angus, Frederick Ball, Wendy Boucher, Kathryn Bourn, John Bueker, George Caballero, Deborah Chen, Gillian Crenshaw, Susan Emenegger, Steven Nadel, Phuong Pham, Patrick Rao, William Reynolds, and Carol Timm.

Karen Wilson provided excellent word processing assistance throughout, and she prepared the final manuscript for printing.

My wife, Betsy Hillman, suffered with me through this project more than anyone could appreciate. Thanks to her are hardly adequate compensation.

My colleague and friend, Robert Summers, not only offered his comments on the manuscript, but also provided support and general counseling throughout the project. His aid has been much appreciated.

I wish to thank the following publishers for permission to reprint (in edited form) excerpts of some of my articles: Cornell Law Review and Fred B. Rothman & Co. for permission to publish Robert A. Hillman, Debunking Some Myths About Unconscionability: A New Framework for U.C.C. Section 2-302, 67 Cornell Law Review 1 (1981), copyright 1981 by Cornell University; Duke Law Review for permission to publish Robert A. Hillman, Court Adjustment of Long-Term Contracts: An Analysis Under Modern Contract Law, 1987 Duke Law Journal 1; Duncker & Humblot GMBH for permission to publish Robert A. Hillman, Good Faith Performance of Contracts in Late Twentieth-Century American Law, in Prescriptive Formality and Normative Rationality in Modern Legal Systems (1994); Northwestern University Law Review for permission to publish Robert A. Hillman, The Triumph of Gilmore's The Death of Contract, 90 Northwestern Law Review 32 (1995), copyright 1995 by Northwestern University; and Texas Law Review for permission to publish Robert A. Hillman, The Crisis in Modern Contract Theory, 67 Texas Law Review 203 (1988), copyright 1988 by the Texas Law Review Association.

PREFACE

In 1987, I wrote an article entitled *The Crisis in Modern Contract Theory*, which analyzed and critiqued modern American theories of contract law. These theories, which continue to flourish, have deepened the understanding of, and stimulated reflection on, the nature and functions of modern contract law. Yet, many of the theories seemed to me too critical or too inflexible or too narrow. In response, I offered a perspective that emphasized contract law's richness and importance and questioned the utility of overly abstract unitary theories. Judged from the reaction, the article met a receptive audience of lawyers, judges, and theorists, both in the United States and around the world.

This book greatly expands and updates my analysis of the theories studied in the *Crisis* article and surveys and evaluates many additional theories. The book also explains more fully my own view of contract law and supplies numerous references to additional sources. More than the article, the book emphasizes and amplifies what is valuable in the various theories.

I hope the book will appeal widely--to law professors, law students, lawyers in practice, and others interested in legal theory--and not only in the United States but around our shrinking world. Theorists may be especially interested in the comparison of contract theories and in the book's general criticism of abstract unitary theories. Lawyers can utilize the book as a research tool or as general reading that exposes the theoretical side of American contract law. Law students will find useful the descriptions and explanations of the theories they encounter in the classroom. The discussion of theories should also help students put the contract cases they study in perspective. Readers generally interested in the law should find the presentation of contract theories illuminating as well.

I have sought, in the book's structure, to facilitate the presentation of the theories and my responses. Each chapter includes a set of contrasting theories to bring out the range of views on contract law and to identify a pragmatic middle ground. Moreover, I analyze the various theories within the context of a few concrete problems to avoid the sweeping and highly abstract generalizations that sometimes plague theoretical work. The problems addressed represent important issues of contract law, but the problems are not too technical.

I have enjoyed reading and studying the theories presented here, and I have learned a great deal in the process of translating the material into book form. I hope the reader agrees with me that contract law and theory are, indeed, rich!

INTRODUCTION

General conceptual accounts of the nature and role of contract law in modern society flourish.[1] Such theoretical work, filled with insights and ideas, deepens understanding of the law of promises and agreements and stimulates reflection and the creation of new hypotheses. In celebrating the relevance and importance of such work, this book surveys, analyzes, critiques, and synthesizes the rich array of modern theories of contract law.

Some of the theories included herein are largely identified with the work of individual scholars, such as Fried, Gilmore, or Macneil. Others are the product of a school of influential writers whose work shares a common theme, such as the theories of Critical Legal Studies (CLS), legal economists, relationalists, and empiricists. Although analysts associated with these and other movements do not always agree, I have tried to meet the challenge of capturing accurately the essence of, and what is best and most interesting about, a particular theory.

Along the way, I also offer my own perspective on modern contract law. I hope to persuade readers of contract law's many dimensions, yet relative objectivity, relevance, and usefulness--the richness of contract law. This effort conflicts with some of the theories to be discussed in this book. For example, critical theorists generally assert contract law's indeterminacy--contract rules do not dictate any particular result in a case--and its tendency in operation to "legitimate" or help support a corrupt status quo. By contrast, some scholars focus on the parties' promises or on the goal of efficiency and minimize the importance of competing principles. These writers assert the overall integrity of contract law. Some empiricists and relationalists announce that contract law is irrelevant or unsuitable for modern society.

I respond to these themes by underscoring contract law's relative predictability and importance, but I also acknowledge its flaws and inconsistencies. I utilize the insights of various theories and my own analysis of case and statutory law to demonstrate that contract law is an

---

1 *See generally* Robert A. Hillman, *The Crisis in Modern Contract Theory,* 67 TEX. L. REV. 103 (1988). *See also* Jay M. Feinman, *The Significance of Contract Theory,* 58 U. CIN. L. REV. 1283 (1990).

intricate and often conflicting set of rules, principles, and policies, governing diverse transactions and applied by judges of many different minds.[2] Nevertheless, I conclude that, on the whole, contract law suitably promotes the formation and enforcement of private arrangements and ensures some degree of fairness in the exchange process. Moreover, contract law largely succeeds because it is the product of the legal system's reasonable and practical compromises over conflicting values and interests.

Although I will insist that no unitary theory adequately captures the entire contract-law field, my message is not an "anti-theoretical counter-attack,"[3] but rather a pragmatic synthesis of the conceptual and the concrete. I acknowledge the great importance of theory in explaining our world, but also am wary of theory's potential for rigid ordering and "excessive abstraction."[4]

The book's structure facilitates the presentation of my thesis. Each chapter presents a pair of largely contrasting theories to enable the reader to understand the central issues of contract law, to appreciate the range of views, and to help identify a practical middle ground. Moreover, I analyze the various theories in the context of concrete fact situations, involving hypothetical television production and performance agreements. We will meet MDM Enterprises, XYZ Television Network, and various actors and actresses. By introducing specific problems, I hope to avoid sweeping and highly abstract generalizations that sometimes plague theoretical work. I choose the television industry because it is a more interesting and less shopworn analytical tool than other contract

---

2 Patrick Atiyah, *Contracts, Promises and the Law of Obligations,* 94 L.Q. Rev. 193, 199 (1978), *reprinted in* A CONTRACTS ANTHOLOGY at 45 (P. Linzer ed., 1989).

3 Feinman, *supra* note 1, at 1284.

4 *See* Steven D. Smith, *The Pursuit of Pragmatism,* 100 YALE L.J. 409, 430, 433 (1990). *See also* Chapter 8.

settings.[5] Nevertheless, the problems analyzed and the arguments made within this context are generally applicable.

Chapter 1 first considers the leading promissory theory of Charles Fried, which stresses the primacy of the parties' promises as the basis of contract law. The chapter then contrasts the contending "death of contract" thesis of the late Grant Gilmore, which posits that fairness principles have "swallowed up" contract law. I conclude that neither vision adequately captures the law of contract because each emphasizes certain principles at the expense of others. In reality, the promise principle and fairness concerns, along with still other precepts, share the spotlight in governing private relations practically and flexibly.[6]

Beginning in 1926 with the now famous Williston-Coudert dispute,[7] controversy has surrounded the theory of promissory estoppel. Williston and Coudert disagreed over whether promise or reliance constitutes the substantive core of promissory estoppel and whether damages should be based on the promisee's lost expectancy or induced detriment. Many recent studies have revisited these issues, and they are the subject of Chapter 2. I argue that the fog over promissory estoppel precipitates a quarrel of theorists that mirrors the general debate about the nature of contractual obligation discussed in Chapter 1. I argue that

---

5 For example, scholars have already analyzed aspects of the long-term supply contract. *See* Robert A. Hillman, *Court Adjustment of Long-Term Contracts: An Analysis Under Modern Contract Law,* 1987 DUKE L. J. 1; Richard E. Speidel, *Court-Imposed Price Adjustments Under Long-Term Supply Contracts,* 76 NW. U. L. REV. 369 (1981).

6 This position is not "neoclassical" as some scholars use the term because it stresses the importance of both freedom of contract and other principles, without finding that one set of principles dominates another. *See, e.g.*, Chapters 1 and 5. According to some scholars "neoclassical" contract law recognizes the limits of freedom of contract, the cornerstone of "classical" contract law, but only diverges partially and incompletely from that "misguided" vision. *See* Feinman, *supra* note 1, at 1285 ("The word 'neoclassical' suggests the partial nature of the accommodation, indicating that neoclassical contract has not so far departed from classical law that a wholly new name is appropriate.").

7 *See* 4 AMERICAN LAW INSTITUTE PROCEEDINGS, 98-99, 103-04 app. (1926), *reprinted in* ROBERT S. SUMMERS & ROBERT A. HILLMAN, CONTRACT AND RELATED OBLIGATION 294-95 (2d. ed. 1992).

promise and reliance share prominence in promissory estoppel cases and that remedies should reflect the nature of the particular case.

Chapter 3 considers how analysts apply contract theory to special relations, namely marriages and corporations. Some theorists claim that a private contract or set of contracts constitutes the core of each of these relations. Nevertheless, marriage contractarians posit that a contractual perspective promotes marital equality, whereas corporation contractarians assert that the perspective justifies broad delegations of power by shareholders to managers. The chapter investigates the broad range of issues raised by contractualism as illustrated in this dichotomy. The chapter also considers theorists of marriages and corporations skeptical of contract models. These theorists assert that such models fail to clarify special relations and only emphasize contract law's complexity. I argue that the debate between contractarians and their critics reproduces in specialized contexts the dialogue considered in Chapter 1 concerning the role of principles of autonomy and fairness in the administration of contract law. I end the chapter by offering some practical suggestions for reforming marriage and corporation law based on modern values and the need to promote greater equality and fairness in these relations.

Chapter 4 focuses on the theoretical debate over the relative merits of standards and rules in contract law. The chapter first considers contextualists who lean toward the use of flexible standards such as good faith and unconscionability in deciding contract cases and who develop frameworks for applying the standards. The chapter then turns to feminist legal writers who have begun to offer a new perspective on contract law. One prominent feminist view also emphasizes the importance of fairness and flexibility in contract law. Chapter 4 then compares the neo-formalists, who focus on the importance of certainty and clarity in contract law and therefore prefer distinct rules over standards. Between these positions, I argue, lies the reality that judges continue to attempt to clarify the law even as they apply broad standards and continue to exercise discretion even as they apply narrow rules.

Chapter 5 compares the Critical Legal Studies (CLS) school with "mainstream" contract scholars, who, according to CLS's own definition of the mainstream, hold the "dominant" view of contract law. Mainstream scholars assert that contract law is not too ad hoc and uncertain despite the breadth of contract rules, principles, and goals.

Even in "hard" cases, when various principles conflict, contract law establishes a range of possible choices and rationales that guide and restrict a court's decision. Moreover, contract law is sufficiently flexible to help promote fairness and equality in the contracting process. CLS scholars, on the other hand, assert that contract doctrine has too many dimensions and is unsystematic, thereby allowing judges to decide cases as they choose. Legal decisions are often predictable, however, because the legal establishment conceals contract law's indeterminacy and endorses results that perpetuate the social status quo. This process depletes resources otherwise available to improve society. Despite the apparent distance between the mainstream and CLS theories, they share some common ground, at least as the theories have evolved. This is true both as to issues relating to contract law's predictability and to its role in society. I take up this theme at the end of the chapter.

Chapter 6 discusses theories of legal economists of contract law. Observing that people enter exchange relations because they value what they get more than what they give up, one major school of legal economists posits that free contracting moves goods and services to "higher-valued uses." These scholars measure contract law against the end of enforcing people's private preferences to achieve what the writers call "allocative efficiency." Economic analysts also assert that the efficiency norm explains existing contract doctrine, which, when observed through the economic filter, proves to be objective and determinate. The chapter also considers critics of this form of economic analysis, who resist the allure of "scientific" but, in their view, unrealistic and impractical models. Although economic approaches lose their predictive value when legal economists increase the complexity and sophistication of their models, recent contributions, focusing on the reduction of the costs of transactions and deterrence of advantage-taking by one side ("opportunism"), demonstrate the value of introducing a social science such as economics into legal analysis.

Chapter 7 discusses two theories that posit a limited role for contract law in modern society, but for different reasons. The chapter first turns to the thesis that contract law is largely irrelevant, a conclusion drawn from empirical studies of actual business practices. The empiricists report that business parties comfortable with their contracting counterpart, familiar with the subject matter of their deals, and eager to do additional business in the future, believe that flexibility and negotiation, not resort to formal legal procedures, will ensure a successful business relationship. Taking these fact-findings at face value, I nevertheless note the importance of contract law even within these business cultures. Contract law defines the outer boundaries of permissible behavior between the business parties and reinforces their expectations of performance. Moreover, the parties can and do turn to contract law when informal methods fail to serve their purposes. In fact, recent empirical studies suggest that business people increasingly turn to litigation to enforce their contract rights.

The conclusion that contract law ultimately is important contrasts with the perspective that contract doctrine is unsuitable in today's "relational" world. Chapter 7 next turns to this subject. Relationalists assert that most exchange occurs within a process of continuous interaction of parties who make incomplete promises at best. Instead of "discrete" or specific promises, relational norms such as cooperation and compromise govern parties' dealings. According to the relationalists, contract rules do not capture this reality. Although the relational perspective offers a largely accurate view of many business customs and dealings, some relationalists overstate the unsuitability of modern contract law. Focusing on the meaning of contract terms such as "agreement" and "good faith," I conclude that modern contract law is not oblivious to the needs of a relational world.

Chapter 8 summarizes my view of the richness and vitality of contract law, derived from studying the various contract theories and doctrine. The chapter also discusses both the importance and the limitations of contract theory. Contract law includes a rich combination of normative approaches and theories of obligation. It is divided by special rules for distinct kinds of contracts and is subject to many exceptions and counter-principles. Despite its many dimensions, contract law is a credible, if not flawless, reflection of the values of the surrounding society. A highly abstract unitary theory illuminates contract law, but it cannot explain the entire sphere.

CHAPTER 1

THEORIES OF CONTRACT: PROMISE AND NON-PROMISSORY PRINCIPLES

The tension between freedom of contract and non-promissory principles such as reliance and unjust enrichment, which legitimize judicial intervention in agreements, preoccupies many contract analysts.[1] Among the subjects of this book are several distinct theories emphasizing one approach or the other. This chapter, for example, compares Charles Fried's promise theory and Grant Gilmore's hypothesis of the "death-of-contract."[2] Professor Fried posits that freely made promises of contracting parties constitute contract law's core, whereas Professor Gilmore insisted that non-promissory principles "swallowed up" private contract law. The debate is not merely descriptive. Promise theorists champion individual choice and urge government not to intercede in private relations. Death-of-contract analysts, on the other hand, support the use of non-promissory principles to assure fairness in the contracting process.

This chapter's thesis is that neither school has offered a compelling and definitive theory. Although based in part on promissory principles, modern contract law is also tempered both within and without its formal structure by principles, such as reliance and unjust enrichment, which focus on fairness and the interdependence of parties rather than on parties' actual agreements or promises. Contract law is complex, contradictory, and, ultimately, inconclusive on what the relationship of these principles is and should be. Moreover, by ignoring or downplaying counter-principles and theories, some theorists camouflage contract's complexity and hence disguise its true nature.[3] The theoretical debate

---

1 *See, e.g.*, Robert A. Hillman, *The Crisis in Modern Contract Theory*, 67 TEX. L. REV. 103 (1988).

2 CHARLES FRIED, CONTRACT AS PROMISE: A THEORY OF CONTRACTUAL OBLIGATION (1981); GRANT GILMORE, THE DEATH OF CONTRACT (1974).

3 *See, e.g.*, Ian R. Macneil, *Relational Contract: What We Do and Do Not Know*, 1985 WIS. L. REV. 483, 508 ("[Promise-centered] theories tend to decrease . . .

therefore diverts the focus from the reality that promissory and non-promissory principles share the contract law spotlight, and that this is all that we can and need to know.[4]

A. Contract as Promise

Problem 1: On April 1, 1990, MDM Enterprises and XYZ Television Network enter a written contract in which MDM licenses the television series, "Why Spy?" to XYZ Television Network for one year and gives XYZ a series of options for up to seven additional years. The licensing fee is $650,000 per episode for twenty-two episodes and escalates ten percent over the course of the seven years. On April 15, 1990, before MDM has invested any resources in the "Why Spy?" agreement or has foregone other opportunities, XYZ repudiates.[5]

Can MDM recover from XYZ even though MDM has not relied on the agreement? Admirers of contractual freedom--the freedom to enter binding contracts without the interference of (but enforced by) the state[6]--support the law's affirmative response.[7]

---

knowledge of relations . . . by blinding us to our errors and omissions.").

4 Hillman, *supra* note 1, at 133. *See also* Robert C. Clark, *Contracts, Elites and Traditions in the Making of Corporate Law*, 89 COLUM. L. REV. 1703, 1726 (1989) ("A good society depends on both autonomy and heteronomy, each present in large measure. Theorists ought to face up to this point . . . .").

5 Most of the problems in this book are based on Thompson, *The Prime Time Crime*, ENT. L.J., July 1982, at 1; Letter from Dixon Q. Dern to Robert A. Hillman (Aug. 5, 1985) (letter from a lawyer in the television industry for more than 20 years). The amounts in question and many of the details have been simplified for discussion purposes.

6 Ian R. Macneil, *Values in Contract: Internal and External*, 78 NW. U. L. REV. 340, 370 (1983).

7 *See* FRIED, *supra* note 2, at 19.

Several distinct theories justify the general principle of freedom of contract. For example, the centrality of contractual freedom in American jurisprudence derives in part from society's fervent respect for individual freedom and strong faith in limited government.[8] Nineteenth-century politicians and theorists, influenced by the governmental tenets of contemporary England and by the writings of social critics and economists of the time, came to believe that individual freedom was both a natural and moral right[9] and that "laissez faire" would best enable people to achieve their potential.[10] By the mid- to late nineteenth century, a new, thriving, and dominant middle class in a now industrialized America adhered strongly to that view.[11] In the twentieth century, the role of the individual declined as "urbanization, massive immigration, and industrialization . . . placed enormous stress" on society's belief in "a neutral, non-redistributive state."[12] Administrative processes came to

---

8 For example, some refer to private contracting as "natural" and needing no justification and to regulation as "unnatural" and demanding explanation. Victor Brudney, *Corporate Governance, Agency Costs, and the Rhetoric of Contract*, 85 COLUM. L. REV. 1403, 1408-09 (1985). *See also* Clark, *supra* note 4, at 1715-16 (power of the autonomy principle); LENORE J. WEITZMAN, THE MARRIAGE CONTRACT 137 (1981).

9 Samuel Williston, *Freedom of Contract*, 6 CORNELL L.Q. 365, 366 (1921) (discussing Jefferson, Mill, Smith, and Bentham). *See also* Roscoe Pound, *Liberty of Contract*, 18 YALE L.J. 454, 457 (1909) [hereinafter Pound, *Liberty*] (common law "had become thoroughly individualistic . . . partly as a result of the course of thought in the eighteenth and nineteenth centuries."); *id.* at 459.

10 Pound, *Liberty, supra* note 9, at 456-57, 459; Williston, *supra* note 9, at 366.

11 BERNARD SCHWARTZ, THE LAW IN AMERICA 85, 116-18 (1974). *See also* P. S. ATIYAH, *Freedom of Contract and the New Right, in* ESSAYS ON CONTRACT 355 (1990) (describing the situation in England); MORTON J. HORWITZ, THE TRANSFORMATION OF AMERICAN LAW, 1870-1960: THE CRISIS OF LEGAL ORTHODOXY 33 (1992); JAMES W. HURST, LAW AND THE CONDITIONS OF FREEDOM IN THE NINETEENTH-CENTURY UNITED STATES 14 (1956).

12 HORWITZ, *supra* note 11, at 4.

dominate the resulting "welfare state."[13] Nevertheless, individualism has reemerged, energized by a general disillusionment with unsuccessful social policies and the wave of deregulation implemented by President Reagan in the United States in the 1980s.[14]

As a result of this heritage and the current proclivities of the government, it is no surprise that Americans value the right to order their own affairs[15] and to employ fully their economic resources.[16] In fact, some individualists believe that the interests of the state are rarely "important enough to supersede individual rights to privacy and freedom,"[17] and equate the public good with safeguarding private rights.[18] A logical corollary of these values, of course, is support for the extension

---

13 P. S. ATIYAH, THE RISE AND FALL OF FREEDOM OF CONTRACT 716-18 (1979) [hereinafter ATIYAH, RISE AND FALL]. The rise of the welfare state in America began with "factory laws and workmen's compensation laws" designed to "safeguard the individual against the uncertain nature" of industrialized society. SCHWARTZ, *supra* note 11, at 163-64. *See also* KARL POLANYI, THE GREAT TRANSFORMATION 149-50 (1944) ("countermove against economic liberalism and laissez-faire" was a "spontaneous reaction" to protect against destruction of the social order).

14 Thomas W. Merrill, *Public Contracts, Private Contracts, and the Transformation of the Constitutional Order*, 37 CASE W. RES. L. REV. 597, 627 (1987).

15 *See, e.g.*, FRIED, *supra* note 2, at 20 (enforcing the moral obligation that arises out of promise-making enables people to "determine their own values").

16 John Dalzell, *Duress by Economic Pressure I*, 20 N.C. L. REV. 237, 237 (1942).

17 WEITZMAN, *supra* note 8, at 137. "[U]nless some countervailing interest must come into account which would be sacrificed in the process, it would seem that the individual interest in promised advantages should be secured to the full extent of what has been assured to him by the deliberate promise of another." ROSCOE POUND, AN INTRODUCTION TO THE PHILOSOPHY OF LAW 133 (1922). *See also* William James, *The Moral Philosopher and the Moral Life, in* THE WRITINGS OF WILLIAM JAMES, 617-622. (John J. McDermott ed., 1967), *quoted in* ROBERT S. SUMMERS, INSTRUMENTALISM AND AMERICAN LEGAL THEORY 43 (1982); Morris R. Cohen, *The Basis of Contract*, 46 HARV. L. REV. 553, 575 (1933) (will theory).

18 Pound, *Liberty, supra* note 9, at 461.

and promotion of contractual rights and obligations.[19] I pursue the theme of individualism and freedom of contract in Chapters 3, 5, and 6.

Some also posit that contractual freedom helps ensure equality and social justice: "[F]reedom of contract on the whole genuinely expresses social and economic liberation from traditional inequality and immobility."[20] According to this view, contractual obligation derives, not from the parties' social status or caste, but from freely-made agreements between parties of equal bargaining power, such as MDM and XYZ in Problem 1.[21] In Chapter 3, I focus on the equality theory, not in the context of business arrangements, however, but in the setting of intimate agreements, where the theory currently enjoys prominence.

Contractual freedom also appeals to instrumentalists. Legal economists, for example, maintain that free contracting increases social welfare[22] because people left to their own devices make agreements that make at least one of them better off and neither worse off.[23] For example, in Problem 1, MDM values the agreed compensation more than the television series, and XYZ values the series more than the money. Each is better off as a result of the exchange. Free contracting therefore enables

---

19 "Freedom of contract is an aspect of individual liberty, every bit as much as freedom of speech, or freedom in the selection of marriage partners or in the adoption of religious beliefs or affiliations. Just as it is regarded as prima facie unjust to abridge these liberties, so too is it presumptively unjust to abridge the economic liberties of individuals." Richard A. Epstein, *In Defense of the Contract at Will*, 51 U. CHI. L. REV. 947, 953 (1984).

20 Wolfgang G. Friedmann, *Some Reflections on Status and Freedom, in* ESSAYS IN JURISPRUDENCE IN HONOR OF ROSCOE POUND 236 (Ralph A. Newman ed., 1962).

21 HENRY S. MAINE, ANCIENT LAW 141 (New Universal Library ed. 1905) (1864) ("[T]he movement of the progressive societies has hitherto been a movement *from Status to Contract.*") (emphasis in original). *See also* HUGH COLLINS, THE LAW OF CONTRACT 138 (1986) ("Far from refusing to develop a theory of distributive justice and fairness in contracts, classical law, through its rules about consideration and strict liability, states a clear preference for the distributive outcome of a largely uninhibited market.").

22 ATIYAH, RISE AND FALL, *supra* note 13, at 292-330.

23 Clark, *supra* note 4, at 1714.

goods and services to move "from less to more valuable uses."[24] It also facilitates the division of labor because parties can arrange to buy and sell future goods and services.[25] Government is unlikely to achieve a more efficient distribution of goods and services because it has less incentive than the parties to increase their welfare and less information about their needs and desires.[26] A constantly expanding market system with "infinite number[s] of atypical transactions"[27] demands self-regulation[28] by parties who know their interests better than public officials do.[29] Because of the continuing prominence of the economic approach, I focus on the theory in Chapter 6.

Freedom of contract also attracts moralists, whom I shall scrutinize here. According to Charles Fried, a leading figure in this field, the moral obligation from making a promise is the key to contract enforcement.[30] Morality requires a regard for the interests (including the person and property) of others. A promise creates a moral obligation because the promisor purposefully invokes the "convention of

---

24 RICHARD A. POSNER, ECONOMIC ANALYSIS OF LAW 79 (3d ed. 1986).

25 Friedrich Kessler, *Introduction: Contract As A Principle of Order, in* FRIEDRICH KESSLER ET AL., CONTRACTS (3d ed. 1986), *reprinted* in PETER LINZER, A CONTRACTS ANTHOLOGY 5 (1989). *See also* ROBERT S. SUMMERS AND ROBERT A. HILLMAN, CONTRACT AND RELATED OBLIGATION 7-8 (2d ed. 1992).

26 Clark, *supra* note 4, at 1714-15.

27 Friedrich Kessler, *Contracts of Adhesion--Some Thoughts About Freedom of Contract*, 43 COLUM. L. REV. 629, 629 (1943).

28 *Id.*

29 WEITZMAN, *supra* note 8, at xxi; Lucian A. Bebchuk, *Limiting Contractual Freedom in Corporate Law: The Desirable Constraints on Charter Amendments*, 102 HARV. L. REV. 1820, 1827 (1989).

30 FRIED, *supra* note 2, at 17 ("But since a contract is first of all a promise, the contract must be kept because a promise must be kept."). *See also* PATRICK ATIYAH, PROMISES, MORALS, AND LAW (1981). For a general discussion of theories about promising, *see* Richard Craswell, *Contract Law, Default Rules, and the Philosophy of Promising*, 88 MICH. L. REV. 489, 491-503 (1989).

promising." A convention is a "system of rules" governing the making of commitments that others can "count on."[31] In fact, the very purpose of the convention of promising is to confer on the promisee "moral grounds . . . to expect the promised performance."[32] For example, although MDM has not detrimentally relied on the contract and has not benefitted XYZ, MDM has reason to trust XYZ and to expect performance by virtue of XYZ's promise. In other words, MDM has moral grounds to expect XYZ to perform.

Although Fried's discussion of the moral force of promising is the foundation for what follows, Fried's focus is on the centrality of promise as a theory of contractual legal obligation. According to Fried, we should enforce moral obligations arising from promises because enforcement enables promisors to "determine their own values."[33] Put another way, enforcement affords promisors the freedom to bind themselves to others when promisors choose to do so. Fried would therefore advocate the enforcement of XYZ's promise in Problem 1 to ensure the freedom of parties such as XYZ to make promises.[34]

Fried's conceptualization accounts for various contract rules, such as the law of offer and acceptance and the doctrine of duress. According to Fried, a promise is not complete unless it is communicated to and "taken up" by the promisee.[35] Until MDM communicates its promise to XYZ to produce "Why Spy?," for example, MDM has made only a

---

31 FRIED, *supra* note 2, at 7, 12-13.

32 *Id.* at 16.

33 *Id.* at 20. *See also id.* at 20-21 ("If we decline to take seriously the assumption of an obligation . . . to that extent we do not take [the promisor] seriously as a person.").

34 Professor Atiyah chastises Fried for focusing on purely executory exchanges, which, according to Atiyah, are rare and unimportant. P. S. Atiyah, *Contracts, Promises and the Law of Obligations*, 94 L.Q. REV. 193, 201-02 (1978) [hereinafter Atiyah, *Contracts*].

35 FRIED, *supra* note 2, at 41.

personal commitment or vow.[36] By requiring communication to and acceptance by the promisee, Fried's notion of a promise ensures that contracting is "voluntary on both sides."[37] Moreover, a promise procured by a threat to harm the promisor has no moral force and is therefore unenforceable under the doctrine of duress.[38]

To Fried, the promise principle is paramount; he dismisses conflicting principles or theories either as "unsystematic" or as applying only "when promise gives out."[39] As an example of an unsystematic competing theory, Fried cites the "bargain theory" of consideration. Under the bargain theory, broadly recognized in the common law, a promise is enforceable only if supported by consideration. Consideration is a promise or an act by one party that induces a return promise or act by another party. In Problem 1, the consideration given by MDM--its promise to produce "Why Spy?"--induces XYZ to promise to pay the licensing fee in return. A bargain thus consists of "a negotiation resulting in the voluntary assumption of an obligation by one party upon condition of an act or forbearance by the other."[40]

Gift promises are unenforceable under the bargain theory for several policy reasons. They are relatively unimportant to society; they are often made heedlessly or ill-advisedly; they are difficult to prove.[41]

---

36 *Id.* at 42.

37 *Id.* at 43.

38 *Id.* at 98-99.

39 *Id.* at 69. For a discussion of Fried's treatment of unconscionability, *see* Chapter 7. *See also* Macneil, *supra* note 3, at 496 (arguing that the nonpromissory aspects of promise-focused scholarship must be "fitted around promise").

40 Baehr v. Penn-o-tex Oil Corp., 258 Minn. 533, 104 N.W.2d 661 (1960). *See also* RESTATEMENT (SECOND) OF CONTRACTS § 71 (1979).

41 "The existence of some kinds of consideration may evidence an intention to be legally bound or a serious intention to keep the promise." 1 ARTHUR CORBIN, CORBIN ON CONTRACTS, § 111, at 496 (1963). *See also* Lon L. Fuller, *Consideration and Form*, 41 COLUM. L. REV. 799 (1941); Lon L. Fuller & William R. Perdue Jr., *The Reliance Interest in Contract Damages*: 1, 46 YALE L.J. 52 (1936).

The bargain theory generally functions smoothly "due to the high degree to which it conforms with the pattern of exchange which permeates social and business relations."[42] Although it bars some promises from enforcement, the bargain theory is highly individualistic because it allows parties to define their performance rights and obligations without the intrusion of judges--courts do not decide the "adequacy" of consideration.[43]

The requirement of consideration obviously conflicts with Fried's focus solely on promise. Fried must explain why courts enforce promises supported by consideration but not gift promises, which also raise a moral obligation in the promisor to perform. Fried acknowledges consideration's role in contract doctrine but denies its validity because, he argues, courts do not apply the bargain theory consistently.[44] For example, courts sometimes delve into the adequacy of consideration.[45] They also enforce promises without consideration, such as a promise that induces reliance,[46] or a promise made after the promisor already has received a benefit,[47] or a promise that modifies a contract.[48] Based on such inconsistencies, Fried writes that "the life of contract is . . . promise, but this conclusion is not exactly a statement of positive law. . . . [T]he

---

42 Stanley D. Henderson, *Promissory Estoppel and Traditional Contract Doctrine*, 78 YALE L.J. 343, 347 (1969).

43 "[T]he consideration doctrine was forced to pay tribute to the great principle of freedom of contract and the adequacy of the quid pro quo was (in theory at least) left to free bargaining." Kessler, *supra* note 25, *reprinted in* LINZER, *supra* note 25, at 8. But Kessler also remarked that courts saw the potential of the doctrine "as an instrument of social control." *Id.*

44 FRIED, *supra* note 2, at 35.

45 *Id.* at 30.

46 *Id.* at 25.

47 *Id.* at 31-32.

48 *Id.* at 33-34. For a discussion of this phenomenon, *see* Chapter 3.

doctrine of consideration offers no alternative basis for the force of contracts . . . ."[49]

Although Fried acknowledges the importance of reliance, restitution, and other equitable principles and theories, he insists that they supplement, not dominate, contract law. For example, Fried would urge that XYZ's moral obligation arising from its promise would form the basis for enforcing the promise in Problem 1, even if MDM had relied on the agreement.[50] After all, XYZ's promise justified MDM's reliance in the first place.[51] Moreover, judicial enforcement of promises that induce reliance but are unsupported by consideration under the doctrine of promissory estoppel demonstrate only "a belated attempt to plug a gap in the general regime of enforcement of promises, a gap left by the artificial and unfortunate doctrine of consideration."[52]

Fried also responds to the claim that the objective interpretation of contracts removes the focus from the parties' promises. Under an objective interpretation, a party's actual intentions are irrelevant--courts enforce a reasonable person's understanding of the meaning of contract language, not what a promisor actually intended.[53] In Problem 1, for example, suppose at the time of contracting XYZ had a secret intention to pay MDM less than the agreed-upon licensing fee based on an incorrect interpretation of a trade practice. XYZ would be bound to the contract price despite its contrary intention.

One commentator characterizes the objective methodology as the "greatest" of "legal fictions expanding the scope of 'consent' far beyond

---

49 FRIED, *supra* note 2, at 37-38.

50 *Id.*

51 *Id.* at 10-11.

52 FRIED, *supra* note 2, at 25 n*. For a discussion of promissory estoppel, the theory plugging the gap, *see* Chapter 2.

53 FRIED, *supra* note 2, at 87. *See, e.g.*, Hotchkiss v. Nat'l City Bank, 200 F. 287, 293 (S.D.N.Y. 1911) (Learned Hand, J.). "We ask judges or juries to discover that 'objective viewpoint'--through their own subjective processes." Zell v. American Seating Co. 138 F.2d 641, 647 (2d Cir. 1943) (Frank, J.); *rev'd,* 322 U.S. 709 (1944) (per curiam).

anything remotely close to what the parties had in mind."[54] Fried points out, however, that "promises, like every human expression, are made against an unexpressed background of shared purposes, experiences, and even a shared theory of the world."[55] This "congruence of background" of the parties is supposed to ensure that a court's objective interpretation coincides with the parties' actual intentions.[56] For example, XYZ and MDM are engaged in the same trade and should be aware of the objective meaning of any trade language they employ. Fried's thesis, of course, depends on the assumption that contracting parties are generally members of the same "community of discourse"[57] and have not made a mistake about the meaning of their contract language.[58]

Fried also admits that courts must fill gaps in incomplete agreements with terms unrelated to the parties' promises. For example, under the rubric of the excuse doctrines--mistake, impracticability, and frustration--courts fill gaps with respect to the allocation of the risk of unanticipated contingencies that make a promisor's performance much more onerous than expected. But Fried asserts that judicial gap-filling supplements the contract-as-promise idea, it does not compete with or overwhelm the idea. Courts fill gaps in contracts only when the parties

---

54 Ian R. Macneil, *Contracts: Adjustment of Long-Term Economic Relations Under Classical, Neoclassical, and Relational Contract Law*, 72 NW. U.L. REV. 854, 884 (1978).

55 FRIED, *supra* note 2, at 88.

56 *Id. See also* Randy E. Barnett, *Conflicting Visions: A Critique of Ian Macneil's Relational Theory of Contract*, 78 VA. L. REV. 1175, 1176 (1992) ("default rules based on the common-sense or conventional understanding of persons belonging to the parties' community of discourse").

57 *Id.*; FRIED, *supra* note 2, at 88 ("the congruence of background between two persons is never more than partial").

58 *See also* Fuller & Perdue, *supra* note 41, at 808. Fuller viewed objective interpretation as a "corollary" of autonomy because it enhanced the "security of transactions." James Boyle, *Legal Realism and the Social Contract: Fuller's Public Jurisprudence of Form, Private Jurisprudence of Substance*, 78 CORNELL L. REV. 371, 386 & n. 67 (1993).

have made no promises.[59] Fried therefore argues that gap filling does not "threaten" promise's dominance because parties can choose to include their own terms at the time of bargaining.[60] Fried concedes, as he must, that at some point "contract gives out" and outside principles take over because of the limitations of parties' planning and drafting skills. Nevertheless, he concludes that this is the exception and not the rule, and he fails to offer an account of how courts should select the outside principles.[61]

Fried's main contribution is his recognition of the strong influence of morals on contract doctrine. Nevertheless, his insistence that the promise principle overshadows other principles and values[62] understandably unsettles many theorists. In fact, I shortly hope to persuade the reader that Fried's vision of contract as promise leads to an inevitably inconclusive theoretical debate.

---

59 FRIED, *supra* note 2, at 69-73.

60 *Id.* at 73.

61 *Id.* at 88-89. For an analysis maintaining that Fried's theory fails to develop a coherent approach to default rules, *see* Craswell, *supra* note 30, at 517-523.

For another unitary theory of contract based on consent, *see* Randy E. Barnett, *A Consent Theory of Contract*, 86 COLUM. L. REV. 269 (1986); Randy E. Barnett, *The Sound of Silence: Default Rules and Contractual Consent*, 78 VA. L. REV. 821 (1992). In Barnett's view, the element distinguishing enforceable from unenforceable promises is whether the promisor "manifested intention to be legally bound." Randy E. Barnett, *Some Problems With Contract as Promise*, 77 CORNELL L. REV. 1022, 1029 (1992). According to Barnett, his view explains the bargain theory of consideration, for example, because "the existence of a bargain so frequently corresponds to the existence of a manifested intention to be legally bound." *Id.*

62 *See, e.g.*, two reviews of Fried's Contract As Promise: P. S. Atiyah, Book Review, 95 HARV. L. REV. 509, 516-524 (1981) (asserting the limited role of contract under Fried's view); Daniel A. Farber, Book Review, 66 MINN. L. REV. 561, 564 (1982) ("[T]he validity of the promise principle does not alone establish its primacy."). *See also* JOHN P. DAWSON, GIFTS AND PROMISES 3-4 (1980).

B. Non-Promissory Principles

Problem 2: Assume that XYZ and MDM resolve their differences, MDM produces "Why Spy?," and a year later the parties begin negotiations for the production of a spin-off series, "Journey." The parties tentatively agree on a licensing fee of $750,000 per episode for twenty-two episodes of the new series. The parties discuss a five-year license, with the network to have the right to cancel at any time. They also discuss a ten percent escalation of the licensing fee over the five-year period. The network requests that MDM begin producing the series and promises to compensate MDM for its efforts, although the parties have signed no documents and have not concluded an enforceable contract. MDM produces three episodes at a cost of more than $2 million before negotiations break down. MDM seeks compensation for these expenses when no other network is interested in the new series.

In his provocative book, *The Death of Contract*, Grant Gilmore also dismissed the bargain theory of consideration, but for reasons very different than Professor Fried's. Instead of focusing on the centrality of promise and the bargain theory's incoherence, Gilmore posited that nonconsensual tort law[63] steadily absorbed the bargain theory and permitted recoveries in the absence of an enforceable contract, such as in favor of MDM in Problem 2. Influenced by the legal realists, who generally posited a lack of objectivity and determinacy in our legal system,[64] Gilmore asserted that the "death of contract" was inevitable. The bargain theory was an artificial and narrow construct improvised by Langdell in his famous casebook, nurtured by Holmes in *The Common Law*, and restated by Williston, to reflect late nineteenth- and early twentieth-century society's flirtation with free market economics and individualism.[65]

---

63 GILMORE, *supra* note 2, at 87, 94.

64 For a discussion of the realists, see Chapter 5.

65 GILMORE, *supra* note 2, at 6-8, 98. *But see* Richard E. Speidel, *An Essay on the Reported Death and Continued Vitality of Contract*, 27 STAN. L. REV. 1161, 1162

According to Gilmore, Langdell "launched the idea that there was . . . a general theory of contract"[66] in his 1871 casebook, which, for the first time, collected "all the important contract cases."[67] The casebook approach reflected the notion that a set of legal rules could be applied mechanically and scientifically to deduce decisions from the facts.

The bargain theory of consideration, the heart of the general theory (or as Gilmore better put it, "the balance-wheel of the great machine"),[68] reflected Holmes's individualist view that legal liability to others discourages socially useful activity and that promissory liability therefore should be as narrow as possible.[69] Prior to Holmes's formulation, consideration consisted of a benefit to the promisor or a detriment to the promisee, but the benefit or detriment did not have to induce the promise.[70] Holmes's approach reduced liability by including the latter as a requirement: consideration demanded "reciprocal

---

(1975) (book review) (describing Gilmore's view of bargain theory as being "rooted in [neither] case law [nor] the real world"). Gilmore's history is suspect. Professor Speidel asserts that Gilmore ignored almost three hundred years of economic and legal history. *Id.* at 1167-68. According to Speidel, the bargain theory was "a very natural adaptation of prevailing economic attitudes to serve important legal needs." *Id.* at 1170. *See also* William M. McGovern Jr., Book Review, 66 MINN. L. REV. 550 (1982) (reviewing P. S. ATIYAH, THE RISE AND FALL OF FREEDOM OF CONTRACT (1979)).

66 GILMORE, *supra* note 2, at 13-14.

67 *Id.* at 13. The casebook is C. LANGDELL, CASES ON THE LAW OF CONTRACTS (1st. ed. 1871).

68 GILMORE, *supra* note 2, at 18.

69 Gilmore cited Justice Holmes' THE COMMON LAW, in which Holmes asserted that "'[t]he general principle of our law is that loss from accident must lie where it falls . . . .'" GILMORE, *supra* note 2, at 16.

70 Prior to Holmes, "'[a] valuable consideration [was] either a benefit to the party promising, or some trouble or prejudice to the party to whom the promise is made.'" GILMORE, *supra* note 2, at 111 n.34 (*quoting* 2 KENT, COMMENTARIES ON AMERICAN LAW 465 (4th ed. 1840).

conventional inducement . . . between consideration and promise,"[71] an idea later adopted by both contract Restatements.[72] In this guise, the bargain theory could explain several rules narrowing contractual liability, such as the revocability of offers and the unenforceability of unilateral contract modifications, agreements to agree, and arrangements lacking mutuality of obligation.[73] Gilmore asserted that this framework reflected and supported the dominance of free-market values in the late nineteenth century.[74]

Gilmore also claimed that, within the limited boundaries of the bargain theory as conceived by Holmes, liability was to be absolute.[75] Although seemingly contradictory (why confine liability on the one hand and limit grounds for avoiding it on the other?), Gilmore surmised that both thrusts narrowed the scope of fact issues, thereby reducing the costs and uncertainties of litigation.[76] As to absolute liability, if a party made a bargained-for promise, the party had to perform the promise or pay damages. Courts would not entertain excuses.[77] This approach would reduce the need for meddlesome judicial intervention, such as factual inquiries into the parties' motives.[78] Gilmore also characterized the shift from subjective to objective interpretation of contracts as an example of the move to absolute liability. Interpreting contracts objectively--according to a reasonable construction of the language--narrowed the

---

[71] *Id.* at 20 (*quoting* OLIVER WENDELL HOLMES, THE COMMON LAW 227-30 (Howe ed. 1963) (1881).

[72] *See* RESTATEMENT (FIRST) OF CONTRACTS § 75 (1932); RESTATEMENT (SECOND) OF CONTRACTS § 75 (1981).

[73] GILMORE, *supra* note 2, at 21-22, 33.

[74] *Id.* at 95-96.

[75] *Id.* at 14.

[76] *Id.* at 47-48.

[77] *Id.*

[78] *Id.* at 42.

potential grounds of avoiding liability for a bargained-for exchange by eliminating the excuse that a promisor was subjectively mistaken about contract terms, was otherwise careless about the use of language, or had a good reason for not performing.[79]

It was left to Williston to collect the cases that supported the new contract theory, to reject those that contradicted it, and to restate the cases in "meticulous although not always accurate, scholarly detail" in the Restatement of Contracts.[80] But the theory was already crumbling, and the end-product of Williston's efforts could not avoid reflecting the forces of change.[81]

Not surprisingly, Gilmore attributed the demise of the Holmes-Williston construct to its shaky origins. According to Gilmore, the theory began to disintegrate when it no longer served business and social interests in the twentieth-century welfare state.[82] Legal reaction was swift. The "tide of codification" in projects such as the Uniform Commercial Code centered analysis on legislative policy adverse to contract theory's paradigm of limited liability.[83] Analysts found inconsistencies in and alternative explanations for the cases supposedly

---

[79] *Id.* at 44. *See also id.* at 48: "To the extent that a theory of excuse from a contractual obligation is admitted, it becomes necessary to take particular factual situations into account."

Gilmore disapproved of contract law's move from subjective to objective interpretation of contracts, from "extended factual inquiry into what was 'intended,' 'meant,' [and] 'believed,'" to an abstract focus on "precedents about recurring types of permissible and impermissible 'conduct.'" *Id.* at 42.

[80] *Id.* at 14, 22.

[81] *See infra* notes 82-87 and accompanying text.

[82] GILMORE, *supra* note 2, at 94-96. *See, e.g.*, Kurt A. Strasser, *Contract's "Many Futures" After Death; Unanswered Questions of Scope and Purpose*, 32 S. C. L. REV. 501, 509 (1981).

[83] For example, the Uniform Commercial Code enforced promises modifying existing contracts. GILMORE, *supra* note 2, at 69, 77.

supporting the theory.[84] Judges refused to follow the theory in difficult cases, creating an "explosion of liability"[85] and requiring the recognition of additional theories of obligation in the Restatements and case law.[86] At the same time, courts also increasingly entertained claims of excuse once a bargain was found.[87]

We shall now consider two important illustrations of Gilmore's "death of contract," namely the expansion of theories of obligation and the rise of law excusing performance. We shall see that Gilmore strongly disagreed with Fried's view of the modest significance of these phenomena. In subsequent chapters, we shall see further evidence of the limits of freedom of contract.

1. The expansion of theories of obligation

Unlike Fried's focus on promise, Gilmore insisted that theories of obligation based on detrimental reliance or unjust enrichment dominate contract law.[88] For example, Gilmore pointed out the "paradox" between Section 75 of the first *Restatement of Contracts*, which incorporates the

---

84 *Id.* at 58, 64. For example, analysts found liability in cases lacking "mutual conventional reciprocal inducement." *Id.* at 63.

85 *Id.* at 57, 62, 65. For example, Gilmore pointed to the increase in products liability cases under the RESTATEMENT (SECOND) OF TORTS. *Id.* at 94. *See* Speidel, *supra* note 65, at 1165.

86 *See infra* notes 88-103, and accompanying text.

87 *See infra* notes 126-141, and accompanying text.

88 GILMORE, *supra* note 2, at 70-73, 77-84. For example, according to Gilmore, promissory estoppel in section 90 dominates the second Restatement. *Id.* at 70-72. *See also* Speidel, *supra* note 65, at 1166. RESTATEMENT (SECOND) OF CONTRACTS § 90(1) (1981) provides:

> A promise which the promisor should reasonably expect to induce action or forbearance on the part of the promisee or a third person and which does induce such action or forbearance is binding if injustice can be avoided only by enforcement of the promise. The remedy granted for breach may be limited as justice requires.

Holmesian bargained-for-exchange consideration requirement,[89] and the promissory estoppel theory of Section 90. The latter section enforces promises that induced reasonable reliance, such as XYZ's promise in Problem 2, even when the promise is not supported by consideration.[90] Section 90 came to be known as the doctrine of promissory estoppel.[91]

Gilmore perceived not only that promissory estoppel filled a gap in promise enforcement,[92] as Fried suggested, but that it had usurped the bargain theory's dominant role in that process. Gilmore claimed that the expansion of Section 90 in the second Restatement, evidenced primarily by its "elaborate [c]ommentary," demonstrated the triumph of promissory estoppel.[93] As particular proof, he pointed to the following comment to Section 90 in the second Restatement:

> Certainly . . . reliance is one of the main bases for enforcement of the half-completed exchange, and the probability of reliance lends

---

89 RESTATEMENT (FIRST) OF CONTRACTS § 75 (1932) provided:

> (1) Consideration for promise is
> (a) an act other than a promise, or
> (b) a forbearance, or
> (c) The creation, modification or destruction of a legal relation, or
> (d) a return promise,
> bargained for and given in exchange for the promise. . . .

90 Unlike Fried, for Gilmore the core component of promissory estoppel was detrimental reliance, not the promise itself. Recent work on promissory estoppel replicates this disagreement. *See* Chapter 2.

91 *See* Chapter 2 for a focused discussion of the doctrine.

92 GILMORE, *supra* note 2, at 70-71.

93 *Id.* at 71. RESTATEMENT (SECOND) OF CONTRACTS § 90(1) (1981) provides:

> A promise which the promisor should reasonably expect to induce action or forbearance on the part of the promisee or a third person and which does induce such action or forbearance is binding if injustice can be avoided only by enforcement of the promise. The remedy granted for breach may be limited as justice requires.

> support to the enforcement of the executory exchange. . . . This Section thus states a basic principle which often renders inquiry unnecessary as to the precise scope of the policy of enforcing bargains.[94]

Gilmore therefore concluded that,

> [t]he wholly executory exchange where neither party has yet taken any action would seem to be the only situation in which it would be necessary to look to [Section] 75 - and even there, as the Comment somewhat mysteriously suggests, the 'probability of reliance' may be a sufficient reason for enforcement without inquiring into whether or not there was any 'consideration.'[95]

Students of contract law probably recognize that Lon Fuller's seminal work on the reliance interest inspired the Comment's "mysterious" reference to the "probability of reliance" supporting the enforceability of executory exchanges.[96] Fuller maintained that reliance on a promise presented a stronger reason for enforcing promises than a mere expectation. He reasoned that reliance entails a change of position to the promisee's detriment, which often also unjustly benefits the other party.[97] A mere unfulfilled expectation, on the other hand, leads only to disappointment.[98] Nevertheless, Fuller believed that reliance may be difficult for a party to prove and to quantify. If contract law required proof of reliance, business people might hesitate to rely on their agreements. Courts must therefore enforce agreements without proof of reliance (but with the likelihood that it occurred) in order to encourage

---

94 GILMORE, *supra* note 2, at 71 (*quoting* RESTATEMENT (SECOND) OF CONTRACTS § 90 cmt. at 165-66 (Tentative Draft No. 2, 1965).

95 GILMORE, *supra* note 2, at 72.

96 Fuller & Perdue, *supra* note 41.

97 "[T]he restitution interest is merely a special case of the reliance interest . . . ." *Id.* at 55.

98 *Id.* For further elaboration, see Chapter 2.

it.[99] Fuller's reasoning thus suggested that the primary justification for enforcing purely executory exchanges, such as in Problem 1, is based on reliance, not on bargain or promise.

Just as reliance usurped the role of consideration when a promisee suffers a detriment, the theory of restitution or quasi-contract, according to Gilmore, diminished the importance of consideration when a promisor receives a benefit.[100] Under quasi-contract, a party can recover the value of a benefit conferred on another when the party did not intend to make a gift and did not foist the benefit. The benefit does not have to be part of a bargain.[101] Gilmore pointed out that Section 86 of the second Restatement, governing promises made after the promisor receives a benefit, was "schizophrenic" in its tendency both to broaden and to confine unjust enrichment theory. Nevertheless, he predicted that by affording "overt recognition" to the theory,[102] Section 86 ultimately would precipitate the expansion of unjust enrichment, just as Section 90 laid the foundation for detrimental reliance.[103]

---

99 "To encourage reliance we must . . . dispense with its proof." Fuller & Perdue, *supra* note 41, at 62.

100 GILMORE, *supra* note 2, at 73-74.

101 E. ALLAN FARNSWORTH, 1 FARNSWORTH ON CONTRACTS § 2.20 (1990).

102 GILMORE, *supra* note 2, at 75-76.

103 *Id.* at 74. RESTATEMENT (SECOND) OF CONTRACTS § 86 (1981) states:

> (1) A promise made in recognition of a benefit previously received by the promisor from the promisee is binding to the extent necessary to prevent injustice.
>
> (2) A promise is not binding under Subsection (1) (a) if the promisee conferred the benefit as a gift or for other reasons the promisor has not been unjustly enriched or (b) to the extent that its value is disproportionate to the benefit.

Other examples of the expansion of liability beyond the Holmes-Williston construct include the enforcement of contract modifications without fresh consideration, the enforcement of bare offers, and the "exploded" theory of mutuality of obligation. *Id.* at 76-77.

Despite misgivings about Gilmore's history of the rise of contract,[104] experience supports his view of the importance of alternative theories of obligation, both in supplying rationales for promise enforcement when bargain theory fails to do so and in offering alternative justifications for enforcement when the parties made a bargain. As to the latter role of non-bargain theories, for example, Fuller's explanation of the importance of reliance in bargain settings is widely accepted by theorists and courts.[105] Perhaps more important, alternative theories continue to grow in importance in non-bargain settings. More and more contracts are only part of complex, continuing relations of long duration, sometimes called "relational contracts."[106] For example, in Problem 2, XYZ and MDM already had joined forces on a series and presumably expected to continue their "relation" in the future. In this context, they were unlikely to reach a formal agreement on all elements of their relation in any one contract.[107] Nevertheless, their relation gave rise to significant restitution, reliance, and expectation interests on the part of both parties. To appraise these interests, lawmakers must focus on the social conditions supporting relations and the fairness of creating, or declining to create, an obligation in a particular context, not solely on whether the parties had formally made a bargain.[108]

---

104 *See supra* note 65.

105 *See, e.g.*, Sullivan v. O'Connor, 363 Mass. 579, 296 N.E.2d 183 (1973). *See also* Chapter 2.

106 *See* Chapter 7. *See also* IAN R. MACNEIL, THE NEW SOCIAL CONTRACT (1980); Hillman, *supra* note 1, at 124; Jay M. Feinman, *The Significance of Contract Theory*, 58 U. CIN. L. REV. 1283, 1301-02 (1990).

107 Hillman, *supra* note 1, at 124.

108 The modern concept of "agreement," for example, directs courts to examine the contextual realities supporting a relation. This inquiry often reveals that contracting parties' minds do not "meet" at one time concerning important terms of agreements. Instead, contract formation is "an incremental process" with the parties "agree[ing] to more and more as they proceed." Ian R. Macneil, *Economic Analysis of Contractual Relations: Its Shortfalls and the Need for a "Rich Classificatory Apparatus"*, 75 NW. U. L. REV. 1018, 1041 (1981).

Assuming that XYZ and MDM's deal was only tentative and that the parties had not entered a "bargain,"[109] then, MDM's ability to recoup its reliance losses in Problem 2 depends on the application of promissory estoppel: Did XYZ make a promise? Should it reasonably have expected the promise to induce action on MDM's part? Will injustice be avoided only by enforcement of the promise?[110] Promissory estoppel obviously increases the regulatory role of contract law.[111]

Despite the importance of these non-bargain theories of obligation, however, one suspects that Gilmore purposefully exaggerated his theme to capture the attention of his audience.[112] The bargain theory of contract retains importance even though it shares the spotlight with other theories.

Although many courts allow recovery by parties such as MDM in Problem 2 on the basis of promissory estoppel,[113] thereby increasing the potential liability of parties at the bargaining stage, many other courts resist the theory. Between 1981 and 1992, in fact, New York courts addressed promissory estoppel in thirty-four cases and rejected the theory

---

109 MDM might attempt to show that the parties already had a binding deal on the basis of an enforceable "agreement to agree" or preliminary contract. *See generally* E. Allan Farnsworth, *Precontractual Liability and Preliminary Agreements: Fair Dealing and Failed Negotiations*, 87 COLUM. L. REV. 217 (1987). Assuming that the facts do not support such a conclusion, MDM could assert promissory estoppel.

110 *See* RESTATEMENT (SECOND) OF CONTRACTS § 90 (1981).

111 I take up the doctrine more fully in Chapter 2.

112 After all, Gilmore alludes to the possible resurrection of contract in the future. GILMORE, *supra* note 2, at 103. *See also* Speidel, *supra* note 65, at 1182-83.

113 *E.g.*, Hoffman v. Red Owl Stores Inc., 133 N.W.2d 267 (Wis. 1965). On reliance theory generally, *see, e.g.*, Michael B. Metzger & Michael J. Phillips, *The Emergence of Promissory Estoppel as an Independent Theory of Recovery*, 35 RUTGERS L. REV. 472 (1983); Daniel A. Farber & John H. Matheson, *Beyond Promissory Estoppel: Contract Law and the "Invisible Handshake,"* 52 U. CHI. L. REV. 903 (1985).

in twenty-nine of them.[114] During the same period, California rejected

---

[114] The New York cases rejecting promissory estoppel were Wurmfeld Assocs., P. C. v. Harlem Interfaith Counseling Servs., Inc., 578 N.Y.S.2d 200 (App. Div. 1992) (no definite promise), *appeal denied*, 594 N.E.2d 933 (N.Y. 1992); Sanyo Elec., Inc. v. Pinros & Gar Corp., 571 N.Y.S.2d 237 (App. Div. 1991) (same); Messina v. Biderman, 571 N.Y.S.2d 499 (App. Div. 1991) (same), *appeal denied*, 580 N.E.2d 1057 (N.Y. 1991); Nicit v. Nicit, 555 N.Y.S.2d 474 (App. Div. 1990) (same); Lerman v. Medical Assocs., 554 N.Y.S.2d 272 (App. Div. 1990) (same); Chem. Bank v. City of Jamestown, 504 N.Y.S.2d 908 (App. Div. 1986) (same); Ski-View, Inc. v. State, 492 N.Y.S.2d 866 (Ct. Cl. 1985) (same); Tribune Printing Co. v. 263 Ninth Ave. Realty, Inc., 452 N.Y.S.2d 590 (App. Div. 1982) (same), *aff'd*, 444 N.E.2d 35 (N.Y. 1982); Clinton v. Int'l Business Machs. Corp., 570 N.Y.S.2d 405 (App. Div. 1991) (no detrimental reliance); Silver v. Mohasco Corp., 462 N.Y.S.2d 917 (App. Div. 1983) (same), *aff'd*, 465 N.E.2d 361 (N.Y. 1984); Dalton v. Union Bank of Switzerland, 520 N.Y.S.2d 764 (App. Div. 1987) (no definite promise and no detrimental reliance); Ripple's of Clearview, Inc. v. Le Havre Assocs., 452 N.Y.S.2d 447 (App. Div. 1982) (same); Advanced Refractory Technologies, Inc. v. Power Auth., 568 N.Y.S.2d 986 (App. Div. 1991) (promissory estoppel not available against governmental agency acting within its statutory authority, absent unusual circumstances), *appeal denied and appeal dismissed*, 578 N.E.2d 440 (N.Y. 1991), *and appeal granted*, 81 N.Y.2d 704 (1993); Modell & Co. v. City of New York, 552 N.Y.S.2d 632 (App. Div. 1990) (same), *appeal dismissed*, 559 N.E.2d 1288 (N.Y. 1990); Cohen v. Brown, Harris, Stevens, Inc., 475 N.E.2d 116 (N.Y. 1984) (no valid promissory estoppel claim to defeat Statute of Frauds defense); Bon Temps Agency, Ltd. v. Towers Org., Inc., 590 N.Y.S. 2d 97 (App. Div. 1992) (same); Gold v. Vitucci, 563 N.Y.S.2d 443 (App. Div. 1990) (same); Cane v. Farmelo, 543 N.Y.S.2d 775 (App. Div. 1989) (same); Aeromar C. Por A. v. Port Auth., 536 N.Y.S.2d 173 (App. Div. 1988) (same); Carvel Corp. v. Nicolini, 535 N.Y.S.2d 379 (App. Div. 1988) (same); Bernard v. Langan Porsche Audi, Inc., 532 N.Y.S.2d 599 (App. Div. 1988) (same); Country-Wide Leasing Corp. v. Subaru of America, Inc., 520 N.Y.S.2d 24 (App. Div. 1987) (same), *appeal denied*, 521 N.E.2d 443 (N.Y. 1988); Tutak v. Tutak, 507 N.Y.S.2d 232 (App. Div. 1986) (same); Klein v. Jamor Purveyors, Inc., 489 N.Y.S.2d 556 (App. Div. 1985) (same); Cunnison v. Richardson Greenshields Sec., Inc., 485 N.Y.S.2d 272 (App. Div. 1985) (same); D & N Boening, Inc. v. Kirsch Beverages, Inc., 471 N.Y.S.2d 299 (App. Div. 1984), *aff'd*, 472 N.E.2d 992 (N.Y. 1984) (same); Long Island Pen Corp v. Shatsky Metal Stamping Co., 463 N.Y.S.2d 39 (App. Div. 1983) (same); Edward Joy Co. v. Noise Control Prods., Inc., 443 N.Y.S.2d 361 (Sup. Ct. 1981) (same); Ginsberg v. Fairfield-Noble Corp., 440 N.Y.S.2d 222 (App. Div. 1981) (same).

Cases upholding the plaintiff's claim as presenting triable issues (*i.e.* stating a valid claim or presenting sufficient evidence to defeat summary judgment) were Urban Holding Corp. v. Haberman, 556 N.Y.S.2d 337 (App. Div. 1990); Allen v. Bd. of Educ., 563 N.Y.S.2d 422 (App. Div. 1990); Buddman Distribs., Inc. v.

promissory estoppel in ten out of thirteen cases.[115] When courts decline to apply promissory estoppel they do so for a variety of reasons: lack of a "clear and unambiguous" promise,[116] unreasonableness of the

---

Labatt Importers, Inc., 458 N.Y.S.2d 395 (App. Div. 1982), *appeal dismissed*, 572 N.E.2d 53 (N.Y. 1991).

Cases actually granting a remedy included Farash v. Sykes Datatronics, Inc., 452 N.E.2d 1245 (N.Y. 1983) (reliance damages); Zimmerman v. Zimmerman, 447 N.Y.S.2d 675 (App. Div. 1982) (same).

[115] California cases rejecting promissory estoppel were Racine & Laramie, Ltd. v. California Dep't of Parks & Recreation, 14 Cal. Rptr. 2d 335 (Ct. App. 1992) (no definite promise); Osborn v. Irwin Memorial Blood Bank, 7 Cal. Rptr. 2d 101 (Ct. App. 1992) (same); Peterson Dev. Co. v. Torrey Pines Bank, 284 Cal. Rptr. 367 (Ct. App. 1991) (same); Smith v. City of San Francisco, 275 Cal. Rptr. 17 (Ct. App. 1990) (no detrimental reliance); Kurokawa v. Blum, 245 Cal. Rptr. 463 (Ct. App. 1988) (same); Hoover Community Hotel Dev. Corp. v. Thomson, 213 Cal. Rptr. 750 (Ct. App. 1985) (same); Downer v. Bramet, 199 Cal. Rptr. 830 (Ct. App. 1984) (same); San Marcos Water Dist. v. San Marcos Unified Sch. Dist., 720 P.2d 935 (Cal. 1986) (promissory estoppel not available against governmental agency acting within its statutory authority, absent unusual circumstances), *cert. denied*, 479 U.S. 1087 (1987); Malmstrom v. Kaiser Aluminum & Chem. Corp., 231 Cal. Rptr. 820 (Ct. App. 1986) (no valid promissory estoppel claim to defeat Statute of Frauds defense); Munoz v. Kaiser Steel Corp., 203 Cal. Rptr. 345 (Ct. App. 1984) (same).

The one case upholding the plaintiff's claim as presenting triable issues was Sheppard v. Morgan Keegan & Co., 266 Cal. Rptr. 784 (Ct. App. 1990).

The two cases actually granting a remedy for promissory estoppel were Allied Grape Growers v. Bronco Wine Co., 249 Cal. Rptr. 872 (Ct. App. 1988) (expectancy damages); and McClatchy Newspapers v. Superior Court, 209 Cal. Rptr. 598 (Ct. App. 1984) (same), *vacated on other grounds*, 751 P.2d 1329 (Cal. 1988).

[116] *See* Pac. Architects Collaborative v. State, 166 Cal. Rptr. 184, 191 (Ct. App. 1979) (state made no implied promise to award construction contract to lowest bidder); Div. of Labor Law Enforcement v. Transpacific Transp. Co., 137 Cal. Rptr. 855, 861 (Ct. App. 1977) (employer neither expressly nor impliedly promised to pay employee bonuses); Messina v. Biderman, 571 N.Y.S.2d 499, 500 (App. Div. 1991) (city did not promise to sell property, only to negotiate for sale), *appeal denied*, 580 N.E.2d 1057 (N.Y. 1991); Tribune Printing Co. v. 263 Ninth Avenue Realty, Inc., 452 N.Y.S.2d 590, 593 (App. Div. 1982) (lessor did not promise to renew lease, only to bargain for more definite terms), *aff'd*, 444 N.E.2d 35 (N.Y. 1982).

reliance,[117] or absence of injury to the promisee.[118] A court may even excuse the promisor because its conduct was not "unconscionable," such as when a subcontractor honestly, but mistakenly, submits an incorrect price quotation.[119] This survey of cases may show only that litigants in New York and California bring weak promissory estoppel cases.[120] On the other hand, it is at least some evidence that courts do not greet the theory with open arms.

Moreover, the bargain theory of contract still retains importance because it affords parties grounds for avoiding liability.[121] If XYZ had expressly reserved the right not to contract with MDM or the circumstances indicated such an intention, MDM could not claim

---

117 *See* Peterson Dev. Co. v. Torrey Pines Bank, 284 Cal. Rptr. 367, 374 (Ct. App. 1991) (no reasonable reliance where letter of commitment to loan money lacks material terms); Sanyo Elec., Inc. v. Pinros & Gar Corp., 571 N.Y.S.2d 237, 238 (App. Div. 1991) (no reasonable reliance where alleged distributorship promise was not only indefinite, but also contrary to other evidence); Nicit v. Nicit, 555 N.Y.S.2d 474, 476 (App. Div. 1990) (husband "was not justified in relying on his own erroneous interpretation" of wife's representations regarding the sale of marital property).

118 For example, in Hoover Community Hotel Corp. v. Thompson, 213 Cal. Rptr. 750 (Ct. App. 1985), the court refused to enforce a church's promise to sell a parcel of land to the plaintiff because the plaintiff had not detrimentally relied on the promise. *See also* Smith v. City and County of San Francisco, 275 Cal. Rptr. 17, 23 (Ct. App. 1990) (property owners did not detrimentally rely on city's alleged promise "to act favorably on" proposed development plans); Kurokawa v. Blum, 245 Cal. Rptr. 463, 471 (Ct. App. 1988) (where former domestic partner never requested forbearance of legal rights, plaintiff neither alleged nor showed such forbearance or any other act of reliance on partner's alleged promise of financial support); Silver v. Mohasco Corp., 462 N.Y.S.2d 917, 920 (App. Div. 1983) (employee did not suffer "substantial and concrete injury" from employer's breach of alleged promise regarding disclosure of employee's termination), *aff'd*, 465 N.E.2d 361 (N.Y. 1984).

119 Edward Joy Co. v. Noise Control Prods, Inc., 443 N.Y.S.2d 361 (Sup. Ct. 1981).

120 I discuss some of the shortcomings of case counting in greater detail *infra* notes 154-157, and accompanying text.

121 *See* Speidel, *supra* note 65, at 1181.

reasonable reliance and would bear the risk of reliance losses. In addition, although the subject of some controversy (to be taken up in Chapter 2), MDM may have a greater chance of recovering its expectancy,[122] its lost profit on the series for a reasonable period, if it can establish XYZ's breach of bargain. Under promissory estoppel, a court might limit MDM's recovery to the cost of producing the three episodes.[123]

2. The rise of law excusing performance

According to Gilmore, the growing willingness of twentieth-century courts to excuse failure to perform on the basis of unforeseen circumstances or a mistake of fact signaled the demise of Holmes's second tenet of the bargain theory, the promisor's absolute liability within a bargain.[124] Courts were now free to consider excusing a promisor because of a mistake or because performance was impractical or frustrated.[125] Such activity would tempt courts to apply principles far removed from the parties' bargain, such as the fairness of compelling performance under the circumstances.

As previously noted, excuse law comes into play when the parties have left a gap in their agreement concerning the allocation of the risk of an occurrence that makes performance very onerous.[126] Although Fried downplayed the problem, incomplete agreements arise for a host of

---

[122] Or at least expectancy tempered by such rules as foreseeability and certainty.

[123] *But see* Jay M. Feinman, *Promissory Estoppel and Judicial Method*, 97 HARV. L. REV. 678, 688-89 (1984) (suggesting that courts sometimes limit recoveries in contract cases to reliance damages and sometimes give expectancy recoveries in promissory estoppel cases). *See also* Edward Yorio & Steve Thel, *The Promissory Basis of Section 90*, 101 YALE L.J. 111 (1991).

[124] GILMORE, *supra* note 2, at 77-84.

[125] *Id.*

[126] *See supra* notes 58-60, and accompanying text.

reasons and often cannot be avoided.[127] For example, the parties may not anticipate future circumstances because of a contract's long duration or because of the drafters' limited vision.[128] Alternatively, an event may be too costly to dicker over in the contract.[129] The parties may depend on mutual trust and cooperation to see them through anticipated or unforeseen rocky times.

The judicial method of gap filling should depend on the reasons for a gap. For example, courts fill gaps concerning the allocation of risk of onerous circumstances most comfortably by searching for the parties' intentions through tests such as the foreseeability of risk. Courts theorize that a promisor must have intended to assume all foreseeable risks in the absence of language to the contrary.[130] But parties may simply have overlooked a foreseeable contingency or may have consciously failed to

---

[127] *See, e.g.*, Alan Schwartz, *Relational Contracts in the Courts: An Analysis of Incomplete Agreements and Judicial Strategies*, 21 J. LEGAL STUD. 271 (1992). For a more complete discussion of gap filling, *see* Chapter 6. *See also* Ian Ayres & Robert Gertner, *Filling Gaps in Incomplete Contracts: An Economic Theory of Default Rules*, 99 YALE L.J. 87 (1989); Chares J. Goetz & Robert E. Scott, *The Limits of Expanded Choice: An Analysis of the Interactions Between Express and Implied Contract Terms*, 73 CAL. L. REV. 261 (1985); Robert A. Hillman, *An Analysis of the Cessation of Contractual Relations*, 68 CORNELL L. REV. 617 (1983); Subha Narasimhan, *Of Expectations, Incomplete Contracting, and the Bargain Principle*, 74 CAL. L. REV. 1123 (1986); *Symposium*, *The Law and Economics of Risk*, 19 J. LEGAL STUD. 531 (1990); *Symposium*, *Default Rules and Contractual Consent*, 3 S. CAL. INTER. L. J. 1 (1993).

[128] The frequency of gaps due to the limited planning capabilities of contracting parties has been well documented. *See, e.g.*, Clayton P. Gillete, *Commercial Relationships and the Selection of Default Rules for Remote Risks*, 19 J. LEGAL STUD. 535, 543 (1990).

[129] For example, in the commercial context, parties sometimes minimize their planning and bargaining to avoid technicalities and "legalese" that might be too costly, cause dissension, and even defeat agreements. *See id.* at 535 (incomplete contracting is not irrational.). *See also* Clayton P. Gillette, *Cooperation and Convention in Contractual Defaults*, 3 S. CAL. INTER. L. J. 167, 172 (1994) ("at some point, it is entirely rational to stop thinking about adverse effects that might subsequently lead one to regret having entered into a contract.").

[130] Hillman, *supra* note 127, at 625.

address it because of the costs of bargaining.[131] To illustrate, in drafting the original "Why Spy?" agreement (Problem 1), XYZ and MDM may have decided to ignore onerous foreseeable risks relating to escalating production expenses because they could not agree on who should bear the risk. Their silence on the issue therefore does not necessarily suggest that they intended MDM to bear these costs. Conversely, the parties may have intended to make MDM an insurer of performance even in the face of unforeseeable production cost increases. Without clear evidence as to the parties' intentions, therefore, an event's foreseeability may say little about risk allocation.[132] With the foreseeability test often unclear, judges must stray from the parties' intentions.[133]

Courts also derive gap-fillers from fairness norms that require the parties to act honestly and reasonably, and to safeguard each other's expectations of enjoying the fruits of their exchange.[134] Such broad directives translate into a rough rule of thumb: Courts excuse performance only when losses to the promisor would be manifestly disproportionate to those contemplated and the promisor has not caused the losses. In the typical case granting an excuse, for example, the

---

[131] *Id.* at 627.

[132] *Id.*

[133] Robert A. Hillman, *Contract Excuse and Bankruptcy Discharge*, 43 STAN. L. REV. 99, 106-07 (1990); Hillman, *supra* note 127, at 624-25; Transatlantic Fin. Corp. v. United States, 363 F.2d 312, 318 (D.C. Cir. 1966) ("Foreseeability or even recognition of a risk does not necessarily prove its allocation."). *See also* Jean Braucher, *Contract Versus Contractarianism: The Regulatory Role of Contract Law*, 47 WASH. & LEE L. REV. 697, 724 (1990) ("[T]he objective approach requires potential promisors to be concerned about how their actions and communications appear to potential promisees and heightens their concern with what meaning a court will consider 'reasonable'.").

[134] *See* Hillman, *supra* note 127, at 629-640. *See also* Gillette, *supra* note 128, at 538 ("[T]he incomplete contract assigns to judges the role of injecting meaning, and hence a normative view of the commercial relationship . . . ."); Wallace K. Lightsey, *A Critique of the Promise Model of Contract*, 26 WM. & MARY L. REV. 45, 50-51 (1984-85).

promisor's costs of performance have been about twice what the parties expected.[135]

Reasons of social policy are, of course, not ignored in judicial gap-filling. For example, courts sometimes justify their decisions, at least in part, on the basis of the economic and social policies of maximizing efficiency and avoiding waste.[136] These are especially important when other reasons do not clearly point the way. We will see in Chapter 6, however, that the efficiency standard is itself complex and confusing and does not always coincide with the parties' intentions.

Legislators also sometimes supply statutory gap-filler provisions for incomplete contracts.[137] For example, among its many gap-fillers, the Uniform Commercial Code provides that the duration of a sales contract indefinite as to time is a "reasonable time."[138] Seeking to supply terms consistent with the parties' goals,[139] lawmakers derive these "off-the-rack" terms by examining the commercial context and using general standards, such as good faith and reasonableness.

Some advocates of freedom of contract seek to minimize the role of gap-filling, not by emphasizing the planning potential of parties as does Fried, but by asserting that parties "consent" in advance to the legal system's default rules. Parties so consent when the costs of learning the rules are not too high so that their failure to expressly displace them represents consent to the rules or when the rules "reflect the tacit understandings of the community of discourse of which the consenting

---

135 Hillman, *supra* note 127, at 652.

136 *See* Chapter 6.

137 *See, e.g.*, U.C.C. Article 2, part III.

138 U.C.C. § 2-309(1).

139 JAMES J. WHITE & ROBERT S. SUMMERS, HANDBOOK ON THE UNIFORM COMMERCIAL CODE § 3-5 at 129-30 (3d ed. 1988) ("What is reasonable will vary with the case depending on such factors as the nature of goods to be delivered, the purpose for which they are to be used, the extent of seller's knowledge of buyer's intentions . . . and so on.").

person is a member."[140] Still, this concept of consent will ring rather hollow to a party who was, at the time of contracting, simply unaware of or mistaken about the gap-filling rules or in no position to bargain to change them.

One can see that gap-filling provides potent ammunition for those, such as Gilmore, who believe that contract is more than bargain or promise. Moreover, Fried may have dismissed gap-filling too easily, by exaggerating the potential of contract planning. Nevertheless, one should not dismiss the significance of contract planning either. Parties *can* limit the courts' interpretation and gap-filling roles by careful planning and drafting. Analysts of judicial decisions must remember that many or even most agreements never break down or, if they do, never reach litigation in part because of successful planning and drafting.[141] It therefore remains to be seen whether judicial gap-filling *subsumes* contract as promise.

Conclusion

Fried's and Gilmore's important theories raise many issues about what contract law is and should be. In conclusion, I want to focus on the descriptive debate to illustrate some of the limits of contract theory. I return to prescriptive issues--what contract should be--in subsequent chapters.

1. The limits of meta-theory

Fried asserts that the promise principle constitutes contract's core.[142] In stark contrast, Gilmore believed that non-promissory

---

140 Barnett, *supra* note 56, at 1185. *See also* Barnett's articles cited *supra* note 61.

141 *See generally* ROBERT S. SUMMERS & ROBERT A. HILLMAN, CONTRACT AND RELATED OBLIGATION 342-60 (2d ed. 1992). Litigation costs and the potential loss of good-will also contribute, of course.

142 *See supra* notes 30-62, and accompanying text. *See also* Feinman, *supra* note 123, at 680, 686. *But see* Joseph William Singer, *The Reliance Interest in Property*, 40 STAN. L. REV. 6ll, 636 (1988) ("Neither torts nor contracts seems to have a core

principles dominate contract law.[143] Who is right? Nothing asserted by either theorist proves definitively whether one theory or another accurately describes contract law.[144] Does "contract as promise" trump other theories because a party, such as XYZ in Problem 2, can avoid an obligation by expressing an intention to be bound only by a signed contract? Or do nonconsensual principles dominate because the law will examine the clarity of XYZ's expression not to be bound and the reasonableness of MDM's reliance on any contrary statements or conduct? Similarly, Fried can assert that gap-filling by courts does not override the promise theory, because judges fill gaps only when parties leave a gap.[145] On the other hand, the inevitability of changed circumstances may make gap-filling unavoidable.

Apart from these conceptual inquiries, one can look to societal trends to ascertain whether one principle or another dominates modern contract law. It is not unreasonable to conclude that contract rules in large measure reflect the attitudes and characteristics of society. For example, consider Gilmore's description of the evolution in society from nineteenth-century individualism to the twentieth-century welfare state,[146] with people now "cogs in a machine, each dependent on the other."[147] Nevertheless, observers such as Gilmore face the challenge of accurately assessing the nature of society and reliably measuring its influence on

---

anymore; rather, every doctrinal issue recreates the contest between the competing social visions of individualism and altruism.").

143 GILMORE, *supra* note 2, at 95-96. *See also* Speidel, *supra* note 65, at 1166. For a theory that modern contract supports "the communitarian values comprising assistance to the weak and handicapped, fairness in the distribution of wealth, and altruistic concern for the interests of others," *see* HUGH COLLINS, THE LAW OF CONTRACT 1 (1986).

144 *But see* DAWSON, *supra* note 62, at 220-21 (describing "bargained for exchange" as an "essential instrument" of contract law and as "subject to [a] few exceptions ... the only recognized reason" for enforcing contracts).

145 *See* FRIED, *supra* note 2, at 73.

146 GILMORE, *supra* note 2, at 95-96.

147 *Id.* at 95.

contract law. In fact, many disagree with Gilmore's account of history and his assessment of the bargain theory: "For purely historical reasons, bargain remains the central concept of contract law; the protection of reliance is an exception or a corrective device."[148] The debate thus remains inconclusive.[149]

Determining whether Fried's or Gilmore's (or someone else's) insights accurately describe contract law may ultimately depend on empirical investigation. Can we derive empirical evidence to support either of the competing visions? Perhaps. Some scholars have investigated the contextual realities of the contracting process and have found evidence of the dominance of Gilmore's collective vision.[150] These scholars point to business norms of sharing and solidarity and to hostile attitudes toward contract law in the business community.[151] As we shall see in Chapter 7, however, the scale of investigation has been limited.[152] Furthermore, these observers concede the importance of contract law in some circumstances even within the contracting societies studied.[153]

Counting the number of cases decided primarily on promise grounds on the one hand and the number decided on the basis of reliance or other nonpromissory principles on the other (or, as described earlier, counting the proportion of successful cases to those brought on a particular theory) provides a different kind of empirical evidence. A

---

148 Feinman, *supra* note 123, at 686.

149 *See supra* notes 3-4.

150 *See* Hillman, *supra* note 1, at 128-132 (discussing theories).

151 *Id.*

152 *See also* Russell J. Weintraub, *A Survey of Contract Practice and Policy*, 1992 WIS. L. REV. 1, 4; W. David Slawson, *Standard Form Contracts and Democratic Control of Lawmaking Power*, 84 HARV. L. REV. 529, 529, 538-39 (1971).

153 *See* Stewart Macaulay, *Non-Contractual Relations In Business: A Preliminary Study*, 28 AM. SOC. REV 55, 62, 65 (1963). *See also* Stewart Macaulay, *An Empirical View of Contract*, 1985 WIS. L. REV. 465, 471; Robert A. Hillman, *Court Adjustment of Long Term Contracts: An Analysis Under Modern Contract Law*, 1987 DUKE L.J. 1, 4-6.

potential flaw in such analyses, however, is the difficulty of characterizing each case correctly.[154] Judges may actually decide some cases portrayed as focusing on a bargained-for-exchange on the basis of detrimental reliance.[155] Conversely, some judges may apply promissory estoppel when they are really moved by the parties' bargain and only some technical defense bars recovery.[156] Furthermore, a court filling a gap in an express contract might rely either on the parties' intentions or on what the judge thinks is fair under the circumstances.

Even if counting cases contributed to our understanding, the investment of time and resources might not be worth the effort. The empirical data might tell us only that parties' actual agreements and fairness principles are both very important. Where would we go from there?[157]

Casual but persuasive empiricism actually suggests the importance of both Fried's and Gilmore's visions. Recoveries abound based on the parties' promises and on other grounds.[158] Despite Gilmore's protestations, the *Restatement (Second) of Contracts* presents

---

154 The point is discussed in Chapter 2.

155 *See, e.g.*, Hamer v. Sidway, 27 N.E. 256, 257 (N.Y. 1891) (enforcing a promise based on the bargain theory, even though the act that formed the consideration did not benefit the promisee or a third party).

156 *See, e.g.*, McIntosh v. Murphy, 469 P.2d 177, 181 (Haw. 1970) (holding that a bargain promise is enforceable despite the statute of frauds if the court can avoid injustice only by enforcing the promise).

157 For discussions of the problems of empiricism, see Chapter 7; WILLIAM TWINING, KARL LLEWELLYN AND THE REALIST MOVEMENT 190-96 (1973); *cf.* William C. Whitford, *Lowered Horizons: Implementation Research In a Post-CLS World*, 1986 WIS. L. REV. 755.

158 One informal study of a randomly selected set of contract cases decided in 1986 included "more cases that at least formally treated contract law strictly as a matter of intent than cases which appeared to construct doctrine to further values other than intent." Jack M. Beermann, *Contract Law as a System of Values*, 67 B.U. L. REV. 553, 74 (1987) (*reviewing* HUGH COLLINS, THE LAW OF CONTRACT (1986)). The reviewer concluded, however, that contract law was "difficult to characterize . . . in general terms." *Id.* at 579.

consideration and promissory estoppel as relatively distinct theories of obligation.[159] Judges fill gaps based on both the presumed intentions of the parties and their own views of fairness. Legal literature is replete with articles, books, and speeches analyzing both the individualist and regulatory tendencies in contract law. People continue both to contract and to rely on promises that fall short of formal contracts.

In light of the substantial roles of both bargain and other principles, one can safely say only that neither the emergence of alternative theories of obligation nor the growth of courts' important gap-filling role has subsumed freedom of contract. Instead, the theories combine to form a set of criteria for determining the rights and obligations of parties engaged in exchange relations in a diverse society.

2. Modern contract's complexity

Taken together, the parties' promises *and* a host of non-promissory principles govern the rights and duties of contracting parties. Courts undoubtedly often engage in less than a systematic inquiry in resolving disputes and do not always establish a clear hierarchy in applying the various elements of contract law. Modern contract law therefore emphasizes the importance of equity and flexibility over certainty. Contract law's complexity belies the simple conclusion that either private ordering or non-promissory, interventionist principles dominates.[160]

Instead, the modern contract-law paradigm encompasses numerous norms and many dimensions. It includes both Gilmore's death-of-contract thesis and, conversely, promissory theories, such as Fried's, that stress the primacy of the parties' promises or intentions.[161] Neither vision alone adequately captures the institution of contract because each

---

159 *See* RESTATEMENT (SECOND) OF CONTRACTS §§ 71, 90 (1981). Admittedly, the Restatement (Second) commentary to Section 90 is not overwhelmingly clear on the relation of promissory estoppel to contract. RESTATEMENT (SECOND) § 90 cmt. a.

160 See the discussion in Pound, *Liberty, supra* note 9, at 462.

161 FRIED, *supra* note 2; GILMORE, *supra* note 2.

emphasizes one view at the expense of the other. In reality, freedom of contract and fairness principles share the contract-law spotlight.[162]

Instead of attempting to find contract law's true core, analysts should investigate the implications of contract law's richness of principles and theories. For example, is contract law objective and coherent? Is the current composition of principle and counter-principle desirable? How should lawmakers determine when the government should intervene in particular contexts? What should be the nature of the intervention? We turn to these questions in subsequent chapters.

---

162 "Is there perhaps, between individual sovereignty of the contract and collective sovereignty of the law, a difference only in degree and in application, and should we finally cease opposing them to each other as if one was destined to triumph over the other?" GEORGES DAVY, LA FOI JUREE--ETUDE SOCIOLOGIQUE DU PROBLEME DU CONTRAT 374 (1922), *quoted in* Lyman Johnson, *Individual and Collective Sovereignty in the Corporate Enterprise*, 92 COLUM. L. REV. 2215, 2249 (1992) (reviewing FRANK H. EASTERBROOK & DANIEL R. FISCHEL, THE ECONOMIC STRUCTURE OF CORPORATE LAW (1991) and ROBERT N. BELLAH, ET. AL., THE GOOD SOCIETY (1991)).

CHAPTER 2

THEORIES OF PROMISSORY ESTOPPEL: RELIANCE AND PROMISE

Despite contract law's modern-day theoretical pluralism, discussed in Chapter 1, the bargain theory of consideration constituted the principal basis for enforcement of promises in the United States from the late-nineteenth to the mid-twentieth century.[1] The bargain theory was underinclusive, however, in part because an assortment of gratuitous promises called out for enforcement.[2] Suppose, for example, a promisee improved land in reliance on a landowner's broken gift promise to convey. Suppose a promisee failed to insure her property in reliance on an insurance agent's gratuitous broken promise to insure the property. Suppose a donor broke a promise to donate money to a charity.[3] Responding to the promisee's hardship or, occasionally, another strong policy such as aiding charitable institutions, courts began to enforce these and other gratuitous promises.[4] Corbin amassed these cases to persuade the drafters of the first *Restatement of Contracts* to recognize justifiable

---

[1] *See* Chapter 1.

[2] *See* Stanley D. Henderson, *Promissory Estoppel and Traditional Contract Doctrine*, 78 YALE L.J. 343, 350 (1969) ("[T]he tradition which produced Section 90 necessitated the extraction of a broad generalization from an assortment of cases which are not reducible to a systematic pattern."); *see also* ROBERT S. SUMMERS & ROBERT A. HILLMAN, CONTRACT AND RELATED OBLIGATION 79-90 (2d ed. 1992) (discussing judicial recognition of the need to enforce relied-upon gratuitous promises).

[3] *See* RESTATEMENT (FIRST) OF CONTRACTS app. (explanatory notes) at 245-50 (Official Draft 1928).

[4] *See, e.g.*, Seavey v. Drake, 62 N.H. 393 (1882); Siegel v. Spear & Co., 138 N.E. 414 (N.Y. 1923); Ryerrs v. Trustees of Presbyterian Church, 33 Pa. 114 (1859); *see also* Jay M. Feinman, *Promissory Estoppel and Judicial Method*, 97 HARV. L. REV. 678, 680 (1984).

reliance on gift promises as a distinct basis of enforcement.[5] Williston, the reporter of the first *Restatement*, responded by setting forth the theory in Section 90:

> A promise which the promisor should reasonably expect to induce action or forebearance of a definite and substantial character on the part of the promisee and which does induce such action or forebearance is binding if unjustice can be avoided only by enforcement of the promise.[6]

Section 90, which attracted major attention because it expanded the category of legally enforceable promises,[7] came to be known as the theory of promissory estoppel.[8]

From the outset, however, controversy surrounded promissory estoppel. We saw in Chapter 1, for example, the uneasy coexistence between promissory estoppel and the bargain theory of consideration.[9] Although I invoke bargain theory from time to time in this chapter, I now focus on the controversy surrounding promissory estoppel's internal conceptual core and, correspondingly, its appropriate remedy. Specifically, I analyze the debate of theorists concerning whether detrimental reliance or promise constitutes the core of promissory estoppel and whether reliance or expectancy damages is the appropriate remedy.

---

5 *See* Feinman, *supra* note 4, at 683.

6 RESTATEMENT OF CONTRACTS § 90 (1932).

7 *See* Feinman, *supra* note 4, at 680, 683. For a more complete history of the section, *see also* E. Allan Farnsworth, *Contracts Scholarship in the Age of the Anthology*, 85 MICH. L. REV. 1406, 1454-1462 (1987).

8 *See* Charles L. Knapp, *Reliance in the Revised Restatement: The Proliferation of Promissory Estoppel*, 81 COLUM. L. REV. 52, 53 (1981) ("[T]he principle of section 90 ... has become perhaps the most radical and expansive development of the century in the law of promissory liability.").

9 *See also* Henderson, *supra* note 2, at 345-50 (discussing assimilation of promissory estoppel theory with bargain principles).

Although Section 90 requires both a promise and reliance induced by the promise, analysts have been debating the relative importance of each since the inception of the section. Some maintain that reliance is the "decisive factor,"[10] while others insist that "issues of . . . liability under Section 90 turn on promise, not reliance."[11] We will see that normative judgments over the respective roles of promise and reliance in part fuel the quarrel. For example, reliance theorists accentuate the fairness of redressing detrimental reliance on a promise, whereas promise theorists focus on individual liberty or the moral significance of promising. Nevertheless, in large part the debate between reliance and promise theorists is descriptive: analysts examining the cases disagree over which element dominates in the courts.

The uncertainty over promissory estoppel's conceptual core also generates confusion over the remedial consequences of promissory estoppel liability. Promise-focused theorists generally believe that courts should enforce promises by awarding expectancy damages to put the injured party in as good a financial position as if the promise had been performed.[12] Reliance-centered analysts generally assert that courts should limit the promisee's recovery to the cost of the detriment incurred.[13]

The famous exchange (at least to American law professors) between Williston and Coudert, a New York lawyer, at the 1926 meeting of the American Law Institute, illustrates the remedial issue. Williston and Coudert discussed the following problem: Nephew tells Uncle that he wants to buy a car. Uncle promises Nephew \$1000. In reliance, Nephew buys a car for \$500, but Uncle will not pay Nephew anything. Under Section 90, Uncle's promise is enforceable if he "should have

---

10 Henderson, *supra* note 2, at 364.

11 Edward Yorio & Steve Thel, *The Promissory Basis of Section 90*, 101 YALE L.J. 111, 167 (1991).

12 *See, e.g.*, Daniel A. Farber & John H. Matheson, *Beyond Promissory: Contract Law and the "Invisible Handshake,"* 52 U. CHI. L. REV. 903 (1985); Yorio & Thel, *supra* note 11.

13 E. ALLAN FARNSWORTH, CONTRACTS § 2.19, at 96 (1982) (discussing theorists).

reasonably expected" his promise to induce Nephew to engage in "definite and substantial" reliance, Nephew actually relied, and justice requires enforcement of the promise.[14] But how much should Nephew recover? Williston thought that the Uncle should be liable for the full $1000, but Coudert challenged that result:

> MR. COUDERT: Would you say, Mr. Reporter, in your case of Johnny and the uncle, the uncle promising the $1000 and Johnny buying the car--say, he goes out and buys the car for $500--that uncle would be liable for $1000 or would he be liable for $500?
>
> MR. WILLISTON: If Johnny had done what he was expected to do, or is acting within the limits of his uncle's expectation, I think uncle would be liable for $1000; but not otherwise.
>
> MR. COUDERT: In other words, substantial justice would require that uncle should be penalized in the sum of $500.
>
> MR. WILLISTON: Why do you say "penalized"?
>
> MR. COUDERT: Because substantial justice there would require, it seems to me, that Johnny get his money for his car, but should he get his car and $500 more? . . .[15]
>
> . . . .
>
> MR. WILLISTON: Either the promise is binding or it is not. If the promise is binding it has to be enforced as it is made.[16]

Analysts considering the Williston-Coudert dispute felt free to choose sides, in part because of the confusion over the substance of promissory estoppel and in part because Section 90 took no clear position

---

[14] RESTATEMENT OF CONTRACTS § 90 (1932).

[15] *Proceedings at Fourth Annual Meeting,* 4 A.L.I. Proc. 98-99 (1926) [hereinafter *Proceedings*], *reprinted in* Yorio & Thel, *supra* note 11, at 116-17.

[16] *Proceedings, supra* note 15, at 103.

on the appropriate remedial response.[17] In 1982, the drafters of the *Restatement (Second) of Contracts* sought to lift the remedial fog in the new Section 90 by granting judges the discretion to award expectancy or reliance damages (or perhaps another remedy) according to the particular equities of the case: "The remedy granted for breach may be limited as justice requires."[18] Reliance theorists posited that the provision's express purpose "is to sanction the use of a reliance measure of damages."[19] Promise theorists did not disagree, but generally claimed that courts have failed to respond to the invitation.[20]

Despite the substantive and remedial confusion, the theory of promissory estoppel gained considerable judicial acceptance. In fact, courts began to apply the theory to commercial promises to remedy defective contracts, such as oral agreements unenforceable under the

---

17 For analysts generally siding with Coudert's position, *see, e.g.*, Benjamin F. Boyer, *Promissory Estoppel: Requirements and Limitations of the Doctrine*, 98 U. PA. L. REV. 459 (1950); Melvin A. Eisenberg, *Donative Promises*, 47 U. CHI. L. REV. 1 (1979); Michael B. Metzger & Michael J. Phillips, *The Emergence of Promissory Estoppel as an Independent Theory of Recovery*, 35 RUTGERS L. REV. 472 (1983); Warren A. Seavey, *Reliance Upon Gratuitous Promises or Other Conduct*, 64 HARV. L. REV. 913 (1951). For theorists supporting Williston, *see, e.g.*, W. David Slawson, *The Role of Reliance in Contract Damages*, 76 CORNELL L. REV. 197 (1990), Yorio & Thel, *supra* note 11.

Some analysts, siding with Williston, interpret the first Restatement's Section 90 to call for expectancy damages. Others interpret the reference to "injustice" in the provision (promises are "binding if injustice can be avoided only by [their] enforcement") to permit courts to grant reliance damages. One commentator, for example, suggested that the purpose of the "injustice" provision was to assuage those who opted for reliance damages, *see* Slawson, *supra*, at 200, and at least one decision relies on the language in awarding reliance damages, *see* Hoffman v. Red Owl Stores, Inc., 133 N.W.2d 267, 275 (Wis. 1965).

18 RESTATEMENT (SECOND) OF CONTRACTS § 90(1) (1981).

19 Eisenberg, *supra* note 17, at 26. The Restatement (Second) also deleted the "definite and substantial" requirement, apparently "to accommodate its policy of permitting partial enforcement of the promise." Metzger & Phillips, *supra* note 17, at 540; *see also* Henderson, *supra* note 2, at 384 n.223.

20 *See* Yorio & Thel, *supra* note 11, at 130-32.

statute of frauds and indefinite agreements,[21] as well as to gratuitous promises. Some courts employed promissory estoppel even when the promisee could also recover on bargain grounds.[22] Notwithstanding the theory's general endorsement, the debate over its theoretical basis and the appropriate remedy still rages seventy years after the Williston-Coudert dialogue.[23]

This chapter examines the current promissory estoppel controversy. We will see that the dialogue resembles the quarrel discussed in Chapter 1 between promise theorists and nonconsensualists over the precise ingredients of contract law.[24] Chapter 2 concludes that neither promise nor reliance enthusiasts have completely won the day. Nevertheless, each school contributes by exploring and accentuating the importance of either promise or reliance. Moreover, the remedial approach in the courts reflects this duality.

A. Reliance Theorists

Problem 3: MDM Enterprises produces the television series "Why Spy?" for XYZ Television Network and later begins negotiations with XYZ for the production of a spin-off series, "Journey." The parties tentatively agree on a licensing fee of $750,000 per episode for twenty-two episodes of the new series. They discuss a five-year license, with the network to have the right to cancel at any time. They also discuss a ten percent escalation of the licensing fee over the five-year period. Before signing any documents or reaching a final agreement on any terms, the network offers MDM $1.5 million to produce two episodes of "Journey." Without

---

21 *See, e.g.*, Farber & Matheson, *supra* note 12, at 907 ("[P]romissory estoppel is regularly applied to the gamut of commercial contexts.").

22 *Id.* at 908; Henderson, *supra* note 2, at 369.

23 *See* supra notes 14-16, and accompanying text.

24 *See, e.g.*, P.S. ATIYAH, THE RISE AND FALL OF FREEDOM OF CONTRACT 777 (1979) (promissory estoppel "indicates a resurgence of reliance-based liability at the expense of consensual liability").

accepting XYZ's offer, MDM produces the episodes at a cost of $1 million. Thereafter, negotiations over the full deal break down. MDM seeks $1.5 million in compensation when no other network shows interest in the new series.

We will see in Problem 3 that MDM may recover under the doctrine of promissory estoppel even though MDM and XYZ have not signed a contract for the production of "Journey," and MDM did not formally accept XYZ's offer to purchase two episodes of the series. Reliance-centered theorists of promissory estoppel would make two arguments, which we shall consider in turn. First, MDM's reliance on XYZ's offer constitutes the "essence" of promissory estoppel and justifies relief.[25] Second, the appropriate remedy is based on MDM's reliance losses.

1. Reliance constitutes the "essence" of promissory estoppel

We begin with a brief discussion of two important articles authored by Lon Fuller that heavily influenced reliance theorists of promissory estoppel. In *Consideration and Form*[26] and in *The Reliance Interest in Contract Damages*,[27] Fuller investigated both the formal and substantive bases for enforcing promises. He pointed out that legal formalities involving the manner of making enforceable promises comprise one set of grounds for determining enforceable promises.[28] For example, the formal requirement of consideration evidences the making of a promise, cautions the promisor about its seriousness, and guides the

---

25 *See* Boyer, *supra* note 17, at 491 "[R]eliance ... is the essence of promissory estopppel.").

26 Lon L. Fuller, *Consideration and Form*, 41 COLUM. L. REV. 799 (1941).

27 Lon L. Fuller & William R. Perdue, Jr., *The Reliance Interest in Contract Damages*, 46 YALE L.J. 52 (1936).

28 Fuller, *supra* note 26, at 800-803.

parties in how to make or avoid enforceable promises.[29] Fuller also stressed substantive reasons for enforcing promises. He suggested that the principle of private autonomy constitutes one basis of contract liability.[30] Contract law gives people the power to "change. . . their legal relations."[31] Reliance on a promise that benefits the promisor and results in the promisor's unjust enrichment comprises a second substantive ground of contract liability.[32] Reliance that fails to benefit the promisor but harms the promisee, such as in Problem 3, forms a third reason for enforcing promises.[33]

Fuller concluded that the formal evidentiary and cautionary reasons for enforcing promises generally do not apply to unrelied-upon gift promises. Moreover, such promises do not unjustly enrich the promisor, nor by definition do they result in detrimental reliance.[34] A broken, unrelied-upon gift promise therefore causes only disappointment.[35] In addition, gift promises play a relatively small role in wealth redistribution or, for that matter, in any other social policy.[36] Such promises are therefore typically not important enough to justify the costs of enforcement.[37]

---

[29] *See id.* at 814-15.

[30] *Id.* at 806.

[31] *Id.*

[32] *Id.* at 812-13.

[33] *Id.* at 810-12.

[34] *Id.* at 815.

[35] Eisenberg, *supra* note 17, at 3.

[36] *Id.* at 4. *But see* Andrew Kull, *Reconsidering Gratuitous Promises*, 21 J. LEGAL STUD. 39, 49-50 (1992) ("The argument that gratuitous promises do not merit enforcement cannot depend . . . on the proposition that the gratuitous transfer is itself unmeritorious.").

[37] Fuller, *supra* note 26, at 815.

Recall that Fuller also explained why courts enforce executory bargained-for

Fuller's work has been remarkably influential.[38] In fact, reliance theorists of promissory estoppel have borrowed Fuller's analysis almost intact. These writers dismiss unrelied-on gift promises on both the formal and substantive grounds suggested by Fuller.[39] Not suprisingly, reliance theorists therefore report "widespread agreement that informal unrelied-upon donative promises should not be legally enforced."[40]

Reliance on gift promises, on the other hand, strengthens the case for enforcement: "Is it not manifest that a person who has actually worsened his position by reliance on a promise has a more powerful case for redress than one who has not acted in reliance on the promise at all?"[41] Reliance is itself some evidence that a promise was made. Moreover, "the prospect of reliance may have a sobering effect on the promisor."[42] In addition, relying parties suffer more than disappointment; reliance

---

exchanges (agreements the parties have not yet performed), which also lack reliance or unjust enrichment. *See* Chapter 1. First, such agreements may satisfy the formal grounds for enforcement. Parties entering exchange agreements tend to create evidence of their agreement and should be alerted to the seriousness of the venture. On the substantive side, Fuller acknowledged a "policy in favor of promoting and facilitating reliance on business agreements." Fuller & Perdue, *supra* note 27, at 61. Nevertheless, he asserted that promisees might encounter difficulty proving and measuring reliance and, therefore, might be unwilling to rely on executory agreements if contract law required proof of reliance. He therefore concluded that to "encourage reliance" the law "must . . . dispense with its proof." *Id.* at 62.

38 *See, e.g.*, Stewart Macalulay, *The Reliance Interest and the World Outside the Law Schools' Doors,* 1991 WIS. L. REV. 247; Todd D. Rakoff, *Fuller and Perdue's The Reliance Interest as a Work of Legal Scholarship,* 1991 WIS. L. REV. 203.

39 *See, e.g.*, Eisenberg, *supra* note 17, at 3. *But see* Kull, *supra* note 36 (little evidence for the proposition that gratuitous promises are less important economically).

40 Eisenberg, *supra* note 17, at 6. What about formal donative promises such as those under seal or in writing? These present a better case for enforcement because such formal devices caution the promisor and provide "evidentiary security." But the question of the social benefit of enforcing such promises remains. *See id.* at 18.

41 P.S. Atiyah, *Contracts, Promises and the Law of Obligations*, 94 L.Q. REV. 193, 202 (1978).

42 Eisenberg, *supra* note 17, at 18.

diminishes their wealth.[43] Such reflections obviously support the approach of both the first and second *Restatement of Contracts* Section 90, which set forth reliance as an independent basis of promise enforcement.[44] In fact, reliance-centered analysts set forth a tort or fairness theory of promissory estoppel that focuses on the promisee's harm: "The wrong is not primarily in depriving the plaintiff of the promised reward but in causing the plaintiff to change position to his detriment."[45] "[P]romissory estoppel is informed by a basic test of fairness."[46]

Influenced at least in part by the "intuitive appeal [of] the justice of compensating reliance"[47] and the absence of any express restriction in Section 90,[48] courts began to apply promissory estoppel not only to gratuitous promises, but also in commercial settings involving reliance on

---

43 *Id.*

44 Henderson, *supra* note 2, at 346. Professor Boyer's reasoning was typical:

> "We begin with a promise, but before liability is imposed for non-performance the promisee must furnish the court with reasons for enforcement. One acceptable reason could be that the promise induced or brought about action or forbearance by the promisee. If one causes another to act in a particular way he furnishes a justifiable basis for intervention by the court. Absent such cause-effect relationship there appears to be no acceptable justification for imposing contractual liability on the gratuitous promisor."

Boyer, *supra* note 17, at 470-71.

45 Seavey, *supra* note 17, at 926; *see also* Randy E. Barnett, *Contract Scholarship and the Reemergence of Legal Philosophy*, 97 HARV. L. REV. 1223, 1241 (1984) (reviewing E. ALLAN FARNSWORTH, CONTRACTS (1982)) (stating that courts may impose promissory liability where promisor's conduct is "blameworthy"). *But see* Slawson, *supra* note 17, at 208 ("The wrong . . . is in not performing the promise after the promisee has relied upon it to his detriment.").

46 Henderson, *supra* note 2, at 383.

47 Feinman, *supra* note 4, at 685.

48 Boyer, *supra* note 17, at 492.

offers (such as in Problem 3), negotiations, indefinite agreements, and illusory promises. The reasonableness of a promisee's reliance posed a conceptual problem, however. In Problem 3, for example, MDM's reliance on XYZ's offer arguably is premature because MDM did not legally bind XYZ first by accepting XYZ's offer: "[A]n offer for an exchange is not meant to become a promise until a consideration has been received, either a counter-promise or whatever else is stipulated. To extend it would be to hold the offeror regardless of the stipulated condition of his offer."[49]

Justice Traynor found a bridge over this conceptual barrier in *Drennan v. Star Paving Co.*[50] In making a bid on a school construction project, Drennan, a general contractor, relied on Star Paving's bid to perform the paving work. The court treated Star Paving's bid as an offer to perform the work upon an acceptance by Drennan. After Drennan was awarded the prime contract but before Drennan accepted Star Paving's bid, Star Paving told Drennan that the bid was a mistake and refused to perform. Although Justice Traynor found that Drennan's use of Star Paving's bid did not constitute an acceptance, the judge held that Drennan's reliance on the bid made it irrevocable under promissory estoppel. Traynor reasoned that Star Paving "had reason to expect that if its bid proved the lowest it would be used by plaintiff," and Drennan did use the bid to its detriment.[51]

Why should Star Paving have reasonably expected Drennan to rely? After all, Drennan did not accept Star Paving's bid before relying, just as MDM did not bind XYZ before producing the two episodes of "Journey." Although not stressed in the case, Traynor apparently believed Drennan followed a custom based on the impracticality of formally accepting the subcontractor's bid when made. According to the custom, subcontractors typically communicated their bids by telephone at the last minute to avoid bid shopping by the general contractor. Similarly, if

---

49 James Baird Co. v. Gimbel Bros., 64 F.2d 344, 346 (2d Cir. 1933).

50 333 P.2d 757 (Cal. 1958).

51 "Reasonable reliance resulting in a foreseeable prejudicial change in position affords a compelling basis also for implying a subsidiary promise not to revoke an offer for a bilateral contract." *Id.* at 760.

MDM can establish a custom in the industry to rely on offers such as XYZ's, then XYZ should reasonably have expected MDM to rely.

Whatever the persuasiveness of Traynor's reasoning, the use of promissory estoppel in commercial settings took hold.[52] Courts began to apply promissory estoppel even in situations lacking a formal offer. In *Hoffman v. Red Owl Stores*,[53] for example, Red Owl's agent told Hoffman that he would receive a Red Owl franchise if he contributed $18,000 and performed other tasks. The agent added conditions as negotiations continued, while he repeatedly assured Hoffman of a franchise. The agent's representations induced Hoffman to take certain actions, including selling his bakery business and buying and selling a small grocery store. Although negotiations ultimately broke down after over two years, the court protected Hoffman's reliance on the basis of promissory estoppel.[54] Other courts have also applied promissory estoppel to enforce indefinite or illusory agreements, such as contracts lacking critical terms[55] and employment or franchise agreements terminable at will.[56]

In sum, reliance on gift promises provided the impetus for *Restatement* Section 90. Courts also carved out considerable territory for the theory in bargain settings. Moreover, analysts found reliance to be the conceptual key to promissory estoppel cases:

> [T]he necessary implication is that the bargain requirement is not as essential in exchange transactions as orthodox doctrine would have us believe. Rather, detrimental reliance emerges as the decisive factor; the promise itself is no longer as significant as the harm it precipitates.[57]

2. The remedy in promissory estoppel cases is reliance damages

---

52 *See* Henderson, *supra* note 2, at 352.

53 133 N.W.2d 267, 267 (Wis. 1965).

54 *Id.* at 274-75.

55 *See, e.g.*, Wheeler v. White, 398 S.W.2d 93 (Tex. 1965).

56 *See* Henderson, *supra* note 2, at 362-364.

57 *Id.* at 364.

Reliance theorists generally support awarding reliance damages in promissory estoppel cases.[58] Siding with Coudert, they believe that to do justice, a legal remedy should reflect the bases for liability: If a promisee's detrimental reliance constitutes the basis of an obligation, then "damages should not exceed the loss caused by the change of position, which would never be more in amount, but might be less, than the promised reward."[59] Especially in light of this argument, Professor Melvin Eisenberg found Williston's exhortations about awarding expectancy "extraordinary" and "counterintuitive."[60]

By awarding expectancy damages and fully enforcing promises in promissory estoppel settings, reliance theorists point out, courts would undermine important policies tied to the enforcement of bargains.[61] Promisees often make promissory estoppel claims in commercial settings because their contract is incomplete, oral (when the statute of frauds requires a writing), or unconsummated, and therefore unenforceable. Courts may justly find an obligation based on the parties' imperfect, but real bargain or one party's promise, either of which induces reasonable reliance. By awarding expectancy damages in these situations, however, courts may undermine the policies behind the defenses (respectively, avoiding judicial interference, deterring fraud, and protecting personal autonomy).[62] For example, courts may diminish XYZ's freedom *from* contract if they grant MDM full expectancy damages in Problem 3, as if

---

58 *See, e.g.*, ARTHUR CORBIN, CORBIN ON CONTRACTS § 1A at 205 (1963); Boyer, *supra* note 17, at 490-91; Eisenberg, *supra* note 17, at 26-27.

59 Seavey, *supra* note 17, at 926.

60 Eisenberg, *supra* note 17, at 24-25.

61

> "[T]he policies which underlie orthodox contract rules are quite relevant to the expansion of Section 90 in commercial cases. No persuasive public policy may preclude a recovery where injury is occasioned by a gratuitous promise. But if a reliance claim arises in the bargain context, policy considerations relating to the security of expectations come into play."

Henderson, *supra* note 2, at 387.

62 *See, e.g.*, Wheeler v. White, 398 S.W.2d 93 (Tex. 1965) (indefinite contract); McIntosh v. Murphy, 469 P.2d 177 (Haw. 1970) (statute of frauds).

a contract had been consummated.[63] XYZ should be liable to MDM for inducing MDM's reasonable reliance, in other words, but XYZ should not be bound to a contract it never intended to make.

Reliance advocates support their view by citing "leading" promissory estoppel cases where courts granted reliance damages, such as *Hoffman v. Red Owl Stores*.[64] Although Hoffman apparently did not ask for expectancy relief,[65] the court intimated that it would not have granted it even if Hoffman had pursued it: "We deem it would be a mistake to regard an action grounded on promissory estoppel as the equivalent of a breach of contract action."[66] The court also relied on Professor Boyer's analysis of promissory estoppel,[67] which urged the award of reliance damages largely for the reasons articulated above.[68]

Reliance theorists also frequently invoke *Wheeler v. White*.[69] In a signed contract, White promised to provide or arrange for a loan to Wheeler so that Wheeler could raze certain buildings on his property and build a new commercial structure. Wheeler demolished the buildings, worth more than $58,000, but White did not procure or make the loan. The court held that the contract was too indefinite to enforce, mainly

---

63 *See* Mary Becker, *Promissory Estoppel Damages*, 16 HOFSTRA L. REV. 131, 148-149 (1987).

64 133 N.W.2d 267 (Wis. 1965).

65 Yorio & Thel, *supra* note 11, at 143.

66 133 N.W.2d 267, 275 (Wis. 1965).

67 *Id.*

68

> It is to be hoped that the trend will be towards a protection of the reliance interest of the promisee . . . . many cases, partial enforcement will prevent injustice to the promisee without the injustice to the promisor that is often patent when complete enforcement is granted. . . . If the courts concentrate their attention on the avoidance of injustice to a promisee who has acted justifiably in reliance on a gratuitous promise, such a trend seems inevitable.

Boyer, *supra* note 17, at 497.

69 398 S.W.2d 93 (Tex. 1965).

because the parties did not specify the interest rate, but still found for Wheeler on the basis of promissory estoppel. Nevertheless, the court denied lost profits to Wheeler "even if . . . provable with certainty" and limited recovery to "no more than reliance damages measured by the detriment sustained."[70]

Despite these and other cases,[71] many, even most, courts appear to award expectancy relief, according to recent studies.[72] Rather than siding with Williston, however, many reliance theorists adopt other explanations for the prevalence of expectancy damages in both donative and commercial promissory estoppel cases.[73] For example, reliance analysts point out that a promise categorized as gratuitous actually may constitute part of a bargain,[74] such as where a disabled family member promises to convey property explicitly or implicitly in exchange for care.[75] As a result, courts conditioned to grant expectancy remedies in bargain settings may reflexively opt for them.

Reliance damages also may be difficult to measure in gift- promise cases.[76] Consider a promisee who improved land over an extended period in reliance on a landowner's broken gratuitous promise to convey.[77]

---

70 *Id.* at 97.

71 *See, e.g.*, Esquire Radio & Elec., Inc. v. Montgomery Ward & Co., 804 F.2d 787 (2d Cir. 1986) (excluding "benefit of the bargain profit" when retailer breaks promise to buy electronic products from importer); Zimmerman v. Zimmerman, 447 N.Y.S.2d 675 (App. Div. 1982) (denying award of expectancy damages for father's promise to pay his daughter's college tuition).

72 *See, e.g.*, Becker, *supra* note 63, at 134-35; Farber & Matheson, *supra* note 12, at 909; Yorio & Thel, *supra* note 11, at 130-31.

73 *See, e.g.*, Eisenberg, *supra* note 17, at 26-28; Henderson, *supra* note 2, at 378-79.

74 Henderson, *supra* note 2, at 378-79.

75 Becker, *supra* note 63, at 137-139 (discussing *In re* Estate of Bucci, 488 P.2d 216 (Colo. Ct. App. 1971)).

76 Eisenberg, *supra* note 17, at 26-28.

77 *See* Becker, *supra* note 63, at 139.

Measuring the value of the improvements may be difficult with the passage of time. Moreover, such a promise may induce the promisee to make important lifestyle decisions, such as where to live and work and what opportunities to pursue.[78] Professor Eisenberg points out that gift promises inducing changes in lifestyle often involve difficult-to-measure costs best approximated by the value of the promise.[79]

Courts also may award expectancy relief as the best strategy for protecting difficult-to-prove reliance in business contexts,[80] such as where the promisee suffers intangible losses[81] or forgoes other opportunities.[82] Courts may grant expectancy damages in the latter context because the value of lost opportunities in a market economy should roughly equal lost expectancy.[83] In Problem 3, for example, no other network showed interest in "Journey." Nevertheless, at least in theory, MDM could have used its resources to produce two episodes of another series worth about $1.5 million. Expectancy damages therefore would put MDM in as good a position as if it had not relied on XYZ's promise. The forgone opportunities rationale for expectancy relief is, of course, not foreign to tort law: "[G]ains prevented may be recovered when A's intentional and

---

78 Boyer, *supra* note 17, at 486.

79 Eisenberg, *supra* note 17, at 28.

80 Feinman, *supra* note 7, at 687. Fuller suggested that courts award expectancy damages to protect the reliance interest because reliance damages are difficult to prove. Although reliance may furnish "the exclusive *raison d'etre* of legal intervention . . . for reasons of convenience and certainty the court may choose [expectancy damages]." Fuller & Perdue, *supra* note 27, at 66-67.

81 *See, e.g.*, Vastoler v. American Can Co., 700 F.2d 916 (3d Cir. 1983).

82 Becker, *supra* note 63, at 139; Boyer, *supra* note 17, at 486; Eisenberg, *supra* note 17, at 26-28.

83 Eisenberg, *supra* note 17, at 26-28; *see also* Metzger & Phillips, *supra* note 17, at 545 (expectancy measure allows "promisee to recover lost profits from foregone opportunities").

wrongful conduct interferes with B's economic opportunities."[84] In fact, many commercial cases expressly invoke the forgone opportunities rationale. Consider *Walters v. Marathon Oil Co.*[85] When Marathon Oil reneged on its promise to provide the Walters with a dealership, the court stated: "[I]t is apparent that [the Walters] suffered a loss of profits as a direct result of their reliance upon the promise made by [Marathon]...."[86]

Grants of expectancy damages in a small group of cases also may reflect other policy concerns.[87] For example, the *Restatement (Second)* specifically exempts charitable institutions from having to prove reliance because of their importance to society.[88] Granting expectancy damages to charities, typically a larger award than reliance damages, also reflects this policy.[89] In addition, courts in promissory estoppel cases may grant employees their promised pension rights because of the importance of safeguarding the retirement prospects of wage earners.[90] Furthermore, some gift-promise cases involve actions against the estate of a promisor who had demonstrated an intention to perform the promise. Courts may grant expectancy damages in such situations for the same reason the law enforces wills, namely to validate testamentary wealth transfers.[91] Despite these instances of awarding expectancy damages, reliance theorists would

---

84 Richard E. Speidel, *The Borderland of Contract*, 10 N. KY. L. REV. 163, 171 (1983).

85 642 F.2d 1098 (7th Cir. 1981).

86 *Id.* at 1100; *see also* Grouse v. Group Health Plan, 306 N.W.2d 114, 116 (Minn. 1981) ("Since . . . the prospective employment might have been terminated at any time, the measure of damages is not so much what he would have earned from respondent as what he lost in quitting the job he held and in declining at least one other offer of employment elsewhere.").

87 Becker, *supra* note 63, at 144-145.

88 RESTATEMENT (SECOND) OF CONTRACTS § 90(2).

89 Becker, *supra* note 63, at 137.

90 *Id.* at 146.

91 *Id.* at 138.

insist that the appropriate remedy in unexceptional cases remains reliance damages.

Although rarely mentioned by reliance theorists, courts may award expectancy damages for still other reasons consistent with a reliance paradigm. For example, courts may wish to punish promisors for harming promisees,[92] just as courts widely recognize and grant punitive damages in tort actions to discourage wrongful conduct.[93] Courts exhibiting little sympathy for XYZ therefore may fine it $500,000 for inducing MDM to incur expenses of $1 million. On the other hand, perhaps history best explains the prominence of expectancy damages. Early promissory estoppel courts, unwilling to cut the apron strings of consideration theory, theorized that a promisee's detrimental reliance literally stopped or barred the promisor from denying that consideration supported the promise.[94] Courts therefore enforced the promise by granting expectancy damages as if it were a contract. Nevertheless, this judicial approach does not mean that reliance was unimportant. Quite the opposite, the detrimental reliance created the basis for the estoppel in the first place.

B. Promise Theorists

Problem 4: Assume as in Problem 3 that MDM produces "Why Spy?" and later begins negotiations with XYZ for the production of "Journey." Unlike Problem 3, however, MDM intended to produce the series regardless of whether XYZ commissioned it. The parties tentatively agree on a licensing fee of $750,000 per episode for twenty-two episodes of the new series. The network promises MDM $1.5 million to produce two episodes of "Journey," although the parties have signed no documents. MDM produces two episodes at a cost of about $1 million before

---

92 *Id.* at 155. Recall Coudert's remark about punishing the Uncle with a $1000 judgment. *See supra* note 15 and accompanying text.

93 *See, e.g.*, United Laboratories Inc. v. Kuyke-dall, 335 N.C. 183, 437 S.E.2d 374 (1993); Reynolds v. Pegler, 123 F. Supp. 36 (S.D.N.Y. 1954).

94 *See, e.g.*, Wheeler v. White, 398 S.W.2d 93 (Tex. 1965).

negotiations break down. MDM seeks compensation when no other network shows interest in the new series.

Promise-focused theorists of promissory estoppel would make two arguments based on Problem 4. First, MDM can recover on XYZ's promise even though MDM would have produced "Journey" anyway because XYZ made a serious business promise.· Second, to enforce XYZ's promise, a court should award MDM $1.5 million, its expectancy.

1. Promise constitutes the substantive core of promissory estoppel

Promise theorists maintain that promise constitutes the core of promissory estoppel. For example, one study concludes that courts enforce promises if "proven convincingly and . . . likely to have been serious and well considered when . . . made."[95] Reliance's diminished role, the study explains, is merely to help prove the promise was "serious and well considered."[96] Under this approach, MDM could recover in Problem 4 without proving reliance on XYZ's serious business promise. Not all promise theorists go this far, but they all proclaim promise's dominance.

Promise theorists make several supporting arguments. One approach simply categorizes promissory estoppel as a contract action,[97] which necessarily focuses on the enforcement of promises: "The subject of contract law is contracts, which are by definition promises or sets of promises the law will enforce. Promissory estoppel concerns the enforcement of a promise on the grounds of reliance."[98]

---

95 Yorio & Thel, *supra* note 11, at 113.

96 *Id.* at 163.

97 Slawson, *supra* note 17, at 208.

98 *Id.*

Individual autonomy and morality, borrowed from Charles Fried,[99] drive another school of promise theorists.[100] Recall from Chapter 1 that Fried posited that a promise creates a moral obligation because the promisor intends to invoke a social convention conferring on the promisee moral grounds "to expect the promised performance."[101] Legal recognition of moral obligations, in turn, enables people to "determine their own values."[102] Enforcing a promise under promissory estoppel reinforces the freedom of a promisor to bind herself and bolsters the promisee's moral grounds for expecting performance.[103] A promise therefore justifies a promisee's reliance and precedes it in importance.[104]

A third approach posits that courts focus on promise in commercial contexts, not because the concept of reliance is unimportant, but to encourage it. Professors Farber and Matheson maintain that the key to enforcement of a promise in promissory estoppel cases is whether a party with authority made a "credible" promise and whether the promisor will benefit "from economic activity."[105] Reminiscent of Fuller, Farber and Matheson assert that courts enforce promises involving economic activity to nurture the promisee's trust in the promisor's performance.[106] Courts therefore enforce promises "entitling" the promisee to rely without requiring proof of reliance in order to encourage it:[107] "[T]he role of reliance in establishing liability and determining damages *in individual*

---

[99] CHARLES FRIED, CONTRACT AS PROMISE (1981); *see* Chapter 1.

[100] Yorio & Thel refer to these grounds. *See* Yorio & Thel, *supra* note 11, at 166 n.363.

[101] FRIED, *supra* note 99, at 16; *see* Chapter 1.

[102] *Id.* at 20.

[103] Yorio & Thel, *supra* note 11, at 166 n.363.

[104] *See*, FRIED, *supra* note 99, at 10-11.

[105] Farber & Matheson, *supra* note 12, at 914.

[106] *Id.* at 905.

[107] *Id.* at 942.

cases is on the decline--but reliance, in the form of trust, is on the rise as the *policy* behind legal rules of promissory obligation."[108] According to Farber and Matheson, courts would therefore enforce XYZ's promise to encourage MDM's trust, regardless of whether XYZ's promise induced MDM's reliance.

Regardless of why courts *should* focus on promise, recent theorists surveying the case law on promissory estoppel report the decline of reliance in the cases. Some proclaim that "reliance is no longer the key to promissory estoppel,"[109] and that "[p]romise-making is the linchpin of liability under both traditional contract doctrine and promissory estoppel."[110] Other theorists even more boldly announce that "[i]ssues of both liability and remedy under Section 90 turn on promise, not reliance."[111] They claim that "the reported cases cannot be explained on the basis of reliance."[112]

Nevertheless, the reports of the downfall of reliance in the cases do not completely persuade. For example, promise theorists report that courts "sometimes allow recovery when the promise has neither induced the promisee to change her behavior, nor caused her to suffer detriment."[113] Moreover, courts "sometimes deny recovery when the promisee has relied to her detriment."[114] But the analyses fail to convey a sense of the frequency of decisions ignoring and requiring reliance. After all, courts "sometimes" require reliance[115] and "sometimes" find

---

108 *Id.* at 929.

109 *Id.* at 904.

110 *Id.* at 914.

111 Yorio & Thel, *supra* note 11, at 167.

112 *Id.* at 161.

113 *Id.* at 151.

114 *Id.*

115 *See, e.g.*, Hoover Community Hotel Corp. v. Thomson, 213 Cal. Rptr. 750 (Ct. App. 1985); Clinton v. Int'l Business Machs. Corp., 570 N.Y.S.2d 405 (App.Div. 1991).

promissory estoppel to apply even without a genuine promise.[116] None of the theorists attempt to prove that *most* cases abandon reliance and, in fact, some intimate that most courts at least invoke the language of reliance.[117] It is difficult to form a judgment about the substantive core of promissory estoppel without more information about what courts are doing.

Promise theorists also employ some less-than-persuasive examples to support their claim of the relative unimportance of reliance in promissory estoppel cases. For example, they concede that many "key" cases allegedly demonstrating the lack of reliance involve imperfect bargains.[118] It is neither suprising nor very significant in this context for reliance to assume a secondary role.

Consider *Vastoler v. American Can Co.*,[119] one study's primary example of the decline of reliance.[120] Based on an employer's promise of certain pension benefits, Vastoler, an employee, agreed to accept a promotion to a supervisory position, which increased Vastoler's responsibility. When the employer broke its promise to extend the benefits, Vastoler brought a claim of promissory estoppel, even though the new position provided better pay and job security. Although the trial court found that Vastoler experienced no detriment, the appellate court reversed, intimating that Vastoler may have forgone other opportunities and finding that "the human dynamics and anxieties" of a supervisory position may cause "stress and emotional trauma."[121]

Vastoler provides only limited evidence that courts do not require reliance for at least two reasons. First, although promise theorists

---

116 Becker, *supra* note 63, at 153 (discussing promises of employers in the context of "at-will" employment).

117 Yorio & Thel, *supra* note 11, at 159 (acknowledging "[t]he many cases that adduce reliance as a reason for enforcing the promise").

118 Farber & Matheson, *supra* note 12, at 913-14 n.43.

119 700 F.2d 916 (3d Cir. 1983).

120 Farber & Matheson, *supra* note 12, at 910.

121 700 F.2d at 919.

downplay the psychological harm that Vastoler experienced in his new position,[122] damage from the job pressure may have been real and significant. In short, the appellate court may have required and found a real detriment. Second, and more important, although the opinion is unclear, apparently Vastoler did not pursue the bargain theory because of a "formal flaw," perhaps the absence of a writing.[123] The court therefore may have been motivated to find for Vastoler principally because of the parties' bargain. *Vastoler* therefore does not prove that reliance is unimportant in promissory estoppel cases lacking a bargain.

An interesting study by Professors Yorio and Thel utilizes *Devecmon v. Shaw*[124] to illustrate the unimportance of reliance.[125] An uncle promised his nephew to pay for a trip to Europe, and the nephew took the trip. The court held that the parties made a bargain and enforced the uncle's promise. Suspicious of the finding that the nephew's trip constituted consideration for the uncle's promise, Yorio and Thel analyze the case on promissory estoppel grounds. They point out that the court apparently did not require the nephew to prove that he would not have gone on the trip but for his Uncle's promise.[126] But it is entirely possible, perhaps probable, that the nephew was induced by the promise.[127] After all, for many people in the United States such a promise would precondition a trip to Europe. Moreover, the court found a bargain, which entails "mutual reciprocal inducement."[128]

---

122 Farber & Matheson, *supra* note 12, at 912.

123 *See id.* at 911 n.31.

124 14 A. 464 (Md. 1888).

125 Yorio & Thel, *supra* note 11, at 155.

126 *Id.*

127 "It might very well be, and probably was the case, that the plaintiff would not have taken a trip to Europe at his own expense." 14 A. 464 (Md. 1888).

128 For a discussion of this term, see Chapter 1.

Promise theorists also invoke cases involving a promise to pay insurance premiums when the insured is unable to pay.[129] Courts have granted promissory estoppel recoveries when the defendant breaks the promise, the insurance coverage lapses, and an otherwise insured event transpires.[130] Promise theorists insist that the promise did not induce the insured to rely. The policy would have expired even without the defendant's promise because the insured could not pay. However, most of the cases do not clearly explain why the insured could not pay and whether the insured could have borrowed or raised the money if necessary.[131] A fair assumption may be that the insured would have somehow made the insurance payment but for the defendant's promise.

Some promise theorists also believe that "there is nothing special about reliance,"[132] based on their assessment of charitable subscription cases. As already noted, the *Restatement (Second)* Section 90(2) specifically exempts charitable institutions from having to prove reliance.[133] Not content with the *Restatement's* explanation for abandoning proof of reliance, namely that charities enjoy a favored position because of their importance,[134] some promise advocates argue that the charitable subscription cases help prove the relative unimportance of reliance in *other* cases.[135] This is an odd treatment of an exception to

---

[129] *See* Yorio & Thel, *supra* note 11, at 155-156.

[130] *Id.*

[131] *See, e.g.*, Spiegel v. Metropolitan Life Ins. Co., 160 N.E.2d 40 (N.Y. 1959); East Providence Credit Union v. Geremia, 239 A.2d 725 (R.I. 1968).

[132] Yorio & Thel, *supra* note 11, at 161.

[133] Comment (f) states that the "probability of reliance" is sufficient in this category of cases. RESTATEMENT (SECOND) OF CONTRACTS § 90 cmt. f (1981). According to Yorio and Thel, the cases "dispense with a requirement of inducement (not just with proof of inducement)." Yorio & Thel, *supra* note 11, at 154.

[134] Yorio & Thel, *supra* note 11, at 153. Yorio and Thel point out the equal importance of other promises that do not receive such treatment. *Id.*

[135] *Id.* ("Charitable subscriptions . . . pose a significant threat to the view that the objective of Section 90 is to protect a promisee who has suffered loss in reliance on

a rule, which is supposed to be *different* from the rule. When the charitable subscription exception does not apply, the implication should be that reliance *is* important.[136]

Some promise theorists admit that courts sometimes "adduce reliance as a reason for enforcing the promise,"[137] that courts appear to deny promissory estoppel claims because of the absence of reliance, and that courts generally "feel constrained to speak the language of reliance."[138] Moreover, some promise theorists "do not claim that all the cases can be reconciled with the conclusion that detrimental reliance is no longer the key to promissory estoppel."[139] Nevertheless, most of the promise theorists do claim that concerns other than reliance better explain most holdings.[140] Professors Yorio and Thel, for example, reason that reliance, like consideration, serves cautionary and evidentiary roles, as if that proved reliance's secondary position.[141] Yorio and Thel also speculate that courts' reference to reliance "'gild[s] the lily' by emphasizing the harm suffered by the promisee in relying on the promise."[142] But the authors do not cite any cases in which a court

---

the promise.").

136 Prior to Restatement Section 90(2), at least some cases involving promises to charities required reliance. *See* Boyer, *supra* note 17, at 471 ("[T]he charity . . . should show that the subscription induced it to change position. If no such change was caused, enforcement is properly denied.").

137 Yorio & Thel, *supra* note 11, at 159.

138 Farber & Matheson, *supra* note 12, at 904.

139 *Id.* at 914.

140 *E.g.*, Yorio & Thel, *supra* note 11, at 158. ("Although courts sometimes give absence of reliance as a reason for refusing to enforce a promise under Section 90, some other factor . . . can usually explain the outcome.").

141 "[Reliance] makes it more likely that the promisor should have expected the promise to induce that action. Substantial action by the promisee also serves an evidentiary function by increasing the likelihood that a promise was in fact made." *Id.* at 159.

142 *Id.*

expressly states that the role of reliance is merely to separate "serious from frivolous promises" or to "gild the lily."[143] Even assuming the truth of these assertions, they prove only the importance of multiple elements in promissory estoppel cases, not the unimportance of reliance.

Nonetheless, Yorio and Thel seek to close the door on the importance of reliance: "[R]eliance theory does not explain why in Section 90 cases courts insist that there be a promise. If the basis of recovery were harm caused by the defendant's conduct, it should not matter whether the conduct constituted a promise."[144] But Section 90 focuses on promise-induced reliance because other theories, such as equitable estoppel and misrepresentation, already protect injured parties from conduct and statements inducing detrimental reliance. Promissory estoppel plugs the gap in liability by creating liability for promise-induced reliance.

Yorio and Thel also point out that courts bar recovery under promissory estoppel when damages are not foreseeable by the promisor. They reason: "If reliance were the basis of Section 90, harm suffered by the promisee would mandate a remedy and foreseeability by the promisor would not matter."[145] No theory of liability is absolute, however. Foreseeability of the reliance seems a reasonable tool for distinguishing detrimental reliance that should and should not be compensated.

In sum, promise theorists' claim of the relative unimportance of reliance seems unconvincing. In fact, some theorists ultimately acknowledge the limitations of an all-or-nothing analysis of the substantive core of promissory estoppel: "[W]e are skeptical of claims that the common law can be reduced to a simple set of rules, as well as claims that the proper resolution of contracts issues can be deduced from some set of abstract principles."[146]

---

[143] *Id.* at 162.

[144] *Id.* at 161-162 (footnote omitted).

[145] *Id.* at 160.

[146] Farber & Matheson, *supra* note 12, at 946.

2. The remedy in promissory estoppel cases is expectancy damages

Some promise theorists unconditionally support the expectation measure. For example, Professor Slawson states that "[a]nalysis of the expectation measure shows it to be superior to the reliance measure in virtually every respect."[147] According to Slawson, the goals of contract remedies are deterrence and punishment of a wrong.[148] "The wrong in a contract case" (including promissory estoppel) is breaking the promise. Expectancy damages "*is* the compensation principle applied to contracts" because this measure will deter and punish.[149] Further, "[t]his application logically applies equally to all contracts, whatever their basis."[150] In Problem 4, therefore, MDM should recover $1.5 million for XYZ's broken promise. But Professor Slawson's conclusions rest on some controversial assertions. Are deterrence and punishment appropriate contract remedial goals? In Chapter 6, we will see that legal economists, for one, strongly disapprove of these goals. Even if deterrence and punishment are appropriate goals, will expectancy damages, full of limitations such as foreseeability, certainty, and causation, accomplish them? Moreover, it is not self-evident why we should treat promissory estoppel as a contract case.

Much recent work by promise theorists focuses not so much on what the appropriate remedy should be, but what it is in the courts. Writers report that courts rarely award reliance damages, but opt for expectancy damages instead: "[C]ourts routinely award expectation damages unless those damages are too speculative, indefinite, or

---

147 Slawson, *supra* note 17, at 217.

148 *Id.*

149 *Id.*

150 *Id.* "[T]he only measure of damages that is designed to compensate" for breaking a promise "is the expectation measure." *Id.* at 208.

otherwise unavailable. . . ."[151] Others are even more adamant: "[T]he remedy for [promissory estoppel] is *invariably* expectancy relief (if measurable). . . ."[152]

If true, the observation that courts award expectancy damages (thereby enforcing the promise) would be some evidence of promise's ascendancy. But some writers reporting the popularity of expectancy damages admit their findings may be misleading because of the non-promissory explanations for the frequency of these recoveries discussed earlier.[153] Undeterred, other analysts attempt to refute some of these explanations. For example, Professors Yorio and Thel dismiss the forgone opportunities explanation for the prominence of expectancy damages. They assert that courts routinely award expectancy damages in donative promise cases, even though the promisee usually has not forgone other opportunities. They therefore reason that courts probably do not base the expectancy remedy on forgone opportunities in commercial cases either.[154] On the other hand, the judicial response in gift-promise cases may not be very probative of their approach in the very different commercial-promise cases. For example, we have seen that the latter involve complex policy issues involving the relationship between promissory estoppel and defenses to bargain-theory claims.[155]

Yorio and Thel admit the difficulty-of-proof explanation for the award of expectancy damages "works reasonably well when reliance

---

151 Becker, *supra* note 63, at 135 (footnote omitted); *see also* Farber & Matheson, *supra* note 12, at 909 ("[r]ecent cases are heavily weighted towards the award of full expectation damages.").

152 Yorio & Thel, *supra* note 11, at 166 (emphasis added).

153 Farber & Matheson, *supra* note 12, at 909 & n.24 ("Depending on how the expectation and reliance interests are conceptualized, the two measures may tend to produce the same results."). For a discussion of the non-promissory explanations for expectancy damages, *see supra* notes 71-94, and accompanying text.

154 Yorio & Thel, *supra* note 11, at 133.

155 *See supra* notes 62-63, and accompanying text.

damages are difficult or impossible to calculate."[156] However, they may not appreciate how frequently this may be true. For example, the authors open their study of promissory estoppel remedies with a quote from *Tomerlin v. Canadian Indemnity Co.*,[157] a promissory estoppel case in which the court nicely set forth the choice of remedies and elected expectancy damages. The court's choice, however, turned on the impossibility of proving reliance damages, not on the basis of the dominance of the promise principle.

In *Tomerlin*, the defendant insurance company's liability policy did not cover the plaintiff for assault. When plaintiff was sued for assault, the insurance company hired a lawyer and obtained a reservation-of-rights agreement from plaintiff permitting the company to investigate without admitting liability. The lawyer falsely represented that the insurance company "would have to afford coverage" in light of another judicial decision concerning the duty to defend.[158] The lawyer later stated that the insurance company "was continuing without a reservation of rights to defend the action."[159] As a result of these representations, the plaintiff's personal attorney withdrew from the case. The insurance company denied coverage, however, after a jury verdict of $15,000 against the plaintiff in the assault case. The court held that the company's lawyer's representations that the policy covered the plaintiff estopped the company from denying liability. The court awarded expectancy damages of the full $15,000 because reliance damages "would impose upon plaintiff the impossible burden of proving, on remand, the precise extent of the loss caused by the withdrawal of his attorney."[160]

Instead of confronting the question of how often courts award expectancy damages because of the difficulty of proving reliance losses, Yorio and Thel simply discuss some cases in which they claim courts

---

156 Yorio & Thel, *supra* note 11, 134.

157 394 P.2d 571, 578 (Cal. 1964).

158 *Id.* at 573.

159 *Id.*

160 *Id.* at 578.

prefer expectancy damages even when reliance damages can be measured. In *Ricketts v. Scothorn*,[161] for example, a grandfather gave his granddaughter a $2000 promissory note and told her she could quit her $10 per week job as a bookkeeper, which she did. She returned to work about a year later, also as a bookkeeper. When her grandfather died, his administrator refused to pay the $2000, but the court enforced the note. Yorio and Thel claim that the court had "a clear choice" between awarding her lost income of about $520 before she took the new job or her expectancy, $2000 plus interest.[162] But the opinion does not indicate how much she earned at the new bookkeeping job or whether the new job, albeit in the same profession, was actually comparable to the original one. If the new job was inferior in pay or otherwise, her reliance damages may have been far in excess of $520.

Yorio and Thel also assert that courts "face a clear choice" between an expectancy remedy in the form of specific performance and reliance damages in promissory estoppel cases involving improvements to land. The authors argue that "[c]ourts routinely grant specific performance."[163] As we have seen, however, these cases often involve imperfect bargains, such as an exchange of land for services.[164] Moreover, reliance damages may be difficult to measure because of changes in lifestyle induced by the promise and the passage of time.[165]

Because some promise theorists insist that courts "invariably" award expectancy damages when measurable, the analysts must explain decisions which seem to grant reliance damages in these circumstances.[166] For example in *Goodman v. Dicker*[167] the court reversed the trial court's

---

161 77 N.W. 365 (Neb. 1898).

162 Yorio & Thel, *supra* note 11, at 134.

163 *Id.* at 135. All but one cited case, however, were decided prior to 1932, when the first Restatement formalized promissory estoppel.

164 *See, e.g.*, Wadsworth v. Hannah, 431 So. 2d 1186 (Ala. 1983).

165 *See supra* notes 76-79, and accompanying text.

166 Yorio & Thel, *supra* note 11, at 139-151.

167 169 F.2d 684 (D.C. Cir. 1948).

award of expectancy damages and granted reliance damages. Yorio and Thel, however, assert that the case involved a misrepresentation, not a promise. They reason that the defendants, distributors of Emerson Radio products who incorrectly told the plaintiffs that they would be granted a dealership, were not agents of Emerson. The plaintiffs therefore could not have reasonably believed that the defendant distributors promised a dealership.[168] Yorio and Thel contrast *Chrysler. Corp. v. Quimby*,[169] where the court granted expectancy damages. They argue that Chrysler's own executives' misrepresentations that Quimby would get a controlling interest in a dealership constituted a promise.[170] Yorio and Thel concede, however, that the *Goodman* court conceptualizes the representations of the distributors as a promise. Moreover, the *Goodman* court's recitation of the facts obscures the relationship of the distributors and dealer and what the plaintiffs knew about the relationship. Perhaps plaintiffs could reasonably have believed that the distributors had authority to bind Emerson and had promised a dealership.

Yorio and Thel also distinguish *Wheeler v. White*.[171] Recall that the court limited Wheeler to reliance damages after he demolished his buildings in reliance on White's promise to procure or grant Wheeler a loan. White's promise was in an agreement unenforceable because the parties failed to specify the interest rate. The court denied lost profits to Wheeler "even if . . . provable with certainty."[172] Despite the court's rather direct language, Yorio and Thel claim the case is an "ambiguous precedent."[173] They speculate that had Wheeler been able to secure an alternative loan, the court probably "would have granted expectation damages under the promissory estoppel count" measured by the difference

---

[168] Yorio & Thel, *supra* note 11, at 140.

[169] 144 A.2d 123 (Del. 1958).

[170] Yorio & Thel, *supra* note 11, at 141-142.

[171] 398 S.W.2d 93 (Tex. 1965).

[172] 398 S.W.2d 03 (Tex. 1965).

[173] Yorio & Thel, *supra* note 11, at 148.

in interest rates.[174] If the parties had specified the interest rate in the agreement so that the court could have ascertained the difference in interest rates, however, the court would have enforced the agreement on contract grounds and expectation damages would have been appropriate. Moreover, the difference in the interest rates is also a fair measure of Wheeler's reliance damages. Assuming that Wheeler would have profited by completing his project, he could have reasonably minimized his reliance damages by securing the substitute higher-interest-rate loan and completing the project. The recoverable reliance damages caused by White's broken promise, in other words, would have been only the difference in the interest rates.[175]

Conclusion

Analysts of promissory estoppel debate the theory's conceptual core. Some theorists champion the reliance interest; others claim that promissory estoppel focuses on promise. Each school contributes by emphasizing the importance of one or the other element. The somewhat stubborn insistence of some writers that everything turns on either reliance or promise,[176] however, diminishes the force of their arguments. The reality of remedial fog and judicial attention to both promise *and*

---

[174] *Id.*

[175] Yorio and Thel also distinguish Hoffman v. Red Owl Stores, 133 N.W.2d 267 (Wis. 1965). They concede that the court held the agent's statements that Hoffman would get a Red Owl store "sufficiently definite to constitute a Section 90 promise." Yorio & Thel, *supra* note 11, at 143. The authors nevertheless claim the opinion "is hardly an endorsement of reliance as the measure of recovery in Section 90 cases," *id.*, in part because Hoffman did not raise on appeal the issue of whether he could recover expectation damages. Yorio and Thel distinguish several other cases granting reliance damages on the same ground. *Id.* at 145, 149. The authors also assert that expectancy damages would be too difficult to determine in *Hoffman*. *Id.* at 143.

[176] *See, e.g.*, Yorio & Thel, *supra* note 11, at 161 ("[T]here is nothing special about reliance."). Yorio and Thel do state that "reliance plays important roles even under a promissory theory of the section." *Id.* at 159. But they consistently stress that promise is the key; reliance plays a secondary role at best.

reliance because of the normative significance of both principles leaves little reason to promote one and demote the other.[177]

As with the general debate between promise theorists and interventionists,[178] excessive categorization causes some of the confusion. The *Restatement (Second)* treats promissory estoppel as a contract claim; some analysts appear to believe a focus on promise and an expectancy measure of damages automatically follows. Other theorists claim that promissory estoppel is at heart a tort theory and urge the courts to award reliance damages.[179] The tort-contract debate arises in many contexts, rarely adds conceptual clarity, and often engenders criticism.[180] The debate is symptomatic of the unwillingness to admit that the law of promises entails multiple norms and goals and therefore reflects both principles of fairness and autonomy. Theorists should accept the reality that the strength of a promissory estoppel claim and the respective roles of promise and reliance depend heavily on the context and that the cases call for diverse remedial responses.[181] As to the latter, analysts should accept the *Restatement (Second)'s* wisdom that "the same factors which bear on whether any relief should be granted also bear on the character and extent of the remedy."[182]

Despite promissory estoppel's complexity and contextuality, the discussion above suggests certain appropriate judicial approaches and portends future directions. Courts should evaluate defenses to bargained-for contracts more fully, for example, before they subvert them by granting expectancy damages under promissory estoppel. A court may conclude that a defense has outlived its usefulness and therefore decide the case on bargain grounds. Alternatively, a court may validate a

---

177 The second *Restatement's* call for remedial flexibility in Section 90 appropriately reflects this view. *See supra* notes 18-20, and accompanying text.

178 *See* Chapter 1.

179 *See* section A.

180 *See* Chapter 1.

181 SUMMERS & HILLMAN, *supra* note 2, at 294-304.

182 RESTATEMENT (SECOND) OF CONTRACTS § 90 cmt. d (1981).

contract defense, but conclude that the promisee's reliance also merits some relief.[183] If the court finds merit in a contract defense and refuses to enforce the bargain, however, it should not then subvert the defense by awarding expectancy damages under promissory estoppel.[184]

Courts should typically grant reliance damages, not only when a contract defense has merit, but also when a promisor breaks a promise made in the context of pre-contract bargaining. In such situations, the court cannot be certain that the parties would have reached an agreement.[185] In Problem 4, for example, MDM and XYZ may never have reached a final agreement on "Journey," even if both parties negotiated in good faith. Notwithstanding the focus on reliance damages in these contexts, courts should be mindful of the possibility that a promise induced a promisee to forgo other valuable opportunities that may closely approximate a promisee's lost expectancy.

Courts should also consider a promisor's good faith, for example, by taking into account the reasons for the broken promise. A court, with some justification, may want to punish a bad faith promisor by awarding expectation damages.[186] Conversely, if a promisor acted in good faith and expectancy damages vastly exceed reliance damages, a court may choose the latter.[187]

---

183 For example, a court may hold that a promisee's reliance on an indefinite contract is reasonable in light of a trade custom.

184 *See, e.g.*, Elvin Assocs. v. Franklin, 735 F. Supp. 1177 (S.D.N.Y. 1990), where the court dismissed a contract claim because the parties did not intend to be bound, but then ordered a trial to determine damages on the basis of promissory estoppel. If the plaintiff ultimately recovers expectancy damages, the court's initial determination of the parties' intentions is irrelevant.

185 *See* FARNSWORTH, *supra* note 13, § 3.26, at 191-92. Farnsworth concludes that the substantive basis for liability in a case such as *Hoffman v. Red Owl Stores* is Red Owl's bad faith. Even if Red Owl had bargained in good faith, however, the parties may not have successfully reached an agreement. Therefore, the expectancy remedy would overcompensate.

186 *See id.* at 189-190; *see also* RESTATEMENT (SECOND) OF CONTRACTS § 90 illus. 9 (1981) (liability for deliberate misrepresentation).

187 FARNSWORTH, *supra* note 13, §3.26, at 100-101.

One final thought: As with charitable subscriptions and marriage settlements, courts may forge additional exceptions to the reliance requirement based on strong policy goals.[188] This would not mean that reliance is unimportant in promissory estoppel cases generally. It would suggest only that reliance theory creates a flexible, evolving, context-dependent obligation.

---

[188] For example, *see* the discussion of plant closings in Chapter 5.

CHAPTER 3

THEORIES OF CONTRACTARIANS AND THEIR CRITICS: MARRIAGES AND CORPORATIONS

Legal scholars increasingly utilize contract "paradigms" or models to analyze diverse relations such as marriages, corporations, creditors and debtors, and private associations.[1] For example, many marriage theorists assert that distinct social norms no longer govern the conduct of marriage.[2] Mandatory state laws regulating the family unit, grounded on general societal norms, are therefore antiquated. The obsolescence of these norms requires a new theoretical structure to govern marriage.[3] Some marriage theorists have set forth a contractarian model to accommodate the idiosyncratic norms of individual marriages. The model recognizes and enforces private agreements made between spouses during marriage, governing marriage support, dispute resolution, lifestyles, or even marriage duration.[4] The model offers a rationale for

---

1 On marriages and corporations, *see* Part II of this chapter. On creditors and debtors, see Thomas Jackson, *Bankruptcy, Non-Bankruptcy Entitlements, and the Creditors' Bargain*, 91 YALE L. J. 857, 860 (1982). On private associations, *see* Gregory Alexander, *Dilemmas of Group Autonomy: Residential Associations and Community*, 75 CORNELL L. REV. 1, 34-39 (1989) (debunking the contractarian view); Note, *Judicial Intervention in the Conduct of Private Associations: Bases for the Emerging Trend of Judicial Activism*, 4 N.Y.U. REV. L. & SOC. CHANGE 61, 64 (1974). Political social contract theory is a broader example of the use of contract paradigms. *See* Elizabeth S. Anderson, *Women and Contracts: No New Deal* (Book Review), 88 MICH. L. REV. 1792, 1794 (1990) (reviewing CAROLE PATEMAN, THE SEXUAL CONTRACT (1988)).

2 *See generally* Marjorie M. Shultz, *Contractual Ordering of Marriage: A New Model for State Policy*, 70 CALIF. L. REV. 204 (1982).

3 *Id.* at 207-08.

4 *Id.* at 219-224.

protecting the economic and social interests of the disfavored spouse under existing state law, typically the wife.[5]

Skeptics of marriage contractualism worry that contractarians too easily dismiss marriage characteristics such as love, loyalty, and trust and doubt that these "can coexist with planning and choice."[6] Doubters also believe that marriage contractarians minimize the problems of overreaching and incomplete planning that would require courts to invoke social norms independent of the parties' agreement to police the quality of the bargaining and to fill gaps. In the marriage context, skeptics insist, such context-dependent, interventionist norms necessarily draw on society's view of suitable marital behavior.[7] Most marriage contractarians are not oblivious to these counterarguments and many concede the need for some regulation. With varying degrees of enthusiasm, they simply advocate greater freedom for marriage partners to contract than currently exists.

Some analysts of corporations also utilize a contractarian model to justify the self-governance of parties comprising corporations. Descriptively, these contractarians view the firm as a "nexus for a set of

---

5 *See, e.g.*, LENORE J. WEITZMAN, THE MARRIAGE CONTRACT 230 (1981) ("Modern-day feminists have . . . embraced the marriage contract as a means of establishing an egalitarian relationship in defiance of the law's sex-based inequalities."); Kris Jeter & Marvin B. Sussman, *Each Couple Should Develop a Marriage Contract Suitable to Themselves*, *in* CURRENT CONTROVERSIES IN MARRIAGE AND FAMILY 283, 283 (Harold Feldman & Margaret Feldman, eds., 1985) ("Today the personal marriage contract bears the potential for couples to form equitable dyadic relationships . . . ."); Shultz, *supra* note 2, at 271. *See also id.* at 316-17 (wife's claim for support to continue her education); Frances E. Olsen, *The Family and the Market: A Study of Ideology and Legal Reform*, 96 HARV. L. REV. 1497, 1504-07 (1983); Marsha Garrison, *Marriage: The Status of Contract,* 131 U. PA. L. REV. 1039, 1043-44 (1983) (reviewing LENORE J. WEITZMAN, THE MARRIAGE CONTRACT (1981)) ("traditional marriage contract . . . perpetuates the subjugation of women," interpreting L. Weitzman).

6 Shultz, *supra* note 2, at 210 (discussing skeptics). *See also* Carol Weisbrod, *The Way We Live Now: A Discussion of Contracts and Domestic Arrangements*, 1994 UTAH L. REV. 777, 779 (discussing skeptics).

7 Ira M. Ellman, *The Theory of Alimony*, 77 CAL.. L. REV. 1, 16-23 (1989).

contracting relations among individual factors of production,"[8] such as shareholders, managers, employees, and creditors. Further, because corporations consist of a series of voluntary exchanges between these rational, self-concerned parties,[9] who have greater incentives than outsiders to create efficient governing rules, contractarians generally reject mandatory, non-consensual, corporate law.[10] Instead, the law should facilitate corporate contracts when the parties leave gaps by supplying the terms the parties would have drafted.[11] Unlike marriage contractualism's goal of leveling the playing field among the parties, the contractarian model of corporations justifies managerial autonomy and power, in the name of maximizing wealth.[12]

As with marriage contractualism, some analysts criticize corporate contractualism. They assert that these contractarians employ problematic empirical descriptions and incomplete contract models involving rather wistful views of the dynamics of bargaining and planning, or of the power

---

8 William W. Bratton, Jr., *The "Nexus of Contracts" Corporation: A Critical Appraisal*, 74 CORNELL L. REV. 407, 409 (1989) (describing contractualism) [hereinafter Bratton, *Nexus of Contracts*].

9 *Id.* at 417. *See also* Frank H. Easterbrook & Daniel R. Fischel, *The Corporate Contract*, 89 COLUM. L. REV. 1416, 1418 (1989) ("[T]he corporate structure is a set of contracts through which managers and certain other participants exercise a great deal of discretion that is 'reviewed' by interactions with other self-interested actors."). For Easterbrook and Fischel's latest view, *see* FRANK H. EASTERBROOK & DANIEL R. FISCHEL, THE ECONOMIC STRUCTURE OF CORPORATE LAW (1991) [hereinafter EASTERBROOK & FISCHEL, ECONOMIC STRUCTURE].

10 *See infra* notes 94-115, and accompanying text.

11 *See, e.g.*, Henry M. Butler, *The Contractual Theory of the Corporation*, 11 GEO. MASON U. L. REV., Summer 1989, at 99, 100.

12 Professor Brudney posits that contractualism "serves the ideological function of legitimating substantially unaccountable managerial discretion to determine corporate activities and to serve itself at the expense of investors." Victor Brudney, *Corporate Governance, Agency Costs, and the Rhetoric of Contract*, 85 COLUM. L. REV. 1403, 1404 (1985). *See also infra* note 73, and accompanying text.

of market or other forces as substitutes for bargaining and planning.[13] Critics doubt that contracting accurately describes existing relations among parties to corporations. They also question the contractarians' reliance on market forces to police managers and believe that contractarians too easily discount the problems of inadequate information and other market failures.[14]

In this chapter, we focus on marriages and corporations to illustrate the nature and broad range of contractarian theory. The discussion reinforces Chapter 1's thesis that consensual and interventionist principles coexist within contract law's intricate structure. Although neither contractarians of marriages and corporations nor their critics generally advocate completely polar views of appropriate governance structures,[15] many legal scholars of these relations spill vast quantities of ink urging greater freedom or regulation without any

---

13 *See* John C. Coffee, *No Exit?: Opting Out, The Contractual Theory of the Corporation, and the Special Case of Remedies*, 53 BROOK. L. REV. 919, 934 (1988) (discussing the view of interventionists) [hereinafter Coffee, *No Exit*].

14 *Id.* at 934 (contractarians "consider[ ] the market and its pricing mechanism as an adequate surrogate for individual bargaining"); Barry D. Baysinger & Henry N. Butler, *The Role of Corporate Law in the Theory of the Firm*, 28 J. L. & ECON. 179, 179-80 (1985) [hereinafter Baysinger & Butler, *Theory of the Firm*].

15 For example, one marriage contractarian desires a "comparatively greater emphasis on private control." Shultz, *supra* note 2, at 305. Corporation contractarians simply remind that "the corporation is a voluntary adventure." Easterbrook & Fischel, *supra* note 9, at 1426. Professor Macey points out that corporate law scholars do not completely dismiss mandatory terms. Jonathan R. Macey, *Courts and Corporations: A Comment on Coffee*, 89 COLUM. L. REV. 1692, 1692 n.1 ((1989). Another contractarian concedes that courts should continue to police corporate contracts for fraud, duress or "some other common-law defense." Fred S. McChesney, *Economics, Law and Science in the Corporate Field: A Critique of Eisenberg*, 89 COLUM. L. REV. 1530, 1536 (1989) [hereinafter McChesney, *Economics*].

resolution in sight.[16] Undaunted, I add my own framework to the debate in the conclusion.

Although the contractarians of marriages and corporations exhibit common tendencies, theorists utilize contract models to advance diverse goals. As noted, marriage and corporation contractarians support respectively, either diminishing or legitimizing one party's power over the other. Another purpose of this chapter is to reflect upon this dichotomy. I show that a nineteenth-century equality paradigm best captures marriage contractualism, whereas a late twentieth-century efficiency model supplies the appropriate metaphor for corporate contractualism.

A. Marriages[17]

Problem 5: Michele Green, an actress appearing in "Why Spy?," and Conrad Argosy, a stage hand preparing to enter law school, fall in love and decide to marry. Green, busy with her career, wants Argosy to be responsible for most of the household obligations and wants to enter a "five-year trial marriage." Argosy seeks Green's promise to support him through law school. They both desire to enter an enforceable contract on these matters.

---

16 Melvin A. Eisenberg, *Contractarianism Without Contracts: A Response to Professor McChesney*, 90 COLUM. L. REV. 1321 (1990) [hereinafter Eisenberg, *Response*]; Fred S. McChesney, *Contractarianism Without Contracts? Yet Another Critique of Eisenberg*, 90 COLUM. L. REV. 1332 (1990) [hereinafter McChesney, *Another Critique*]; Shultz, *supra* note 2; Ellman, *supra* note 7. *See also* MICHAEL TREBILCOCK, THE LIMITS OF FREEDOM OF CONTRACT 23-57 (1993).

17 As with many papers on marriage contracting, I focus on relations between husband and wife and not on the legal ramifications of the interests of children. *See, e.g.*, Ellman, *supra* note 7; Shultz, *supra* note 2. The analysis obviously becomes more complicated when the interests of children are considered. For example, permitting the parties to set their own marriage duration will affect children negatively. Research shows, for example, that fewer children from two-parent families are poor. Whitmire, *Fixing the American Family*, ITHACA JOURNAL, June 22, 1991, at 14B, col. 2.

Traditionally, marriage constitutes a legal status.[18] On the basis of public policy, the state supplies the legal terms that govern a marriage, such as the bases for divorce and the prohibition of remuneration for services within a marriage.[19] Parties who wish to marry have no choice but to accept this "prepackaged relationship."[20] Green and Argosy's plans to contract in Problem 5 would likely be thwarted therefore under traditional marriage law.

Traditionalists reason that the enforcement of private marital agreements would adversely impinge on spousal harmony, trust, and cooperation,[21] thereby destabilizing the core social obligation of our society.[22] In addition, litigation would overburden courts,[23] which are already incompetent to fashion remedies for broken marital agreements anyway.[24] While the marriage-as-status view has softened in the late

---

18 For a history of marriage contracts, *see* Jeter & Sussman, *supra* note 5, at 284-86.

19 Shultz, *supra* note 2, at 230-31.

20 *Id.* at 232. For example, unlike other contracting parties, marriage partners cannot adjust the terms of their ongoing marriage. *See* Jeter & Sussman, *supra* note 5 at 285, quoting Maynard v. Hill, 125 U.S. 190 (1888). *See also* Ellman, *supra* note 7, at 13. Under traditional marital arrangements the husband is head of the household and responsible for support, and the wife is in charge of "domestic services" and child care. Garrison, *supra* note 5, at 1041-43.

21 *See* Shultz, *supra* note 2, at 235. *See also* WEITZMAN, *supra* note 5, at 239.

22 WEITZMAN, *supra* note 5, at 231. For example, contracting partners would likely make unwise arrangements and create legal obligations unintentionally, which would cause dissatisfaction and disharmony. *Id.* at 241. For a discussion of the kinds of situations in which contract law should leave enforcement to nonlegal sanctions, *see* David Charny, *Nonlegal Sanctions in Commercial Relationships*, 104 HARV. L. REV. 373 (1990).

23 *See, e.g.*, Balfour v. Balfour, [1919], 2 K.B. 571, 579.

24 *Id.*; Schultz, *supra* note 2, at 235.

twentieth century,[25] public regulation remains the "primary source of marital obligation."[26]

Despite this heritage, marriage contractarians generally prefer private ordering to the imposition of public norms governing decisions about lifestyles.[27] They make what are essentially empirical claims concerning the evolving structure and mores of marriage to support a move to contractualism.[28] They observe the weakening of religious, communal, familial, and economic marriage standards,[29] as marriage partners increasingly enter arrangements based on personal needs.[30] For

---

25 June Carbone, *Economics, Feminism, and the Reinvention of Alimony: A Reply to Ira Ellman*, 43 VAND. L. REV. 1463, 1469 (1990). *See also* Shultz, *supra* note 2, at 231-32; 280-82. Several states permit spouses to make enforceable agreements concerning property rights and post-separation support. *Id. See, e.g.*, N.M. STAT. ANN. § 40-2-8 (1978) ("A husband and wife cannot by any contract with each other alter their legal relations, except of their property, and except that they may agree in writing, to an immediate separation, and may make provisions for the support of either of them and of their children during their separation."); CAL. CIV. CODE § 4802 (West 1983); NEV. REV. STAT. § 123.080 (1986).

26 Carbone, *supra* note 25, at 1469. For example, although some states permit spouses to negotiate binding agreements concerning the terms of their separation, typically the laws require the separation to be imminent. *See* OHIO REV. CODE ANN. § 3103.06 (Anderson 1989); OKLA. STAT. ANN. tit. 43, § 205 (West 1990); S.D. CODIFIED LAWS ANN. § 25-2-13 (1984). See also WEITZMAN, *supra* note 5, at 342 ("An exception . . . has allowed couples to contract *after* they have decided to separate or divorce . . . . The general rule, however, has been that antenuptial agreements . . . or postnuptial contracts . . . cannot include provisions for divorce.").

27 Shultz, *supra* note 2, at 258. *See also* Carol Rose, Bargaining and Gender, 18 *Harv. J. L.& Pub. Policy* 547, 561 (1995) ("women benefit greatly from their ability to bargain"); Weisbrod, *supra* note 6, at 783 ("everything is discussable in contract terms").

28 Schultz, *supra* note 2, at 249-53.

29 *Id.* at 251. "Family status is no longer the central prestige-conferring mechanism in an age of mobility and urban anonymity." WEITZMAN, *supra* note 5, at 136.

30 *See, e.g.,* Weisbrod, *supra* note 6, at 810. The increasing frequency of divorce with society's approbation underscores evolving marriage mores: "From being a scandalous and sinful rarity, virtually impossible for most people to achieve,

example, as with Green and Argosy, both parties may work, and a spouse's gender less frequently determines who performs domestic chores.[31] In addition, each party may arrange his or her own financial matters.[32]

The possibility of fewer viable generalizations about society's view of marriage and its increasing tolerance of "'pluralism in family forms'"[33] demands, according to the contractarians, the construction of personalized law to facilitate and legitimize individual arrangements.[34] The traditional rigid marriage paradigm therefore must accede to a more flexible contractarian view that allows for diversity[35] and that

---

divorce has become a morally neutral commonplace, available to all." Neil McKendrick, Book Review, N.Y. TIMES, Nov. 4, 1990 § VII (Book Review), at 12, col. 1 (reviewing LAWRENCE STONE, ROAD TO DIVORCE (1990)).

31 Garrison, *supra* note 5, at 1043.

32 Professor Garrison reports the decline of the "nuclear family . . . as a central unit of social and economic organization." *Id.* at 1049. She reports a ten to twenty percent drop in households headed by a husband and wife in the last thirty years (75% to possibly 55%) and a doubling in the number of female heads of households from 1960 to 1980. *Id.* at 1049 n.49, relying on SARA LEVITAN & RICHAD S. BELOUS, WHAT'S HAPPENING TO THE AMERICAN FAMILY? 127 (1981) and census statistics. According to Garrison, statistics support the claim that "individual mobility and satisfaction have replaced family stability as a dominant social ethic." *Id.* at 1056.

33 Shultz, *supra* note 2, at 247 (quoting Sussman, *Family Systems in the 1970's: Analysis, Policies and Programs*, 396 ANNALS 40, 42 (1971)).

34 *Id.* at 314-15; Weisbrod, *supra* note 6, at 815. "[T]he traditional marriage contract is now at odds with social reality." Garrison, *supra* note 5, at 1043.

The message of marriage contractarians includes a prescriptive agenda: "[A] decision to support private decisionmaking might lead the state to encourage the making of such contracts rather than just to tolerate them." Shultz, *supra* note 2, at 281.

35 Shultz, *supra* note 2, at 248. *See also id.* at 274: "If the state no longer asserts that it is in a better position than the spouses to define the characteristics that mark the end of a marriage, then the state can hardly assert that it can best define the characteristics of an existing marriage."

accommodates individual "interests, injuries, and remedies."[36] The law should therefore validate agreements between spouses,[37] such as for support,[38] for dispute resolution, for nontraditional lifestyles, and even for Green and Argosy's particular marriage duration.[39]

By exhorting the privatization of marriage to enable partners to achieve personal fulfillment, marriage contractualism parallels the nineteenth-century move from status and hierarchy to contractual freedom and equality.[40] As mentioned in Chapter 1, optimism about the potential of individuals to understand and accommodate their own interests and a belief in their right to pursue and accomplish their own goals characterized nineteenth-century contractual freedom. Freedom of contract, it was thought, would free people socially and economically.[41] Similarly, a faith in individual expression, fair bargaining, and effective planning characterize marriage contractarians, who posit that contractualism will diminish society's sex-based inequities.[42]

---

36 *Id.* at 280. For a discussion of those areas of marriage that are traditionally regulated, *see id.* at 224-40. "[C]ourts have refused to enforce such agreements between spouses as: payment by one spouse to another for domestic, child care, or other services in the home; planned termination of the marriage after a given period of time; alteration of statutory duties of support; and provision in advance for the eventuality of divorce." *Id.* at 231.

37 *Id.* at 331.

38 WEITZMAN, *supra* note 5, at 339-41.

39 *Id.* at 284, 223, 260-61. Professor Weitzman also offers examples involving agreements as to the frequency of entertaining, attending the ballet, going on vacation, and responsibility for birth control. *Id.* at 298, 304. A few states already enforce antenuptial agreements dealing with post-divorce financial issues. *See, e.g.*, Posner v. Posner, 233 So.2d 381 (Fla. 1970), *rev'd* on other grounds, 257 So.2d 530 (Fla. 1972).

40 *See* Chapter 1.

41 *See id.*

42 *See, e.g.*, WEITZMAN, *supra* note 5, at 230 ("Modern-day feminists have . . . embraced the marriage contract as a means of establishing an egalitarian relationship in defiance of the law's sex-based inequalities."); Shultz, *supra* note 2,

Marriage contractarians are nevertheless not oblivious to the distinctions between traditional contracting and the marriage model. They generally recognize that the "archetypical arena of private contract"[43] is the commercial deal between businesses of equal bargaining power. Marriage contractarians nonetheless deny the depth of the chasm separating marriage and commercial contracting.[44] For example, although they acknowledge the potential for bargaining power disparities in marriage, marriage contractarians rely on mutual love and admiration to level the playing field[45] and find an analogy in the "solidarity norms" that support business contracts.[46] They therefore assert the feasibility of fair bargaining in marriage.[47]

Marriage contractarians also concede that marriage entails intimacy, which, in turn, involves emotions, irrationality,[48] and

---

at 271. *See also id.* at 316-317 (wife's claim for support to continue her education); Olsen, *supra* note 5, at 1504-07; Garrison, *supra* note 5, at 1043-44 ("traditional marriage contract . . . perpetuates the subjugation of women"); TREBILCOCK, *supra* note 16, at 57.

43 Schultz, *supra* note 2, at 216.

44 "Certainly differences exist between marriage and primarily economic realms, but they are matters of degree and emphasis, not of qualitative dichotomy." *Id.* at 262. "[B]oth marriage partnerships and business partnerships combine emotional and practical elements, although certainly in different proportions. Neither is likely to flourish without some attention to both elements." WEITZMAN, *supra* note 5, at 240.

45 *See id.* at 242: "The assertion that equalization is more likely than exploitation rests on the assumption that even though men have more power they nevertheless share an egalitarian ideology and will not think it 'fair' or 'just' to try to impose an exploitative contract on the women they love."

46 *Id.* at 240. The term "solidarity norms" derives from Ian Macneil, *Economic Analysis of Contractual Relations: Its Shortfalls and The Need for a "Pick Classificatory Apparatus*," 75 NW. U. L. REV. 1018 (1981).

47 Shultz, *supra* note 2, at 210.

48 *Id.* at 254.

spontaneity,[49] unlike the self-interested and deliberate planning of commercial contracting.[50] Marriage contractarians insist, however, that "intimate interaction can be predicted and explained by concepts such as reciprocity, cost/benefit analysis, outcome maximization, and interpersonal equity."[51] In addition, these marriage theorists point out that commercial arrangements also often involve complex relations, in which norms such as cooperation, reciprocity, and solidarity govern the parties' inevitably incomplete long-term agreements.[52]

The contractarian view of marriage obviously raises issues requiring additional empirical investigation, such as the frequency of nontraditional marriage and the nature of existing societal marital mores. Today's marital values are undoubtedly in flux,[53] but the extent and nature of change requires more study.[54]

---

49 *Id.* at 242.

50 *Id.* For a recent discussion of the value of intimacy in family relations, *see* MILTON C. REGAN, JR., FAMILY LAW AND THE PURSUIT OF INTIMACY (1993).

51 Schultz, *supra* note 2, at 256. Further, "intimate behavior involves reciprocity and processes analogous to those for assessing personal gain and loss in economic exchange. . . . [S]uch concepts and processes can contribute to both its understanding and its effective functioning." *Id.* at 257. *See also* Weisbrod, *supra* note 6, at 797 ("a focus on the emotional . . . does not tell the whole story").

52 Schultz, *supra* note 2, at 301-03. *See* Chapter 7 for a discussion of relational contracting.

53 Marriage mores are evolving as women pursue their education, enter the work force in large numbers, and postpone marriage. LEVITAN & BELOUS, *supra* note 32, at 23. But postponement does not reflect marriage's rejection. *Id.* at 24. Nor does the vast increase in the numbers of divorces, separations, and families headed by a single female, portend the demise of marriage norms. Two thirds of first marriages entered as of 1981, for example, were forecast to avoid divorce. *Id.* at 30.

54 Marriages are undoubtedly less traditional as we approach the next century, but perhaps they are not radically different: "Today's family . . . is still the center of affectional and emotional life. Indeed, its role as the major source of psychological and emotional support for its members has, if anything, greatly increased." WEITZMAN, *supra* note 5, at 136. "In general, it appears that a variety of family structures prevails at any one time. The idea that mobility is a modern phenomenon

Marriage contractualism also requires additional evaluation of the viability of contracting between intimate partners and its policy implications. For example, do most partners really want to contract in the first place or will they ignore the institution despite its increased availability?[55] Even if marriage partners increasingly contract, what are the psychological and other effects on solidarity and communication?[56]

---

has . . . proved wrong; in preindustrial Europe, it turns out, people moved around from place to place much more than had been believed. Further, generational conflicts, sexual behavior outside prescribed channels, and women's resistance to their traditional roles are not modern innovations." ANTONE S. SKOLNICK, THE INTIMATE ENVIRONMENT 72 (2d ed. 1978). *See also* Inga Markovits, *Family Traits* (Book Review of MARY A. GLENDON, THE TRANSFORMATION OF FAMILY LAW), 88 MICH. L. REV. 1734, (1990) ("Make any assertion about the state of the modern family, and there is a good chance that its opposite will be just as plausible."); LEVITAN & BELOUS, *supra* note 32, at 12: ("The shift in basic values has not been as widespread as anecdotal stories or reports in the media would seem to indicate."); MARY J. BANE, HERE TO STAY: AMERICAN FAMILIES IN THE TWENTIETH CENTURY 70 (1976) ("[M]any of the arguments made by advocates of new family policies are based on incomplete or inaccurate information."); *id.* at 35 ("Taken as a whole, the data on marriage and divorce suggest that the kind of marriage that Americans have always known is still a pervasive and enduring institution."); Carbone, *supra* note 25, at 1465 ("[M]en have assumed only a slightly greater share of domestic responsibilities....").

Interestingly, the explosion in the English divorce rate since 1960 has not changed the length of the traditional marriage, it has merely substituted for mortality as a marriage terminator. McKendrick, *supra* note 30, at 12. "The duration of marriage is remarkable more for its stability than its change in 20th-century England . . . ." *Id.* Another surprise: marriages in England after the parties have lived together end in quick divorce more often than marriages with more traditional courtships. *Id.*

55 Professor Macaulay's study suggests that business people often ignore contract. *See* Stewart Macaulay, *Non-Contractual Relations in Business: A Preliminary Study*, 28 AM. SOC. REV. 55 (1963). Marriage partners may often act like business people who choose to avoid issues that might upset their deal.

56 *See generally* MILTON C. REGAN, JR., FAMILY LAW AND THE PURSUIT OF INTIMACY (1993). Even if parties made marriage contracts, they may not promote more harmonious relations during the marriage. Suppose Green and Argosy marry and Argosy seeks to "enforce" through legal dispute resolution Green's promise to support him while he attends law school. Marriage contractarians assert that this alternative might save the marriage, whereas today the parties will resent each other

Will contracting "[erode] the spirit of romance" and trust[57] and create "anxiety and insecurity,"[58] or will it foster open communication of goals and desires that will improve domestic harmony[59] and thereby decrease the amount of intrafamily quarrels?[60]

Even assuming marital norms no longer support traditional marriage law and that marriage contracting generally is feasible, some marriage theorists doubt that a contractual perspective will improve marriage law. First, critics believe that marriage contractarians' reliance

---

and perhaps divorce. Shultz, *supra* note 2, at 326-27. But in the commercial realm, business people rarely sue each other, preferring to maintain good will and to work out their problems. Macaulay, *supra* note 55. As with business people, Argosy and Green would probably end up resenting each other if a court or other tribunal awarded Argosy damages or specific performance. Argosy would resent the need to vindicate his rights through formal proceedings. Green would dislike being sued and losing. *But see* WEITZMAN, *supra* note 5, at 239-46 (contracting will not increase negative feelings).

57 WEITZMAN, *supra* note 5, at 239.

58 *Id.*

59 "The contracting process . . . helps the parties articulate and clarify their goals and expectations. It stimulates straightforward, open communication . . . ." *Id.* at 232. *See also id.* at 247-48.

Marriage contractarians invoke a commercial contract paradigm: Contract bargaining and planning in the business context facilitate discussions, clarify expectations, and help avoid disputes and conflicts. Borrowing this model, marriage theorists insist that planning and bargaining in marriage may increase communication and help avoid contract breakdown: "Contracts facilitate open and honest communication, and help . . . clarify . . . expectations. . . . In addition, a contract can help a couple to identify and resolve potential conflicts in advance . . . . Finally, contracts increase predictability and security." *Id.* at 228. *See also id.* at 239.

Garrison reports "strong evidence" to support Weitzman's claims. The Conciliation Court of Los Angeles County discussed by Weitzman, *id.* at 235-36, counsels married couples to resolve disagreements by helping the parties negotiate detailed agreements. 75% of such couples were still married a year later. Garrison, *supra* note 5, at 1051. Agreements made after disputes, of course, serve a different purpose than those made when the parties' relations are harmonious.

60 WEITZMAN, *supra* note 5, at 240.

on "solidarity norms" too easily dismisses the problem of unequal bargaining power in marriage.[61] According to Professor Olsen, for example, "the position of women in society may make [contract] rights meaningless."[62] Remaining social inequities severely test the thesis of fair bargaining and ultimately require a more paternalistic approach.[63]

Green and Argosy may be exceptional in Problem 5, for example. Despite positive changes in women's potential to establish successful vocations, the career environment remains much more favorable to men.[64] In addition, marriage prospects diminish more quickly for women as time passes because women outlive men.[65] Accordingly, women may still feel more pressure than men to marry.[66] Moreover, married career women

---

61 Anderson, *supra* note 1, at 1792: "[C]ontracts do not enable men and women to enter into cooperative relations on terms of equality. Rather, their function is to legitimate patriarchal and other forms of domination under the guise of equality." (discussing Pateman's thesis). *See also id.* at 1801: "Expanding the domain of fully contractual relations is not a useful tool for feminists because contracts legitimate the domination of women."

62 Olsen, *supra* note 5, at 1537. *See also* Gail Frommer Brod, *Premarital Agreements and Gender Justice*, 6 YALE J. LAW & FEMINISM 229, 247 (1994) ("There may be a considerable imbalance of power, experience, and resources in favor of the prospective husband.").

63 "Women around the world lag far behind men in power, wealth and opportunity despite some advances in the last 20 years . . ." Women are confined to the lower-status, lower paid positions. *U.N.: World's women underpaid, underrepresented in management*, ITHACA JOURNAL, June 22, 1991, at 1A, col. 16. *See also* Brod, *supra* note 62, at 247.

64 *See generally* TERESA A. SULLIVAN ET AL., AS WE FORGIVE OUR DEBTORS: BANKRUPTCY AND CONSUMER CREDIT IN AMERICA ch. 8 (1989). *See also* Markovits, *supra* note 54, at 1734.

65 Lloyd Cohen, *Marriage, Divorce, and Quasi Rents; or, "I Gave Him the Best Years of My Life,"* 16 J. LEGAL STUD. 267, 280-82 (1987) ("older women have a great deal more competition for potential spouses and have a much smaller possibility of finding a suitable spouse than do older men").

66 WEITZMAN, *supra* note 5, at 247 (women "conditioned to desire marriage more than men"). *See also* Anderson, *supra* note 1, at 1792 (Pateman's thesis is that contracts "legitimate patriarchal and other forms of domination under the guise of equality.").

continue to perform most of the domestic work.[67] Prospective spouses therefore may adopt this expectation as a starting point for negotiations.[68] Even without these hurdles, women may be vulnerable to exploitation by their prospective spouses,[69] who may remain more comfortable with the role of a self-interested bargainer.[70] Relatedly, one prospective spouse's love may be stronger; instead of working to level the playing field, the feelings of the parties toward each other at the time of contracting may increase bargaining imbalances.[71] Because of all of these problems, contracting between spouses may increase the subordination of women, not minimize it: "[I]n the same way that contracts in the marketplace may formalize domination as much as they express the will of the parties, contracts among lovers and friends may reflect the inequalities in their relationships."[72]

Marriage theorists lacking enthusiasm for contractualism also point out that marriage contractarians may overstate the usefulness of contract policing norms, such as "fair bargaining, free consent, and party competence" to regulate disparities in bargaining power.[73] These context-dependent principles necessarily reflect existing attitudes toward

---

67 Ellman, *supra* note 7, at 46. *See also* Carbone, *supra* note 25, at 1465 n.10.

68 Anderson, *supra* note 1, at 1807 ("[P]atriarchal conceptions of gender differences" defeat contractualism as an equalizer).

69 *Id.*; WEITZMAN, *supra* note 5, at 247.

70 Anderson, *supra* note 1, at 1807. *See also* Rose, *supra* note 27, at 550.

71 Garrison, *supra* note 5, at 1058.

72 Olsen, *supra* note 5, at 1537-38. *See also* Brod, *supra* note 62, at 295 ("It is ironic, if not perverse, that in the name of gender equality, premarital agreements that discriminate against women as a class have been made readily enforceable."); CAROLE PATEMAN, THE SEXUAL CONTRACT 187 ("Men exercise their masculine capacity for political creativity by generating political relationships of subordination through contract.").

73 The quote is from Shultz, *supra* note 2, at 315.

marriages and gender roles.[74] For example, traditionalists and reformers may have dramatically different views of whether Argosy "consented" to a five-year marriage or whether he had no choice.[75] We therefore must apply nonconsensual law based on attitudes about marriage regardless of whether our starting point is a traditional marriage paradigm or contractualism.[76]

Despite marriage contractarians' optimism about the problem of contract gaps, other marriage theorists also believe that contractarians minimize the challenges of effective planning and drafting in marriage. These critics point out that even if marriage partners parrot their commercial counterparts, they are unlikely to avoid ambiguous language and incomplete agreements, just as commercial parties rarely successfully draft long-term contracts covering all contingencies despite much more predictable settings.[77] For example, suppose Green and Argosy agree in a contract that Green will support Argosy through law school. When can Argosy return to school? Before the couple has children? Only while Green is employed? How many years may Argosy attend school? In what location? Suppose Argosy is dissatisfied with his first year of law school and decides to go to medical school? Even if some sophisticated marriage partners, such as Green and Argosy, can successfully plan and draft terms dealing with such matters, planning and drafting will remain problematic for less educated and less sophisticated marriage partners.

---

74 Shultz ultimately concedes the impracticality of policing private contracting: "[I]n intimacy no one can say what is 'right' except the parties involved." *Id.* at 333.

75 Moreover, Green's promise to work to support Argosy's legal education may not seem one-sided to a traditionalist judge even if Argosy does not promise to share his potential gains.

76 *See* Ellman, *supra* note 7, at 21-24.

77 *See* Shultz, *supra* note 2, at 302-03. Weitzman acknowledges the problem of gaps, but believes that the problem is no greater in marriage than commercial contracts and that it is not insurmountable in either. WEITZMAN, *supra* note 5, at 248-50. *See also* Weisbrod, *supra* note 6, at 781.

After all, lawmakers should not construct the law focusing only on young urban professionals or other highly-educated people.[78]

Moreover, for some marriage theorists, the relational contracting metaphor[79] may not resolve the planning quagmire. Marriage partners, otherwise inclined toward disharmony, are not likely to avert disputes over omissions in agreements and avoid coercive adjustments resulting from one partner's greater reliance on the marriage simply because the marriage originally called for cooperation and compromise.[80] Moreover, when a dispute leads to litigation, courts necessarily will turn to societal, not contract, norms to complete these standards.[81] In fact, to the extent that evidence confirms the "idiosyncratic" nature of today's marriages, the lack of customary evidence will complicate the inquiry, forcing judges to incorporate their own views of cooperation, compromise, and fairness.[82]

As of yet, parties have been relatively unsuccessful in obtaining relief in the marriage setting for detrimental reliance or for unjust enrichment, probably for many of the reasons that courts have hesitated to recognize marriage contracting in the first place.[83] If a contractual legal structure envelops marriages, however, these avenues of obligation will become more prevalent: Argosy may rely on Green's promise that has not yet ripened into a full-fledged contract; Green may confer a benefit that in a contractual environment appears not to have been a gift.

---

78 *See* Carbone, *supra* note 25, at 1497.

79 *See supra* note 52, and accompanying text. *See also* Chapter 7.

80 Nevertheless, some marriage contractarians posit that current contract law minimizes the problem of changed circumstances. They assert that the law facilitates party adjustment of agreements or that the law helpfully defines when a party is excused in the face of changed circumstances. WEITZMAN, *supra* note 5, at 249. *See generally* Margaret F. Brinig and Steven M. Crafton, *Marriage and Opportunism,* 23 J. LEGAL STUD. 869 (1994).

81 *See* Ellman, *supra* note 7, at 28-29; Shultz, *supra* note 2, at 315.

82 *See*Garrison, *supra* note 5, at 1053 (marriage agreements suggested by Weitzman "pose difficult questions of interpretation.").

83 *See supra* notes 18-26, and accompanying text.

Ironically, resolving claims arising from such incidents will require invoking non-contractual fairness norms in the marriage setting. Recognizing these independent fairness-generated theories of obligation in the contract setting may further subordinate the parties' actual intentions. Of course, accommodating them will increase courts' flexibility and the potential for just results.[84]

Ultimately, marriage contractualism, grounded on individual freedom and faith in contractual processes, is understandably problematic for those who remain unpersuaded by the assertion that marriage partners are likely to plan and bargain over terms to their mutual benefit if the law more fully recognized marriage contracts.[85] By focusing on the question of the optimal mix of freedom and regulation in marriage law, the marriage contracting debate nicely mirrors contract theory's traditional quarrel between individualists and interventionists.[86] We now shall see that a similar dispute preoccupies theorists of corporations.

B. Corporations

Problem 6: MDM Enterprises, a publicly owned corporation with 1,000,000 outstanding shares, is principally engaged in the production of television programming. A provision in MDM's articles of incorporation authorizes the company to invest in television stations and immunizes MDM's directors from breach of loyalty claims for so investing. MDM purchases corporate bonds from BCD television station. At the time, MDM's directors are controlling shareholders of BCD. Because of financial difficulties, BCD would have had to discontinue paying dividends if it had been unsuccessful in selling the bonds.

---

[84] *See infra* notes 175-79, and accompanying text.

[85] Some interventionists also doubt the extent of dissipation of marital norms and suspect that marriage contracting may largely repudiate current marital values. *See supra* notes 53-60, and accompanying text.

[86] *See* Chapter 1.

Have MDM's directors violated the duty of loyalty by investing in BCD? If so, should a court enforce the provision immunizing the directors? Many corporation contractualists would urge courts to find no violation and to uphold the provision.

As with marriage, the dominant model of corporations from early this century until recently[87] entailed active state regulation of management-shareholder relations.[88] The need for intervention arose not because of the intimate relationship between the parties, however, but, quite the opposite, primarily because of the parties' remoteness. According to the corporate interventionist model, management of large public corporations, such as MDM in Problem 6, can exploit its power to increase its gains at the expense of remote, dispersed shareholders.[89] Individual shareholders do not monitor managers because the costs of becoming informed would exceed the benefits--the vote of any particular

---

87 According to Professor Bratton, the "management-centered" model of corporations took hold about 1930. Bratton, *Nexus of Contracts, supra* note 8, at 413.

88 Barry D. Baysinger & Henry N. Butler, *Antitakeover Amendments, Managerial Entrenchment, and the Contractual Theory of the Corporation*, 71 VA. L. REV. 1257, 1269-70 (1985)[hereinafter Baysinger & Butler, *Antitakeover*]; Lucien A. Bebchuk, *Foreward: The Debate on Contractual Freedom in Corporate Law*, 89 COLUML. REV. 1395, 1396 (1989) (mandatory rules "govern most of the important corporate arrangements"); Bernard S. Black, *Is Corporate Law Trivial: A Political and Economic Analysis*, 84 NW. U.L. REV. 542, 547 (1990) [hereinafter Black, *Corporate Law*]. *See generally Symposium, New Directions in Corporate Law,* 50 WASH. & LEE L. REV. 1373 (1993).

I focus here on law involving the duties of managers to investors, not on law governing the duties of managers to other parties such as employees or members of the community. On the latter, *see, e.g.*, Black, *Corporate Law, supra* at 547; Robert B. Thompson, *The Law's Limits on Contracts in a Corporation*, 15 J. CORP. L. 377, 380 (1990). *See also* Bebchuk, *supra* at 1405-06 (discussing possible "externalities").

89 "[T]he separation of managerial decisionmaking from the scrutiny of dispersed shareowners in the large corporation lessened managerial concern for shareholders' interests." Baysinger & Butler, *Antitakeover, supra* note 88, at 1269. *See also* Bratton, *Nexus of Contracts, supra* note 8, at 460.

shareholder would not likely affect a result.[90] Moreover, uninformed shareholders can "free ride" on (use) information investments of others, thereby further encouraging individual apathy.[91] Theorists justify both legislative and judicial lawmaking, such as rules providing for minimum votes of shareholders, intermittent director elections, and the fiduciary duties of care and loyalty of managers,[92] to make managers accountable to shareholders and thereby to rectify the "separation of ownership and control."[93]

Contractarians generally reject the interventionist approach and champion the freedom to "opt out" of corporate law.[94] Although there are many variations and degrees of commitment,[95] the gist of their theory is

---

90 Bernard S. Black, *Shareholder Passivity Reexamined*, 89 MICH. L. REV. 520, 527-29 (1990) [hereinafter Black, *Passivity*].

91 *See id.* at 527-28; Mark J. Roe, *A Political Theory of American Corporate Finance*, 91 COLUM. L. REV. 10, 12 (1991).

92 "The duty-of-care doctrine in state law holds directors and senior management to some degree of competency in guiding the affairs of the corporation. It is not an ordinary negligence test . . . . Courts have usually searched for indicia of gross negligence, or gross inattentiveness to duty . . . ." Nicholas Wolfson, *The Theoretical and Empirical Failings of The American Law Institute's Principles of Corporate Governance in* THE AMERICAN LAW INSTITUTE AND CORPORATE GOVERNANCE 69, 92 (National Legal Center for the Public Interest 1987). The duty of loyalty "comes into operation when the directors or senior management suffers from judicially cognizable conflicts of interest. The classic case is illustrated by a director selling or buying land in a transaction with his corporation." *Id.* at 99. *See also* Black, *Corporate Law, supra* note 88, at 551; Easterbrook & Fischel, *supra* note 9, at 1417-18.

93 *See* ADOLF A. BERLE & GARDINER C. MEANS, THE MODERN CORPORATION AND PRIVATE PROPERTY 124 (1932); William W. Bratton, Jr., *The New Economic Theory of the Firm: Critical Perspectives from History*, 41 STAN. L. REV. 1471, 1494 (1989) [hereinafter Bratton, *New Economic Theory*]. *See also* David Millon, *Theories of the Corporation*, 1990 DUKE L.J. 201, 221 (corporate law's "central concern" is "the accountability problem").

94 Bebchuk, *supra* note 88, at 1396-97. *See also* Wolfson, *supra* note 92.

95 As with any "theoretical school" there are varying degrees of enthusiasm for the contractarian thesis. *See* Bratton, *Nexus of Contracts, supra* note 8, at 419. *See also*

that investment in securities is no different than "ordinary market contracting between any two people."[96] As such, the parties know their interests best and choose optimal terms for themselves and, because their decisions do not adversely affect third parties, for society.[97] The role of the law is predominantly to provide gap filling provisions when the parties fail to contract.[98] Whereas marriage contractarians, inspired by nineteenth-century individualism,[99] focus on the potential of bargaining to enable intimate parties to achieve fair agreements and to realize their self-worth, corporation contractarians, prompted by a twentieth-century deregulation model, count on market forces to police business transactions between remote parties.[100] Despite evoking different stages

---

John C. Coffee, *Unstable Coalitions: Corporate Governance As a Multi-Player Game*, 78 GEO. L.J. 1495, 1496 (1990) (public corporations should be viewed as a "series of coalitions"). *See also infra* note 98, and accompanying text.

96 Armen Alchian & Harold Demsetz, *Production, Information Costs, and Economic Organization*, 62 AM. ECON. REV. 777, 777 (1972). *See also* Easterbrook & Fischel, *supra* note 9, at 1417-18 ("[W]hat is open to free choice is far more important to the daily operation of the firm . . . than is what the law prescribes."); Bratton, *Nexus of Contracts, supra* note 8, at 453-54. Contractualism derives from Coase's 1937 essay, *The Nature of the Firm*, 4 ECONOMICA 386.

97 Easterbrook & Fischel, *supra* note 9, at 1421. *But see* Michael Klausner, *Corporations, Corporate Law, and Networks of Contracts*, 81 VIRGINIA L. REV. 757 (1995) (focusing on "network externalities").

98 Bebchuk, *supra* note 88, at 1397. Even the most enthusiastic contractarians concede the need for some regulation. Judge Easterbrook and Professor Fischel, for example, seem to approve of law forbidding perpetual directorships and "the sale of votes divorced from the investment interest." Easterbrook & Fischel, *supra* note 9, at 1417. They also agree with quorum and disclosure rules. *Id.* at 1417-18. The authors nevertheless insist that "for equity investors, almost everything is open to choice." *Id.* at 1418.

For Easterbrook and Fischel's latest word, *see* EASTERBROOK & FISCHEL, *supra* note 9.

99 *See, e.g.*, WEITZMAN, *supra* note 5, at 229.

100 *See, e.g.*, Bratton, *New Economic Theory, supra* note 93, at 1499. *See also* Brudney, *supra* note 12, at 1410 ("[T]he rhetoric of contract serves to . . . complete the process of legitimating the substantial discretion which corporate management

of contract's evolution, however, both schools ultimately champion greater individual freedom and share a disregard for overregulation.

Corporation contractarians reason that the price of shares and management services are two related provisions within the assortment of terms offered to investors in a competitive market with a sufficient number of "sophisticated" players.[101] Aware of the possibility that managers may "shirk" their responsibilities[102] or usurp corporate opportunities, and of the difficulties of differentiating among firms' general quality of management, some investors will pay more for securities of companies in which shareholders exercise greater control over management.[103] Other investors will contentedly delegate decision-making to management, even waive managerial fiduciary obligations, in order to pay less.[104] In other words, investors do not have to invest in MDM, with its charter provision immunizing directors from certain fair-dealing claims. Investors can shop around and select another production company with the desired amount of delegation to managers and price.[105] Even uninformed investors are protected--an adequate number of

---

has, both to shirk in its performance and to divert corporate assets to its own benefit at investors' expense.").

101 Bebchuk, *supra* note 88, at 1404. Contractarians employ the metaphor of contract or agency to capture the relationship of managers and shareholders. *See* Brudney, *supra* note 12, at 1411-12.

102 The costs of shirking are called "agency costs." Millon, *supra* note 93, at 230.

103 Bratton, *Nexus of Contracts, supra* note 8, at 417-18. *See also* Brudney, *supra* note 12, at 1412 ("[Investor consent] . . . is anchored in the theory that if investors wanted to hold management to stricter, or more favorable terms, they would withhold their investments and wait until other owners or promoters [competing to attract their funds] offered them an arrangement with less managerial discretion and more stockholder power . . . .").

104 Bebchuk, *supra* note 88, at 1397. *See also* Bratton, *Nexus of Contracts, supra* note 8, at 455; McChesney, *Another Critique, supra* note 16, at 1334 ("The contractarian paradigm . . . counts as contracts agreements that specify rules of open-ended, unilateral future performance.").

105 Bratton, *Nexus of Contracts, supra* note 8, at 455.

informed investors ensure that the price will reflect the degree of delegation in particular companies.[106]

In addition to this "fair-pricing" argument, contractarians claim that market constraints of various kinds join the interests of managers and shareholders, thereby "lead[ing] managers to adopt optimal governance structures."[107] For example, inefficient management depresses the price of shares and attracts less capital.[108] Poor management also increases the costs of production. Inadequate finances, in turn, increase the potential for economic disaster, such as insolvency[109] and, in an economic environment such as the 1980s and the mid 1990s, takeover attempts.[110] The threat of economic failure and the concomitant loss of management positions creates incentives for managers to improve the price of shares

---

[106] Bebchuk, *supra* note 88, at 1407. *See also* Easterbrook & Fischel, *supra* note 9, at 1430 ("The price of stocks traded in public markets is established by professional investors."); *id.* at 1435. Professor Black notes, for example, that voting shares cost more than nonvoting shares. Black, *Corporate Law, supra* note 88, at 570.

[107] Baysinger & Butler, *Theory of the Firm, supra* note 14, at 179.

[108] Baysinger & Butler, *Antitakeover, supra* note 88, at 1272.

[109] Melvin A. Eisenberg, *The Structure of Corporation Law*, 89 COLUM. L. REV. 1461, 1489 (1989) (discussing contractarians) [hereinafter Eisenberg, *Structure*].

[110] State antitakeover legislation and the unfavorable economic climate of the early 1990's diminished the number of takeover attempts. But takeovers were back on track by the mid-1990s, financed in part by the increase in value of equity in a bullish stock market. See Stephanie Strom, *This Year's Wave of Mergers Heads Toward a Record,* New York Times, October 31, 1995 at A-1, Col. 5.

Antitakeover legislation confounded contractarians (who assert that corporate law conforms to what the parties would have wanted) because "it is 'difficult to call on the contractual paradigm to explain why managers could have a right to resist their own removal.'" Lyman Johnson, *Individual and Collective Sovereignty in the Corporate Enterprise*, 92 COLUM. L. REV. 2215, 2245 (1992) (Book Review of FRANK H. EASTERBROOK & DANIEL R. FISCHEL, THE ECONOMIC STRUCTURE OF CORPORATE LAW [1991] and ROBERT N. BELLAH, THE GOOD SOCIETY [1991]).

Ironically, many contractarians favored state *regulation* prohibiting antitakeover amendments to corporate charters or by-laws because the amendments would insulate managers from market incentives to perform in the shareholders' interests. *See, e.g.*, Baysinger & Butler, *Antitakeover, supra* note 88, at 1268-69.

by performing optimally[111] and by establishing monitoring devices, such as hiring independent directors.[112] If a manager owns stock or her compensation is tied to the success of the company, inadequate performance more directly diminishes the manager's own wealth.[113] Even apart from the threat of takeovers or concerns about the general success of the company, the personal desire to succeed within an existing hierarchy also constrains managers.[114] After all, managers do not want to lose the perquisites of generous compensation and other benefits of office.[115]

Unlike marriage contractarians' resolute belief in the efficacy of planning, corporation contractarians concede the incompleteness of specific contract terms, without admitting the deficiency of the "nexus of contracts" approach. Although corporate charters are relatively short and simple, omissions in these "contracts" between shareholders and managers are rare, according to contractarians, because shareholders delegate decision-making to managers. Gaps in MDM's charter are inconsequential, in other words, because MDM and its shareholders have agreed in advance for managers to use their discretion when unanticipated circumstances arise.[116] As a fall-back position and to fill out the contours

---

111 *Id.* at 1273.

112 Michael P. Dooley & E. Norman Veasey, *The Role of the Board in Derivative Litigation: Delaware Law and the Current ALI Proposals Compared, in* THE AMERICAN LAW INSTITUTE CORPORATE GOVERNANCE PROJECT IN MID-PASSAGE WHAT WILL IT MEAN TO YOU?, 45, 78 (1991).

113 Thompson, *supra* note 88, at 383.

114 *Id.* at 381. Professor Black asserts that shareholder voting constrains managers because collective action problems are "manageable" today where large institutions, such as banks, insurance companies, and mutual funds, are the "dominant shareholders." Black, *Passivity, supra* note 90, at 608.

115 Easterbrook & Fischel, *supra* note 9, at 1420.

116 John C. McChesney, *Another Critique, supra* note 16, at 1334. *See also* Coffee, *The Mandatory/Enabling Balance in Corporate Law: An Essay on the Judicial Role*, 89 COLUM. L. REV. 1618, 1681 (1989) ("[C]orporate law entrusts authority to the board of directors . . . to resolve all future disputes.") [hereinafter Coffee,

of the delegation to managers, contractarians assert that corporate law appropriately supplies non-mandatory terms to fill gaps based on "what the parties would have wanted," which decreases the costs of contracting and ties corporate law to actual assent and efficiency.[117]

Not only do contractarians believe that the market protects investors,[118] they assert that, whatever the costs of contractualism, it is superior to intervention because lawmakers have fewer incentives than the parties and less information about the parties' goals and needs to create optimal corporate law.[119] In fact, contractarians insist that

---

Mandatory/Enabling]. Professor Macey finds the flexibility afforded by the enabling approach its "most important advantage" over mandatory corporate law. Jonathan R. Macey, *Corporate Law and Corporate Governance: A Contract Perspective*, J. CORP. L. 198 (Winter 1993) (hereinafter Macey, *Corporate Law*).

[117] Easterbrook & Fischel, *supra* note 9, at 1433. Under this approach, the "true ground of authority is not the beliefs of the judge . . . but the will and consent of the contracting parties . . . ." Johnson, *supra* note 110, at 2237. Contractarians recognize that gap filling by means other than "implied contracts" would defeat contractualism. *See* Macey, *supra* note 15, at 1694-95. For an account of gap-filling based on "penalty defaults," *see* Ian Ayres, *Making a Difference: The Contractual Contributions of Easterbrook and Fischel* (Book Review of FRANK H. EASTERBROOK & DANIEL R. FISCHEL, THE ECONOMIC STRUCTURE OF CORPORATE LAW (1991)), 59 U. CHI. L. REV. 1391 (1992). For a discussion of penalty defaults, *see* Chapter 6.

[118] Henry N. Butler & Larry E. Ribstein, *Opting Out of Fiduciary Duties: A Response to the Anti-Contractarians*, 65 WASH. L. REV. 1, 34-35 (1990) ("There is substantial evidence favoring the general efficiency of the securities markets. . . . And because information about contract terms and managers is accurately reflected in market price, investors get what they pay for, and capital is allocated to the most efficient terms."). *See also id.* at 53; Bratton, *New Economic Theory, supra* note 93, at 1480.

[119] Black, *Corporate Law, supra* note 88, at 574; Easterbrook & Fischel, *supra* note 9, at 1432 ("No one argues that regulators are better at valuing terms of corporate governance than are markets."). *See also* Robert C. Clark, *Contracts, Elites and Traditions in the Making of Corporate Law*, 89 COLUM. L. REV. 1703, 1714-15 (1989) ("'[G]overnment,' in the person of judges, legislators, or regulators, is only infrequently likely to do better than A and B on either the incentive or the information dimension."). But Professor Black points out that the power of corporations to incorporate elsewhere may create the correct incentive for regulators. Black, *Corporate Law, supra*, at 574.

incentives lead legislators to favor large, organized, special interests over the public interest.[120] In addition, contractarians point out that lawmakers may be mediocre bureaucrats, unable to gather and process information effectively.[121] Even if generally sophisticated and competent, lawmakers are less qualified than the parties to adapt to unanticipated technological, economic, and other contextual developments. For all these reasons, contractarians generally repudiate mandatory legal rules regulating the firm[122] and urge default provisions reflecting the parties' presumed choices had they bargained over the matter at hand.[123]

As with marriage contractualism, the contractarian model of corporations depends on the accuracy and validity of several assertions and assumptions. Are the relations of managers and shareholders "contracts"? Do markets constrain managerial misconduct?[124] Are political markets deficient? Some scholars of corporations disagree with contractualists in whole or part on all of these issues.

---

120 Fred S. McChesney, *Economics, Law and Science in the Corporate Field: A Critique of Eisenberg*, 89 COLUM. L. REV. 1530, 1544 (1989) [hereinafter McChesney, *Economics*]. *See also* Eben Moglen & Richard J. Pierce, Jr., *Sunstein's New Canons: Choosing the Fictions of Statutory Interpretation*, 57 U. CHI. L. REV. 1203, 1218 (1990) (legislatures favor large organizations over "loose aggregations . . . crippled by relatively high organization and information costs"). The "lack of identity between the interests" of regulators and those regulated, contractarians point out, leads regulators to pursue their own interests instead of those regulated. Clark, *supra* note 119, at 1720.

121 Clark, *supra* note 119, at 1718-19 (discussing contractarians).

122 *Id.* at 1714-15. *See also* Bebchuk, *supra* note 88, at 1397 ("[T]he contractual view of the corporation implies that the parties involved should be totally free to shape their contractual arrangements."); Clark, *supra* note 119, at 1706. Professor Bratton discusses the "institutional variant" of this microeconomic analysis, which describes a more relational view of the nature of contracting between management and shareholders. Bratton, *New Economic Theory, supra* note 93, at 1480.

123 Clark, *supra* note 119, at 1706 (discussing contractarians).

124 Brudney, *supra* note 12, at 1405-06. *See also id.* at 1444 ("Analyzing the corporation in terms of [contract] . . . casts the problem in a framework that implies less managerial discretion and more effective remedial options for investors than institutional impediments permit.").

Echoing the thesis of marriage scholars more comfortable with regulation, corporate interventionists unsurprisingly doubt the workability of the contract paradigm. They insist that remote investors simply "lack the requisite information and . . . institutional mechanisms to bargain effectively" over corporate terms[125] or to shop around for the stock conferring on managers the optimal amount of discretion.[126] Interventionists therefore assert that contractarians fail to persuade that investors seek provisions exculpating managers from fiduciary duties in exchange for lower prices.[127]

Interventionists also claim that stock prices cannot impact effectively on managerial performance even in a market setting with sophisticated investors because too many diverse factors influence prices.[128] Interventionists therefore debate the incentive effect of financial considerations and also doubt the influence of stock ownership,

---

[125] Coffee, *No Exit, supra* note 13, at 933 (discussing Brudney, *supra* note 12). *See also* Bratton, *Nexus of Contracts, supra* note 8, at 460; Brudney, *supra* note 12, at 1421; Roe, *supra* note 91, at 13-14 ("dispersed investors cannot cheaply distinguish egoistic empire-building from a high net present value project").

[126] Brudney, *supra* note 12, at 1420; Eisenberg, *Structure, supra* note 109, at 1515. Professor Coffee points out that exculpatory provisions in corporate charters may be difficult to price because of uncertainty as to how the provision will affect management behavior. Will the manager avoid self-dealing because of non-legal constraints, for example? Coffee, *Mandatory/ Enabling, supra* note 116, at 1667-69.

[127] Professor Eisenberg points out the absence of empirical evidence on whether investors shop around for monitoring devices and for price because fiduciary rules are already largely mandatory and, therefore, investors have no real choice. Eisenberg, *Structure, supra* note 109, at 1515. He also points out that the "pricing" argument cannot apply to charter amendments. *Id.*

[128] Brudney, *supra* note 12, at 1424 ("[T]he choice [to buy or sell] does not permit separation of the treatment ... of the quality of management ... from other factors -- such as the particular industry involved, the accidents of timing, or even those internal matters to the enterprise for which the present management cannot be said to be responsible.").

compensation, and other personal perquisites.[129] Interventionists also question whether shareholders knowingly delegate to managers the discretionary power to fill the gaps in corporate charters.[130] Moreover, judicial gap-filling based on "what the parties would have wanted" requires analyzing too many diverse factors to produce terms realistically based on any notion of individual consent.[131]

Midstream charter amendments particularly concern interventionists because shareholders may be especially vulnerable at this stage to managers who unfairly take advantage.[132] Because of high costs and "free rider" problems, shareholders may fail to learn about or to contest amendments too favorable to management.[133] Moreover, unlike investors who can shop around for the desired package of terms and price, shareholders already own their shares and can sell them only for a price that reflects the new or anticipated amendment.[134] Shareholders also may be coerced by threats at the charter amendment stage (for example, to withhold dividends) or resign themselves to improved but less than

---

129 Eisenberg, *Structure, supra* note 109, at 1488-1515. Managers rarely sell their own shares and, for the most part, actually remain in their jobs until retirement. Black, *Corporate Law, supra* note 88, at 579. *See also* Brudney, *supra* note 12, at 1422 (little relationship "between poor corporate performance and displacement of managers").

130 *See supra* note 116, and accompanying text.

131 Bratton, *Nexus of Contracts, supra* note 8, at 460-61; Brudney, *supra* note 12, at 1415 n.31; Lewis A. Kornhauser, *The Nexus of Contracts Approach to Corporations: A Comment on Easterbrook and Fischel*, 89 COLUM. L. REV. 1449, 1452 (1989).

132 *See generally* Lucien Bebchuk, *Limiting Contractual Freedom In Corporate Law: The Desirable Constraints on Charter Amendments*, 102 HARV. L. REV. 1820 (1989) [hereinafter Bebchuk, *Charter Amendments*].

133 Eisenberg, *Structure, supra* note 109, at 1477-78. "Shareholder consent to rules proposed by top managers in publicly held corporations may be either nominal, tainted by a conflict of interest, coerced or impoverished." Eisenberg, *Response, supra* note 16, at 1328.

134 Bebchuk, *Charter Amendments, supra* note 132, at 1828-29.

optimal terms.[135] In the end, according to critics of contractualism, by labeling corporate relations contractual, the contractarian view obfuscates hard issues concerning the nature of the investors' assent and the efficacy of market incentives[136] and legitimizes managerial power without accountability.[137]

Not surprisingly, interventionists also dispute the alleged general deficiencies of regulation. For example, responding to the admonitions of contractarians to privatize existing law, interventionists stress the probable efficiency and rationality of the status quo and the costs of

---

[135] Eisenberg, *Structure, supra* note 109, at 1477-78.

[136] *See* Jean Braucher, *Contract Versus Contractarianism: The Regulatory Role of Contract Law*, 47 WASH. & LEE L. REV. 697, 701 (1990) (pointing out that a provision entitling managers to act in their own interests would raise issues of consent, such as whether the investors had sufficient information, and whether the term permitted managers to usurp all opportunities). *See also* Manuel A. Utset, *Towards a Bargaining Theory of the Firm*, 80 CORNELL L. REV. 540, 546 (1995) ("market and contractual constraints on managerial discretion . . . are not terribly effective").

[137] Brudney, *supra* note 12, at 1444 ("[I]deologically, the contract analysis' assumption that each of the parties is a knowledgeable consenting participant offers legitimacy for the very condition of corporate management that Berle and Means deplored a half century ago--considerable power with little accountability."); Bratton, *New Economic Theory, supra* note 93, at 1499. *See also* Bratton, *Nexus of Contracts, supra* note 8, at 412 (contractarianism "understates the significance of hierarchical relations"); Lawrence E. Mitchell, *The Cult of Efficiency*, 71 TEX. L. REV. 217, 224 (1992) (reviewing FRANK H. EASTERBROOK & DANIEL R. FISCHEL, THE ECONOMIC STRUCTURE OF CORPORATE LAW (1991)) ("What matters to Easterbrook and Fischel is that corporate relationships be governed by the market, without legal intervention.").

Some theorists concede the potential for bargaining inequality but assert that uninformed or powerless investors can "free ride" on the efforts of expert investors, whose purchases set the price. *See* Black, *Corporate Law, supra* note 88, at 570. *See also* Black, *Passivity, supra* note 90, at 527-28 (free-rider problem in proxy contests). According to some, however, such professionals do not participate in all initial price offerings and, even when they do, may not find investigation of governance terms efficient. Black, *Corporate Law, supra note 88,* at 571.

dismantling existing structures.[138] Interventionists also emphasize the superior resources of lawmakers, their access to technical information, which they can better process and utilize, and the limited foresight, inconsistencies, and irrationalities of individuals.[139] In addition, interventionists point to the many incentives of lawmakers to do a good job.[140]

Ultimately, combatants on both sides have failed to persuade their adversaries on the basis of these arguments or even to explain how the arguments could be weighed accurately and effectively.[141] The debate often reduces to who should have the burden of proof.[142] Contractarians insist that the costs of intervention outweigh the gains and therefore wish to place the burden of persuasion on the interventionists to prove the

---

[138] Clark, *supra* note 119, at 1731 ("Traditions greatly reduce the very high costs of repeated discovery, learning, and rational decisionmaking by individuals"). *See also id.* at 1742.

[139] *Id.* at 1718-19 ("the reason given for resisting paternalism--no information asymmetry exists--is desperately implausible in many real-world contexts"). *See also id.* at 1720 ("the informational advantages of elite rule making may outweigh the agency costs it creates").

[140] *Id.* at 1719. Moreover, logically, some of the criticisms of intervention fall away when the goal is defining minimal levels of reasonable conduct. After all, it is hardly convincing to argue that law mandating good faith and fair dealing may be unwise or inefficient because it may be the product of uninformed or disinterested lawmakers.

[141] *But see* Oliver E. Williamson, *The Logic of Economic Organization*, 4 J. L. ECON. & ORGANIZATION 65, 72-76 (1988) (empirical study). *Cf.* Anderson, *supra* note 1, at 1805 ("argument for a noncontractually based labor system must depend upon an empirical comparison of its advantages to those of the best contractual systems available").

[142] *See, e.g.*, Easterbrook & Fischel, *supra* note 9, at 1442 ("Unless the person challenging a provision of the corporate contract can make a convincing argument that the consequences of that term could not have been appreciated by investors and priced efficiently, there is no reason for intervening to correct a mistake."); Eisenberg, *Response, supra* note 16, at 1324, 1330-31; McChesney, *Another Critique, supra* note 16, at 1335-36.

necessity of intrusion.[143] The latter counter with precisely the opposite recommendation.[144] Neither hears the other.[145]

As a description, then, a corporation may consist of a "nexus of contracts." But the normative conclusions to be drawn from this are, at best, highly controversial and the empirical questions concerning investors' motivations and market effects largely remain unanswered.[146] As with marriage contractualism, the theory of corporation contractualism replays, even accentuates, the debate about the nature of modern contract law, but it fails to resolve most dilemmas.

Conclusion

The discussion above establishes that to label a relation contractual does not end the inquiry, it initiates it.[147] All relations involving the voluntary pursuit of mutual aspirations are contractual in a broad sense. But the context of the "contract," including the nature of the parties, their goals, the structure of their arrangement, the quality of their bargaining,[148] and the attributes of their planning and drafting, determine

---

143 McChesney, *Another Critique, supra* note 16, at 1335.

144 Eisenberg, *Response, supra* note 16, at 1330-31.

145 *Id.* at 1331; McChesney, *Another Critique, supra* note 16, at 1339. Professor Romano questions the centrality of this debate: "The rules that are identified as 'mandatory' . . . are either easily--and legally--side stepped, or they pose nonbinding contraints because there is no burning demand to deviate from them." Roberto Romano, *Answering the Wrong Question: The Tenuous Case for Mandatory Corporate Laws*, 89 COLUM. L. REV. 1599, 1599 (1989).

146 *But see* Macey, *Corporate Law, supra* note 116, at 207-211 (discussing empirical evidence).

147 Bebchuk, *supra* note 88, at 1409 ("[D]eregulators do not have a monopoly over the contractual framework of analysis."). *See also* Bratton, *Nexus of Contracts, supra* note 8, at 416-18.

148 The nature of the parties' bargain involves their wealth, education, and information, among other things.

the appropriate legal governing structure. Moreover, contractualism neither guarantees equality nor justifies domination.

Despite these shortcomings of contractualism, some critics may be overzealous in denying its contribution.[149] Instead of drawing battle lines over whether the net benefit of contractualism exceeds the net benefit of intervention,[150] contractarians and their critics should focus on the appropriate relationship between freedom of contract and intervention in particular relations.[151] Although many scholars of marriages and corporations do just that, too many attempt to "hose down" their opponents with arguments and counterarguments championing one broad paradigm or the other.[152]

This chapter's discussion of marriage and corporate contractualism suggests a more practical approach.[153] The following discussion merely attempts to emphasize the nature of thinking that in the long run may prove more profitable than the kind of debate that currently rages.

---

149 Coffee, *No Exit, supra* note 13, at 951: "[W]hile the 'rhetoric of contract' may legitimate excessive managerial discretion, 'fiduciary rhetoric' could equally justify unthinking devotion to anachronistic legal dogma."

150 Eisenberg, *Response, supra* note 16, at 1330-31.

151 *See* Clark, *supra* note 119, at 1726 ("A good society depends on both autonomy and heteronomy, each present in large measure. Theorists ought to face up to this point and then see what headway, if any, can be made in devising principles for setting the optimal mix."). Of course, this will be a difficult task. "[I]dentifying theoretically justified and practically useful criteria for distinguishing between waivable and nonwaivable rules [has] proven to be extraordinarily difficult." *Id.* at 1708.

152 *Id.* at 1707. That is not to say that centrists have failed to present proposals. Dean Clark's essay is a fine example of the latter. *See also* Shultz, *supra* note 2, at 328: "While selective reduction of legal control is appropriate and essential, wholesale delegalization is not ultimately a tenable strategy for state governance of marriage."

153 Others who have proceeded in this fashion include Clark, *supra* note 119; Jeffrey N. Gordon, *The Mandatory Structure of Corporate Law*, 89 COLUM. L. REV. 1549, 1554-55 (1989); Coffee, *Mandatory/Enabling, supra* note 116, at 1621. *See also* Garrison, *supra* note 5, at 1061-62.

1. A preliminary agreement model of marriage

We have seen that nineteenth-century individualism best captures marriage contractualism. It seeks to free partners from the shackles of caste to enable them to achieve their goals and to realize their self-worth within a relationship that benefits both parties. How best to achieve this goal?

Although all of the facts are not in, the irrefutable weakening of traditional marriage mores, society's growing tolerance of nontraditional relationships, and the shortcomings of the legal status quo, especially its tendency to impede marriage equality, suggest the need to modernize marriage law, including to grant greater freedom of contract between the parties.[154] Legislators therefore should loosen their grip somewhat and increase the opportunity for marriage contracting, but without abandoning the parties.[155] Legislators should set forth minimum standards to govern marriage consistent with enduring societal mores, just as they have utilized principles such as public policy, unconscionability, and good faith to set limits in general contract settings. These standards should promote communication, trust, cooperation, and, ultimately, marriage equality.

Of course, such value-laden parameters will remain obtuse, will continue to promote contention, and will necessitate judicial activism. Still, some limited steps should not be too controversial. Marriage law should no longer use gender-based stereotypes for determining marriage

---

154 *See* TREBILCOCK, *supra* note 16, at 43: "The goal of reform has been to affirm in women the ability to operate as fully autonomous and self-determining agents, free to bargain and enjoy all the rights and freedoms previously held only by men."

"Many systems provide for almost complete freedom of the spouses to arrange their affairs to suit themselves, subject only to the limitation that the arrangements so made must not contravene some important public policy of the jurisdiction . . . ." Max Rheinstein & Mary Ann Glendon, *Interspousal Relations*, *in* IV INTERNATIONAL ENCYCLOPEDIA OF COMPARATIVE LAW 148-49, (A. Chloros, chief ed. 1980).

155 "[U]nlimited freedom of contract . . . does not necessarily lead to public or individual welfare . . . the only ultimate test of proper limitations is that provided by experience." Samuel Williston, *Freedom of Contract*, 6 CORNELL L. Q. 365, 374 (1921).

roles, but the law should strike one-sided agreements that unfairly burden only one partner.[156] In Problem 5, an agreement assigning Argosy all of the domestic chores if both parties work an equal time outside of the home, for example, might be unenforceable. In addition, marriage law should not automatically renounce unusual agreements, such as for particular modes of dispute resolution, or agreements concerning the more business-like aspects of marriage, such as those involving finances and property.[157] But marriage law should carefully police or even prohibit terms that may tend to reduce personal trust and nurturing, such as those licensing extra-marital relations or, as in Problem 5, setting forth a finite duration for the marriage. Perhaps the state could best effectuate marriage contracting limits, and at the same time alleviate some of the impediments to effective bargaining, by setting forth approved "marriage packages"--off-the-rack terms, such as for separate or joint property and finances, from which Green and Argosy could choose.[158]

But helping marriage partners realize their self-worth depends on fostering solidarity norms such as compromise and cooperation. For many of the reasons expressed by the skeptics of marriage contractualism--intimate partners' reluctance and inability to plan and draft viable contracts, unequal bargaining relations, changed circumstances--contracting may nurture unity norms ineffectively or not at all.[159] In fact, the difficulty of constructing viable contract rules to

---

[156] Garrison, *supra* note 5, at 1046.

[157] Some states have already made similar advances. *See supra* notes 24-25 and accompanying text.

[158] *See* Shultz, *supra* note 2, at 305; Weisbrod, *supra* note 6, at 810-811. "Some systems . . . facilitate the spouses' choice by providing statutory models of the most commonly desired alternative regimes and statutory guides to varying the details of the basic regime. This is the scheme of French law . . . and also that of the Netherlands." Rheinstein & Glendon, *supra* note 154, at 149. *See also id.* at 56 (The Holland "Civil Code supplies authoritative explanations for frequently used designations of contractual regimes:" for example, "community of fruits and income" and "community of gain and loss.").

[159] "Contracts are not worth the paper they are printed on unless there is trust, commitment, and a developing flexibility in role relationships." Jeter & Sussman,

replace traditional assent-based ones in the context of long-term flexible commercial arrangements bears out this skepticism.[160] What alternative but related structures may foster solidarity norms?

State law could promote disclosure of the expectations of the parties without, necessarily, inviting formal contracting.[161] The law could adopt a procedure facilitating the parties exchange of detailed written explanations of their expectations, both immediate and specific--who will go to graduate school, who will work--and long-term.[162] These writings would not bind the parties legally to any explicit representation. The goal of the writings would be to increase communication between the parties, to help them comprehend underlying, possibly unformed, suppositions about the relationship,[163] to allow them to face their differences,[164] and to create a moral, if not legal, infrastructure for conducting the marriage.[165]

The disclosure process would not be unlike that of commercial contracting parties who create preliminary writings that memorialize precursory understandings, structure future negotiations, and foreshadow

---

supra note 5, at 291. *See also* Williston, *supra* note 155, at 374.

160 *See generally* Chapter 6. *See also* William C. Whitford, *Ian Macneil's Contribution to Contracts Scholarship*, 1985 WIS. L. REV. 545.

161 *See, e.g.*, Lynn A. Baker, *Promulgating the Marriage Contract*, 23 U. MICH. J. L. REF. 217 (1990).

162 *See, e.g.*, Jeter & Sussman, *supra* note 5, at 287-90.

163 Not only would one partner learn the expectations of the other, but the disclosing party would better understand his or her own perspective. Disclosing one's thoughts and beliefs allows one to perceive, reconsider, and understand one's own point of view. *See* William B. Stiles, *"I Have to Talk to Somebody": A Fever Model of Disclosure*, *in* SELF-DISCLOSURE: THEORY, RESEARCH, AND THERAPY, at 264 (Valerian J. Derlega & John H. Berg eds., 1987) [hereinafter SELF-DISCLOSURE].

164 Susan Edmiston, *How to Write Your Own Marriage Contract*, *in* PEOPLE AS PARTNERS 107, 108, 116 (Jaqueline P. Wiseman, ed., 2d ed. 1977).

165 Jeter & Sussman, *supra* note 5, at 287 ("Contract functions as a moral or ethical basis for a relationship in terms of reciprocal expectations and responses to expectations.").

the ultimate terms of their deal, but which the parties intend either to have no legal effect or to require only further negotiation in good faith.[166] Although these commercial parties may intend to conclude an enforceable contract, in many instances the nature of their preliminaries--whether they foster communication, trust, and cooperation, and therefore commit the parties to the deal,[167] or, on the other hand, create an adversarial atmosphere--may be more important in determining success than the ultimate terms of the deal.[168] Similarly, disclosing marriage expectations may be more crucial than the governing terms of the marriage in building a viable relationship[169] or in convincing some that they should not marry.[170] In conjunction with this disclosure approach and to enhance the parties' understandings of what is to follow, the state could supply detailed written guidance about the legal ramifications of the parties' marriage.[171]

At the time of any conflict in the marriage, and certainly prior to any divorce filing, state law also could require the parties to engage in good-faith discussions, mediation, or some other form of dispute

---

166 *See* E. Allan Farnsworth, *Precontractual Liability and Preliminary Agreements: Fair Dealing and Failed Negotiations*, 87 COLUM. L. REV. 217, 249-251 (1987).

167 *See* Charles L. Knapp, *Enforcing the Contract to Bargain*, 44 N.Y.U. L. REV. 673, 681 (1969).

168 Macaulay, *supra* note 55, at 60-62.

169 Intimacy develops through the *process* of communicating as well as through the exchange of views. Gordon J. Chelune, *A Neuropsychological Perspective of Interpersonal Communication*, *in* SELF-DISCLOSURE, *supra* note 163, at 9, 12.

170 *See, e.g.*, Jeter & Sussman, *supra* note 5, at 287; *see also supra* note 161, and accompanying text.

171 There is some evidence that prospective spouses need such guidance. For example, some apparently blindly assume that divorce courts balance the needs of the parties on some equitable basis. *See* Baker, *supra* note 161, at 232-33. *See also id.* at 237-42 (discussing Lenore J. Weitzman & Ruth B. Dixon, *The Alimony Myth: Does No-Fault Divorce Make a Difference*? 14 FAM. L. Q. 141 (1980)).

resolution,[172] similar to the modern judicial propensity to enforce preliminary commercial agreements to negotiate in good faith.[173] Although dispute resolvers should treat the parties' pre-marital written declarations only as aspirations, and the marriage itself may generate few concrete expectations, the goal of conflict resolution should be to invigorate solidarity norms such as good faith, trust, and cooperation. In short, mediators or others can seek to resolve differences by suggesting how these norms should play out in the context of particular disputes arising during the marriage.[174]

State law also should recognize and enforce restitution and reliance theories of obligation in marriage, just as contract law increasingly recognizes these theories in pre-contract commercial negotiations.[175] Of course, these flexible theories require faith in judicial administration. For example, under restitution law, the intent to confer a benefit as a gift is generally a complete defense to an unjust enrichment claim.[176] Within the context of marriage, courts historically have found

---

[172] *See* Garrison, *supra* note 5, at 1055. *See also* FED. R. CIV. P. 16(c); Robert A. Hillman, *Court Adjustment of Long-Term Contracts: An Analysis Under Modern Contract Law*, 1987 DUKE L.J. 1, 19 n.97. "ADR rejects traditional win-or-lose outcomes in favor of compromises, tries to develop 'a consensus about future conduct rather than [assign] responsibility for events in the past,' views personal conflicts as embedded in social contexts, and looks to the satisfaction of needs rather than the vindication of rights." Markovits, *supra* note 54, at 1753 (quoting Susan Silbey & Austin Sarat, *Dispute Processing in Law and Legal Scholarship: From Institutional Critique to the Reconstruction of the Juridical Subject*, 66 DEN. U. L. REV. 437, 453 (1989)). But Professor Markovits doubts the benefits of ADR. *Id.* at 1753-54.

[173] *See* Hillman, *supra* note 172, at 18 n.93 and cases cited therein.

[174] *See id.* at 6-8 for the commercial analogy.

[175] On marriage, *see* Susan W. Prager, *Shifting Perspectives on Marital Property Law*, *in* RETHINKING THE FAMILY: SOME FEMINIST QUESTIONS 125, 126 (B. Thorne & M. Yalom eds. 1982). On commercial negotiations, *see infra* note 176, and accompanying text.

[176] DAN B. DOBBS, HANDBOOK ON THE LAW OF REMEDIES 299 (1973).

"all services . . . to be gratuitous."[177] But courts should be more open to proof of contrary intentions, explicit or implicit, in the context of modern marriage where economic realities, such as the prevalence of families with two wage earners, make arrangements between parties, if not contractual, at least more business-like.[178] For the same reason, courts also should be more receptive to claims of reasonable reliance on spousal representations even when the promisor may not have envisioned creating a legal obligation, similar to court enforcement of ex ante representations in commercial settings.[179]

2. A commercial-contextual model of corporations

Recall that unlike marriage contractualism, a modern deregulation paradigm best captures the corporate branch of contractualism. This model relies not on faith in personalized bargaining to enable individuals to realize their self-worth, but on organized markets to create choices for investors and appropriate incentives for managers to whom investors delegate power. Lawmakers therefore should step in only when the market fails to achieve these purposes.[180] If nothing else, however, the debate between contractarians and interventionists demonstrates that ascertaining when markets falter challenges lawmakers. Nevertheless, some observations are possible.

First, what are the appropriate roles of legislator, judge, and the parties in making corporate law? Legislators are probably even less adept

---

177 Carbone, *supra* note 25, at 1483.

178 *See, e.g.*, Lenore J. Weitzman, *The Economics of Divorce: Social and Economic Consequences of Property, Alimony and Child Support Awards*, 28 U.C.L.A. L. REV. 1181, 1211 (1981) ("Even though both spouses may have worked during the marriage, it is likely that, as a marital unit, they have chosen to give priority to one spouse's career in the expectation that both will share in the benefits of that decision.").

179 Hoffman v. Red Owl Stores, 26 Wis. 2d 683, 133 N.W. 2d 267 (1965) is the leading case. *See also* Skycom Corp. v. Telstar Corp., 813 F.2d 810 (7th Cir. 1987).

180 Coffee, *Mandatory/Enabling, supra* note 116, at 1665 (case for unconscionability weakest in commercial setting).

at addressing transaction-specific problems of parties to corporations and at assessing the influences of markets than they are at formulating marriage standards consistent with society's convictions.[181] Nevertheless, even some ardent corporation contractarians concede the need for minimal structural and antifraud rules to protect shareholders when market forces fail.[182] Legislators can appropriately promulgate basic structural rules, such as shareholder approval, voting rights, and disclosure edicts,[183] and can prescribe standards, including the duties of managerial loyalty and care, encompassing the "necessary minimum area of protection" for shareholders.[184] Painting in broad strokes empowers courts to ascertain in particular cases whether managers have abrogated these standards. But courts ordinarily should defer to particular corporate definitions of the protective rules and standards, provided that the definitions do not nullify the protection, they are consistent with trade practice, and they are promulgated in good faith.

The commercial law counterpart of this technique lends support and illustration. The Uniform Commercial Code (U.C.C.) allows commercial parties to personalize, but not obliterate, general standards such as good faith, diligence, and reasonableness,[185] even in the context

---

181 Easterbrook & Fischel, *supra* note 9, at 1418 ("No one set of terms will be best for all; hence the 'enabling' structure of corporate law."); PRINCIPLES OF CORPORATE GOVERNANCE: ANALYSIS AND RECOMMENDATIONS, Introductory Note to Part IV (Tentative Draft No. 11, 1991) ([a]pplication of general legal standards "will involve subtle evaluations of specific facts and circumstances").

182 *See, e.g.*, Easterbrook & Fischel, *supra* note 9, at 1436-37 ("unless legal rules set up a requirement of reciprocal disclosure no firm may find it optimal to disclose information that is valuable to investors").

183 "In publicly held corporations core structural rules . . . should be mandatory" because they "double as fiduciary rules." Eisenberg, *Structure, supra* note 109, at 1480. An analog is Article 9 of the Uniform Commercial Code, which sets forth mandatory rules for creating and disclosing security interests.

184 *See* Rudolf B. Schlesinger, *The Uniform Commercial Code in the Light of Comparative Law*, 1 INTER-AM. L. REV. 11, 33 (1959).

185 U.C.C. § 1-102(3) provides in part: "[O]bligations of good faith, diligence, reasonableness and care prescribed by this Act may not be disclaimed by agreement

of standard-form contracts, which obviously raise parallel questions concerning the market incentives of merchants and the quality of consumer assent.[186] The law should utilize this approach not because shareholders or consumers clearly shop around or barter for particular terms in form contracts or even understand them or because the market without question adequately polices managers or merchants, but because the strategy probably represents the most sensible compromise between proponents of market forces and champions of intervention. The methodology decreases the importance of legislative mandates and empowers the parties, but it also protects them through active judicial review of particular provisions in context.[187]

How would courts determine in particular cases whether corporate provisions abrogate managerial duties such as loyalty and care, instead of define them? Under the U.C.C., typical cases include those in which a

---

but the parties may by agreement determine the standards by which the performance of such obligations is to be measured if such standards are not manifestly unreasonable."

See also U.C.C § 2-719(2), discussed *infra* note 186.

[186] For example, the U.C.C. authorizes parties to shape their own remedies. U.C.C. § 2-719. Because of modern-day form contracting, in which consumers must "adhere" to the standard form's terms, however, many consumers cannot dicker over remedial provisions and sellers often severely limit them. If a remedy "fails of its essential purpose," however, the buyer is free to pursue additional remedies. U.C.C. § 2-719(2). For example, a buyer can pursue additional remedies when the exclusive remedy of repair and replacement of defective parts fails because repairs are never satisfactorily completed. *See generally* ROBERT A. HILLMAN ET AL., COMMON LAW AND EQUITY UNDER THE UNIFORM COMMERCIAL CODE at 9-43 (1985).

[187] "The existence of some mandatory rules may lead to better contracts. In other words, the mixed system of optional and mandatory legal rules . . . may be best even from an essentially contractarian perspective." Gordon, *supra* note 153, at 1554. In adopting a similar approach, Professor Coffee suggests permitting parties to set the minimum level of responsibility of managers at the "level of good faith," which, according to Coffee, permits a manager to pursue her own interests, instead of at the level of fiduciary responsibility, which does not. Coffee, *Mandatory/Enabling, supra* note 116, at 1658-59. He argues that fiduciary duties are "geared to the preindustrial, hierarchical society, . . . not the entrepreneurial and egalitarian society of the late twentieth century." *Id.* at 1659.

secured or other creditor holds the collateral of a debtor or surety.[188] Courts generally strike a contractual provision "defining" the standard of care of a creditor toward the collateral only when the standard absolves the creditor from all liability, such as a term that waives misfeasance as well as nonfeasance,[189] or a term that waives the statutory requirement of a commercially reasonable disposition of the collateral.[190] But courts uphold waivers that delimit or spell out duties when the evidence suggests that knowledgeable parties attempted to tailor the provision to their particular needs in accordance with industry practice and in good faith.[191]

Following the U.C.C. strategy,[192] courts would evaluate the substance of a corporate provision, including its purposes and effects, and the term's derivation.[193] The best case for striking a provision would involve both a serious and unusual encroachment into shareholder rights and formative difficulties demonstrating the lack of shareholder assent.

Concerning the substance of a provision, courts should be wary of terms largely annulling traditional managerial duties, but they should enforce provisions responsive to a company's particular needs.[194] For example, courts should suspiciously eye a general provision authorizing

---

188 *See, e.g.*, American Bank of Commerce v. Covolo, 88 N.M. 405, 540 P.2d 1294 (1975); Federal Deposit Insurance Corp. v. Forte, 94 A.D.2d 59, 463 N.Y.S.2d 844 (1983); Continental Bank and Trust Co. v. Utah Security Mortgage, Inc., 701 P.2d 1095 (Utah 1985).

189 *See, e.g.*, Congress Financial Corp. v. Sterling-Coin Op Machinery Corp., 456 F.2d 451 (3d Cir. 1972); Toomey Equipment Co., Inc. v. Commercial Credit Equipment Corp., 386 So. 2d 1155 (Ala. Civ. App. 1980).

190 May v. The Women's Bank, 807 P2d 1145 (Colo. 1991).

191 *See, e.g.*, Brodheim v. Chase Manhattan Bank, 75 Misc. 2d 285, 347 N.Y.S.2d 394 (N.Y. Sup. Ct. 1973). *See also In re* East Coast Brokers & Packers, Inc. 120 BR 221 (1990) (parties can agree to a term requiring inspection of perishable goods within 24 hours).

192 *See* U.C.C. § 1-203 (good faith); U.C.C. § 2-302 (unconscionability).

193 *See* Hillman, *supra* note 172.

194 *See supra* notes 185-86, and accompanying text.

management to coopt corporate opportunities; nonetheless, courts generally should permit a corporation to approve particular management ventures in which individual managers may gain and preclude others.[195] Under this approach, a court might approve the charter provision authorizing MDM to invest in television stations substantially owned by the managers of MDM, when a purpose of MDM is to invest in television stations.[196] Courts also should distrust omnibus exculpatory clauses that conflict with other express charter provisions or are unusual in the industry, such as terms that exonerate managers who consciously or recklessly disregard specific managerial obligations.[197]

Courts should not ignore that, in particular cases, a term may carve rather deeply into traditional managerial duties but still offer a net benefit to investors. For example, a provision authorizing MDM's managers to gain from a corporate venture, such as authorizing MDM to invest in television stations owned by MDM's managers, may benefit shareholders by depressing the managers' salaries or by encouraging them to look for new corporate opportunities.[198] In addition, a term narrowing the duty of care to encompass only willful or reckless conduct may ensure that managers are not overly cautious[199] and may help avoid abusive

---

[195] Coffee, *Mandatory/Enabling, supra* note 116, at 1668-69; Eisenberg, *Structure, supra* note 109, at 1469-70 (discussing closely held corporations).

[196] But a court would strike a provision permitting directors to create secret salaries. *See* Coffee, *Mandatory/Enabling, supra* note 116, at 1649-50, discussing Irwin v. West End Development Co., 342 F. Supp. 687 (D. Colo.), *aff'd in part*, 481 F.2d 34 (10th Cir. 1972), *cert. denied*, 414 U.S. 1158 (1974) and Everett v. Phillips, 288 N.Y. 227, 43 N.E.2d 18 (1942).

[197] PRINCIPLES OF CORPORATE GOVERNANCE, ANALYSIS AND RECOMMENDATIONS § 7.17 (Tentative Draft No. 9, 1989).

[198] Easterbrook & Fischel, *supra* note 9, at 1433.

[199] Dooley & Veasey, *supra* note 112, at 75. Professor Coffee reports that most states permit charter terms exculpating manager negligence. Coffee, *Mandatory/Enabling, supra* note 116, at 1650.

stockholder derivative suits.[200] Some posit that market forces constrain managerial incompetence more effectively than they deter self-dealing--for example, with the potential for a large payoff, managers may be willing to "take the money and run" after running afoul of the duty of loyalty.[201] This supposition, of course, reinforces deferring more readily to corporate definitions watering down the duty of care than to those diminishing the duty of loyalty.

Before deciding whether a corporate provision should be enforced, courts also should consider its derivation. For example, courts should appraise the nature of the corporation enacting the controversial charter term. One's view of the formation process is likely to change as we move from large to small public corporations to closely-held corporations. Stock prices rarely will accurately reflect broad delegations

---

200 *See* Clark, *supra* note 119, at 1707 (discussing Daniel R. Fischel & Michael Bradley, *The Role of Liability Rules and the Derivative Suit in Corporation Law: A Theory and Empirical Analysis*, 71 CORNELL L. REV. 261, 277-83, 286 (1986)). Following this logic, several states have enacted provisions limiting liability for duty of care violations. For a discussion, *see, e.g.*, PRINCIPLES OF CORPORATE GOVERNANCE: ANALYSIS AND RECOMMENDATIONS § 7.17, cont. a at 116-117 (Tentative Draft No. 9, 1989).

> The rationale for [the] difference in the treatment of due care and loyalty cases is explained not only by the greater need for a litigation remedy to enforce the duty of loyalty, but also by the greater vulnerability of due care cases to abusive litigation. Virtually any corporate transaction can be challenged on due care grounds, and the risk of delay . . . can often have very costly consequences for the corporation. Thus, in a duty of care case, unless some unusual factor calls the board's or committee's judgment into question . . . the court should accept adequately supported findings as to business matters, even if the court itself could not conclude that it would reach the same judgment on the same record, unless the findings are so clearly unreasonable as to fall outside the bounds of the directors' discretion.

PRINCIPLES OF CORPORATE GOVERNANCE: ANALYSIS AND RECOMMENDATIONS § 7.08, cont. c at 121-122 (Tentative Draft No. 8, 1988).

201 EASTERBROOK & FISCHEL, ECONOMIC STRUCTURE, *supra* note 7. *See also* PRINCIPLES OF CORPORATE GOVERNANCE: ANALYSIS AND RECOMMENDATIONS § 7.08, cont. c at 120 (Tentative Draft No. 8, 1988).

to managers in the context of large public corporations because of the lack of information as to how managers would use the authorization.[202] Suppose, for example, a provision in MDM's charter immunized its directors from most breach of loyalty claims. The difficulties for investors, even institutional ones, of predicting how managers might utilize such an empowerment makes it unlikely that the price of shares would accurately reflect the provision.[203] Of course, prices of shares may more accurately reflect provisions particularizing managerial discretion, but only if properly disclosed by the corporation so that investors could decide whether to purchase with some sophistication as to the term's likely effect.[204]

The limited numbers of parties to closely-held corporations and the greater likelihood of effective monitoring by shareholders increase the possibility of traditionally-bargained specific agreements devoid of delegation and gap problems.[205] Still, courts must be wary of terms largely *invalidating* managerial duties even in this context for any of the reasons courts police contract formation generally: the possibility of uninformed or naive shareholders, the difficulty of predicting the effect of broad provisions, and so on.[206]

Courts should delve further into a provision's derivation. Particularly, did the parties include the term in the original charter or was it an amendment? For example, suppose MDM's articles of incorporation did not include a general authorization to invest in television stations, but MDM's directors proposed a charter amendment authorizing MDM to loan money to BCD television station. As discussed, theorists have urged

---

202 *But see* Gordon, *supra* note 153, at 1562-64.

203 Coffee, *Mandatory/Enabling, supra* note 116, at 1668-70.

204 *See id.* at 1667-71. For example, consider a term authorizing managers to purchase surplus corporate property at market value. *See* PRINCIPLES OF CORPORATE GOVERNANCE: ANALYSIS AND RECOMMENDATIONS 5.02, illustration 1 at 281 (Tentative Draft No. 11, 1991). Arguably, if properly disclosed, the price of shares will reflect the provision.

205 Thompson, *supra* note 88, at 392-93.

206 Eisenberg, *Structure, supra* note 109, at 1469-70.

that a greater opportunity exists for management self-dealing in this situation, where information may be more costly to gather[207] and managers can exploit shareholders, such as by withholding dividends if they do not approve an amendment.[208] But courts should consider whether institutional or other investors with sufficient clout had appropriate incentives to investigate and to withstand any threats even in the context of charter amendments.[209]

It remains only to consider the appropriate methodology when a corporation fails to promulgate any provisions defining general fiduciary standards. In other words, how should courts proceed when shareholders assert that managers usurped a corporate opportunity, competed with the corporation, or failed to exercise reasonable business judgment, and the governing standards simply require loyalty and care? Again, contractualism supplies no ready-made answers. Filling out the standards based on "what the parties would have wanted" will continue to challenge courts.[210] Instead of that approach, courts likely will persist in doing what they do best--in conjunction with existing law, they will develop the meanings of managerial good faith,[211] fairness,[212] and reasonableness [213]

---

207 *See* Gordon, *supra* note 153, at 1575-76. *See also* Clark, *supra* note 119, at 1725.

208 Eisenberg, *Structure, supra* note 109, at 1477. *See also* Romano, *supra* note 145, at 1607 (characterizing the "crucial premise" of the charter amendment problem as the "rational apathy" of shareholders). For a detailed account of the issue, *see* Gordon, *supra* note 153, at 1573-85.

209 Romano, *supra* note 145, at 1607 ("The characterization of shareholders as rationally apathetic . . . is . . . highly problematic."). *But see* Gordon, *supra* note 152, at 1576 ("Since [the large public shareholder's] expected returns from the combined costs of acquiring and disseminating information will probably be negative, he too will follow a course of rational apathy.").

210 *See supra* note 131, and accompanying text.

211 *See, e.g.*, PRINCIPLES OF CORPORATE GOVERNANCE: ANALYSIS AND RECOMMENDATIONS § 5.05, reporter's note 2, at 381 (Tentative Draft No. 11, 1991) (citing Morad v. Coupounas, 361 So. 2d 6 (Ala. 1978)).

212 *See, e.g., id.* at 382 ("Some courts have declined to articulate a precise definition of a corporate opportunity, and have simply concluded that the matter is one of

in transaction-specific settings, forming over time situation-specific presumptions to guide but not to handcuff them.[214] Corporate law therefore will remain complex and, to a degree, uncertain, whether we call it contractual or something else.

---

fairness, to be decided on the facts of the particular case.").

213 *See id.* § 4.01(a) at 177 (a manager must "perform his functions in good faith, in a manner that he reasonably believes to be in the best interests of the corporation, and with the care that an ordinarily prudent person would reasonably be expected to exercise . . . .").

214 *Id.*, Part IV Introductory Note at 171 ("It should be emphasized at the outset . . . that [the duty of care and the business judgment rule] are general legal standards and that their application . . . will involve subtle evaluations of specific facts and circumstances.").

CHAPTER 4

THEORIES OF CONTEXTUALISTS AND NEO-FORMALISTS

This chapter begins the discussion of the role of judicial discretion in applying contract law. I focus here on the normative debate over the relative merits of standards and rules in contract law.[1] I leave for the next chapter the claim that contract law as a whole contains a "fundamental contradiction"[2] that enables judges to decide cases at their discretion.

The standards-rules debate in contract law mirrors the general jurisprudential dialogue on this matter.[3] Recently one theorist characterized rules as consisting of "an advance determination of what conduct is permissible, leaving only factual issues for the adjudicator."[4] Rules therefore narrow the decisionmaker's inquiry to a range of preestablished elements.[5] Standards, on the other hand, "entail leaving both specification of what conduct is permissible and factual issues for the adjudicator."[6] Although, as we shall see, much of law falls

---

1 *See generally* Duncan Kennedy, *Form and Substance in Private Law Adjudication*, 89 HARV. L. REV. 1685 (1976).

2 *See* Chapter 5.

3 *See generally* P.S. ATIYAH & ROBERT S. SUMMERS, FORM AND SUBSTANCE IN ANGLO-AMERICAN LAW: A COMPARATIVE STUDY IN LEGAL REASONING, LEGAL THEORY AND LEGAL INSTITUTIONS (1987); FREDERICK SCHAUER, PLAYING BY THE RULES: A PHILOSOPHICAL EXAMINATION OF RULE-BASED DECISIONMAKING IN LAW AND IN LIFE (1991); Louis Kaplow, *Rules Versus Standards: An Economic Analysis*, 42 DUKE L.J. 557 (1992); Kennedy, *supra* note 1; Kathleen M. Sullivan, *Foreword: The Justices of Rules and Standards*, 106 HARV. L. REV. 22 (1992).

4 Kaplow, *supra* note 3, at 560.

5 *Id.* at 589. *See also* Duncan Kennedy, *Legal Formality*, 2 J. LEGAL STUD. 351, 355 (1973).

6 Kaplow, *supra* note 3, at 560. *See also* Kennedy, *supra* note 1, at 1688: "The application of a standard requires the judge both to discover the facts of a particular situation and to assess them in terms of the purposes or social values embodied in the standard."

somewhere between these poles,[7] rules and standards tend to conflate in actual operation, and the above definitions omit many of their attributes,[8] the definitions serve as a helpful starting point.

Theorists preferring law located towards the standards end of the continuum, whom we shall refer to as "contextualists," assert that flexible and adaptable standards encourage judges to appraise all of the circumstances and equities of individual cases in context-dependent situations.[9] Standards also ensure the continuity of the rule of law because they "enable the content of legal norms to change while ensuring that the legal order continues as an unbroken unity."[10] Because rules bind judges to decide in a particular manner, based on a set of "triggering facts"[11] and regardless of the equities, contextualists claim that rules inevitably lead to judicial manipulation and obfuscation to reach just results.[12]

Despite the decline of nineteenth-century legal formalism,[13] proponents of rule-like law remain prominent today. Unlike

---

7 A rule can be very general, for instance, and a standard quite specific. Professor Kennedy notes that "[a] rule setting the age of legal majority at 21 is more general than a rule setting the age of capacity to contract at 21." Kennedy, *supra* note 1, at 1689. Moreover, "[a] standard of reasonable care in the use of firearms is more particular than a standard of reasonable care in the use of 'any dangerous instrumentality.'" *Id.*

8 *See infra* notes 224-35, and accompanying text. *See also* Kaplow, *supra* note 3, at 560-61.

9 Sullivan, *supra* note 3, at 66.

10 M. P. Ellinghaus, *In Defense of Unconscionability*, 78 YALE L.J. 757, 760 (1969) (quoting JULIUS STONE, LEGAL SYSTEM AND LAWYERS' REASONINGS 25 (1964)).

11 Sullivan, *supra* note 3, at 58. Standards tend "to collapse decisionmaking back into the direct application of the background principle or policy to a fact situation." *Id.*

12 *See infra* notes 53-61, and accompanying text.

13 *See* Chapter 5.

contextualists, these writers, whom I shall call "neo-formalists,"[14] advocate the use of rules because rules require judges to "treat [ ] like cases alike,"[15] thereby helping to eliminate judicial bias and arbitrariness.[16] Rules narrow the factors judges legitimately employ, thereby helping to reduce judicial usurpation of power[17] and poor evaluations of social policy issues better left to the legislature.[18] Under a regime of rules, judges also decide cases more efficiently, avoiding the costs of a case-by-case resolution of an issue.[19] Relatedly, parties can better predict outcomes and plan coherently[20] and freely[21] when governed by "forward-looking" rules.[22] This, in turn, leads parties to pay attention

---

14 We will encounter the school of theorists denominated "legal formalists" in Chapter 5. I use "neo-formalists" here to describe recent theorists who advocate a system of rules.

15 Sullivan, *supra* note 3, at 62.

16 *Id.* Arbitrary decisionmaking "means the sub rosa use of criteria of decision that are inappropriate in view of the underlying purposes of the rule." Kennedy, *supra* note 1, at 1688. Arbitrariness can be "mechanical" as when a rule dictates a result conflicting with its own purpose or "biased" as when a judge applies a standard in a manner inconsistent with its purpose. *Id.* at 1695.

17 Sullivan, *supra* note 3, at 64-65.

18 *See* Robert L. Hale, *Bargaining, Duress and Economic Liberty*, 43 COLUM. L. REV. 603, 625 (1943); Kennedy, *supra* note 1, at 1752; Arthur A. Leff, *Unconscionability and the Crowd--Consumers and the Common Law Tradition*, 31 U. PITT. L. REV. 349, 356-57 (1970).

19 Sullivan, *supra* note 3, at 63. *See also* Kaplow, *supra* note 3, at 563.

20 Sullivan, *supra* note 3, at 62.

21 *Id.* at 64 ("rules . . . make it possible to foresee with fair certainty how the authority will use its coercive powers in given circumstances, and to plan one's individual affairs on the basis of this knowledge.").

22 Frank H. Easterbrook, *Foreword: The Court and the Economic System*, 98 HARV. L. REV. 4, 5 (1984). "[J]udges who look at cases merely as occasions for the fair apportionment of gains and losses almost invariably ensure that there will be fewer gains and more losses tomorrow." *Id.* at 10-11.

to the law and to conform their behavior to desired activity.[23] In short, neo-formalists favor rules because they believe rules "serve valuable objectives such as avoiding abuses of power and promoting certainty and predictability in human affairs."[24]

In this chapter, I focus on the debate between contextualists and neo-formalists of contract law. I begin by considering two schools of contractual contextualism. First I examine theorists whose work clarifies the meaning of and justifies the use of specific standards, namely unconscionability and good faith. These theorists acknowledge the open-endedness of certain standards, but they are little troubled. The theorists of unconscionability and good faith assert the value and inevitability of these legal safety-valves. Moreover, they believe that judges can and will develop subsidiary principles to clarify the meaning of these standards, thereby diminishing the concerns of neo-formalists. Second I turn to feminist contract theorists for another approach to contextualism. Although feminists write with many voices, one prominent view in the contract field emphasizes the importance of fairness, flexibility, and contextuality in applying contract doctrine.

I contrast the contextualists with the neo-formalists of contract law, who criticize standards such as good faith and unconscionability and generally bemoan the turn to contextualism in contract law.[25] Neo-formalists also laud the certainty and determinacy of contract rules, a subject taken up in detail in Chapter 5.

A. Theories of Contextualists

Problem 7: Michele Green, out of work and rather desperate, interviews for the job of assistant producer of "Journey," one of the few television shows then being cast. Floyd Webb, president of

---

23 Kennedy, *supra* note 1, at 1688-89, 1698. *See also* SCHAUER, *supra* note 3, at 139.

24 Steven D. Smith, *The Pursuit of Pragmatism*, 100 YALE L.J. 409, 428 (1990) (discussing Frederick Schauer, *Formalism*, 97 YALE L.J. 509 (1988)).

25 On unconscionability, *see generally*, Arthur A. Leff, *Unconscionability and the Code--The Emperor's New Clause*, 115 U. PA. L. REV. 485 (1967).

MDM Enterprises, the producer of the series, is impressed with Green's credentials and offers her a contract on the spot. Green reads through the contract quickly, but asks for time to consult a lawyer. Webb exhibits impatience at Green's reluctance to sign immediately. Although uncomfortable with a provision in fine print that expressly authorizes MDM to decrease her salary (initially $5000 per episode for one year) "without notice and for any reason," Green signs the contract. Six months after "Journey" premieres, Webb elects to decrease Green's salary by forty percent even though the show is a success.

Can Green successfully contest the salary cut? Contract doctrines such as unconscionability and good faith and the feminist contract perspective inform the decision.

1. Unconscionability

a. History and justifications

All legal systems include some method of introducing ethics and fairness in law.[26] In the commercial realm, the Civil Codes of Europe contain "general clauses" providing, for example, that "all immoral transactions are void," or that obligations be performed in good faith.[27] The civil law doctrine of *laesio enormis* is based on the policy of avoiding oppressive bargains.[28] In England, equity grew in part because of the failure of English law courts to employ fairness principles.

The American unconscionability standard can be traced to the Chancery court of England.[29] Prior to the merger of law and equity, the English Chancery court administered a body of equitable rules and

---

26 *See* Ralph A. Newman, *The Hidden Equity: An Analysis of the Moral Content of the Principles of Equity*, 19 HASTINGS L.J. 147 (1967).

27 RUDOLPH B. SCHLESINGER, COMPARATIVE LAW 282 (4th ed. 1980).

28 Leff, *supra* note 25, at 539.

29 See the discussion in Ryan v. Weiner, 610 A.2d 1377 (Del. Ch. 1992).

remedies that developed in part because of the absence in the law courts of principles based on general moral values.[30] As the result of criticism of their discretionary powers,[31] an increase in the case load,[32] and the growth of legally trained chancellors,[33] however, the chancellors began to consider the larger implications of their jurisprudence[34] and gradually began to create and follow their precedents. Substantive rules of fraud, mistake, trusts, and mortgages crystallized, and remedial principles such as estoppel, clean hands, laches, and unconscionability emerged. These rules and principles reflected the importance of principles of fairness in the early Chancery court and preserved the early court's flexibility.[35] The United States inherited the equity/law distinction, and American equity

---

[30] JOHN H. BAKER, AN INTRODUCTION TO ENGLISH LEGAL HISTORY 118 (3d ed. 1990); John L. Garvey, *Some Aspects of the Merger of Law and Equity*, 10 CATH. U. L. REV. 59 (1961); RALPH A. NEWMAN, EQUITY AND LAW: A COMPARATIVE STUDY 30 (1961). By barring new writs, the Provisions of Oxford in 1258 ended the flexibility of the common law. William F. Walsh, *Equity Prior to the Chancellor's Court*, 17 GEO. L.J. 97, 104-05 (1928). The early Chancellors were mostly members of the Church who believed they were not bound by precedent. *See* NEWMAN, *supra*, at 26-28.

[31] *See, e.g.*, O. METCALFE, GENERAL PRINCIPLES OF ENGLISH LAW 29 (8th ed. 1967); NEWMAN, *supra* note 30, at 255.

[32] Roger L. Severns, *Nineteenth Century Equity: A Study in Law Reform, Part II -- Maturity and Reform*, 13 CHI-KENT L. REV. 305, 309 (1935).

[33] *See* Charles A. Keigwin, *The Origin of Equity*, 18 GEO. L.J. 215, 233-34 (1930).

[34] *Id.*; BAKER, *supra* note 30, at 121, 126-27.

[35] NEWMAN, *supra* note 30, at 261-63; BAKER, *supra* note 30, at 127-128 ("equity has remained more flexible than the common law"). Professor Newman isolated certain principles that developed in equity courts:

> [R]ights should be based on substantial factors rather than on form[,] . . .the law should not aid the unscrupulous[,]. . .fully intended agreements should be carried out[,]. . .advantages gained through accident or mistake should be relinquished, and . . .hardship arising from accident or mistake should be fairly distributed . . . .

Id. at 19.

courts employed equitable principles similar to those of their English counterparts.[36]

The chancellors employed the doctrine of equitable unconscionability most often, although not exclusively, in cases involving specific performance of land sales contracts.[37] Courts denied specific performance on the basis of unconscionability if the exchange was deemed inadequate; conflicting authority developed on whether improprieties in the bargaining process were required as well. Some equity decisions required a degree of bargaining unfairness, such as concealment of facts or trickery, in addition to a finding of unfair terms.[38] Other decisions in equity found a contract (or the offending part) unenforceable on fairness grounds even when the contracting process seemed fair.[39] Still other courts found a contract unenforceable without emphasizing the fairness of the exchange if, as a result of fraud, misrepresentation, duress, undue influence, or the like, the bargaining conduct itself was sufficiently egregious.[40]

Section 2-302 of the Uniform Commercial Code (U.C.C.) codified the equitable unconscionability doctrine in the United States, authorizing courts to distinguish between fair and unfair sales agreements in order to

---

36 NEWMAN, *supra* note 30, at 33-34.

37 *See, e.g.*, Campbell Soup Co. v. Wentz, 172 F.2d 80 (3d Cir. 1948); Texas Co. v. Central Fuel Oil Co., 194 F. 1 (8th Cir. 1912); Eastern Rolling Mill Co. v. Michlovitz, 157 Md. 51, 145 A. 378 (Md. 1929). *See also* Leff, *supra* note 25, at 534 & n.209.

38 Herzog v. Gipson, 185 S.W. 1119, 1120 (Ky. 1916); Banaghan v. Malaney, 85 N.E. 839, 840 (Mass. 1908). *See also* Leff, *supra* note 25, at 538-39; John A. Spanogle, Jr., *Analyzing Unconscionability Problems*, 117 U. PA. L. REV. 931, 949 (1969).

39 *E.g.*, Campbell Soup Co. v. Wentz, 172 F.2d 80, 83 (3d Cir. 1948); Koch v. Streuter, 83 N.E. 1072, 1077 (Ill. 1908). *See also* 3 JOHN N. POMEROY, A TREATISE ON EQUITY JURISPRUDENCE § 928, at 639 (5th ed. 1941). In some cases, courts assumed unfair bargaining on the basis of the status or class of the weaker party. Spanogle, *supra* note 38, at 949.

40 *E.g.*, Jaeggi v. Andrews, 200 A. 760, 764 (N.J. Ch. 1938) (fraud); McDougall v. O'Hara, 276 P.2d 6, 7 (Col. Dist. Ct. App. 1954) (false representations); Margraf v. Muir, 57 N.Y. 155 (1874) (undue influence).

prevent "oppression and unfair surprise."[41] The section provides in part:

> If the court as a matter of law finds the contract or any clause of the contract to have been unconscionable at the time it was made the court may refuse to enforce the contract, or it may enforce the remainder of the contract without the unconscionable clause, or it may so limit the application of any unconscionable clause as to avoid any unconscionable result.

Many courts have applied unconscionability by analogy to other categories of contracts as well.[42] The modern formulation of unconscionability in the Code and courts, we shall see, reflects the Chancery courts' imprecision on the necessary mix of bargaining problems and unfair terms.

Despite the appeal of freedom of contract,[43] the unconscionability provision of the Code obviously affords judges great power to police agreements without offering very explicit guidance on how to accomplish the task.[44] Contextualists nevertheless make several arguments in support of unconscionability. First, they assert the *need* for an overriding policing device because unequal wealth and power and imperfect markets decrease the allure of the private-contracting paradigm[45] and permit one party to

---

41 *See* U.C.C. § 2-302 cmt. 1 (1962); Waters v. Min Ltd., 587 N.E.2d 231 (Mass. 1992).

42 *See, e.g.*, Ryan v. Weiner, 610 A.2d 1377 (Del. Ch. 1992); Waters v. Min Ltd., 587 N.E.2d 231, 233 (Mass. 1992).

43 *See* Chapters 1, 3, and 5.

44 *See, e.g.*, Robert A. Hillman, *Debunking Some Myths About Unconscionability: A New Framework for U.C.C. Section 2-302*, 67 CORNELL L. REV. 1 (1982).

45 *See* Friedrich Kessler, *Contracts of Adhesion--Some Thoughts About Freedom of Contract*, 43 COLUM. L. REV. 629, 640-41 (1943). *See also* Jean Braucher, *Contract Versus Contractariarism: The Regulatory Role of Contract Law*, 47 WASH. & LEE L. REV. 697, 712 (1990) ("'Consent' occurs in the context of a prior distribution of entitlements and abilities."); Robert L. Hale, *Coercion and Distribution In a Supposedly Non-Coercive State*, 38 POL. SCI. Q. 470, 471-73 (1923).

Professor Kennedy saw connections between individualistic law and rules and

dictate disadvantageous terms in a myriad of situations.[46] Contextualists often point to take-it-or-leave-it standard-form contracts between consumers and large companies to illustrate.[47] They paint a bleak picture of the quality of consumer assent: Confronted by industry-wide form contracts and lacking information and sophistication, consumers have little choice but to accede to boiler-plate terms that are often heavily one-sided.[48] They must rely on industry to draft forms fairly and reasonably.[49] Even when specific terms of an agreement are disclosed, unsophisticated and uneducated consumers may not understand them.[50] Moreover, consumers faced with the concerted practices of industry lack the aggregate strength to combat these terms.[51] Even outside form-contract settings, one party may be able to dictate terms because of the other's lack of market alternatives, education, information, resources, or time.[52] Witness the plight of Michele Green in Problem 7. Contextualists argue that legal intervention is necessary in such circumstances and is, in fact, inevitable.

---

altruistic law and standards. Kennedy, *supra* note 1, at 1685-87; 1737-1751. Professor Kelman evaluates the argument with some skepticism in MARK KELMAN, A GUIDE TO CRITICAL LEGAL STUDIES 56-59 (1987).

46 Freedom of contract therefore "can ring very hollow when used to defend a grossly unfair contract secured at the expense of a person of little bargaining skill." P.S. Atiyah, Book Review, 95 HARV. L. REV. 509, 527 (1981) (reviewing CHARLES FRIED, CONTRACT AS PROMISE: A THEORY OF CONTRACTUAL OBLIGATION (1981)).

47 *See* W. David Slawson, *Standard Form Contracts and Democratic Control of Lawmaking Power*, 84 HARV. L. REV. 529 (1971).

48 Hillman, *supra* note 44, at 25-26.

49 Williams v. Walker-Thomas Furniture Co., 350 F.2d 445, 449-50 (D.C. Cir. 1965); Gladden v. Cadillac Motor Car Div., 416 A.2d 394, 402 (N.J. 1980).

50 Richard E. Speidel, *Unconscionability, Assent and Consumer Protection*, 31 U. PITT. L. REV. 359, 363-64 (1970).

51 Kessler, *supra* note 45, at 631-32.

52 *See, e.g.*, Waters v. Min Ltd., 587 N.E.2d 231 (Mass. 1992); Hillman, *supra* note 44, at 25-26.

Contextualists advocate the use of unconscionability because it allows judges to police the quality of assent and the fairness of the terms directly, rather than covertly by manipulating an existing rule,[53] by purposefully applying a particular interpretive approach (including literal, purposive, contextual, or historical interpretation),[54] or by selecting a different rule when an applicable rule leads to an unjust result.[55] Contextualists argue that even the most clearly expressed rules fail to deter judicial creativity. No matter how artfully drafted, they point out, static and abstract rules rarely suitably fit the particular circumstances.[56] Moreover, nonlegal factors, such as the respective wealth of the parties and the general attractiveness of their positions, unavoidably influence judges.[57] The use of unconscionability averts the "corruption" of rules[58] and the creation of overly complex rules.[59] "Corrupted" or overly complicated rules, of course, are themselves ambiguous or unclear and, therefore, less helpful in subsequent cases.[60]

Consider, for example, the provision in Problem 7 entitling Webb to decrease Green's salary "for any reason." Without unconscionability, a court might avoid enforcement of the harsh provision by labeling it

---

53 *See, e.g.*, Ellinghaus, *supra* note 10; John E. Murray, Jr., *Unconscionability: Unconscionability*, 31 U. PITT. L. REV. 1, 4-5 (1969); Slawson, *supra* note 47, at 563.

54 *See infra* note 61, and accompanying text for some examples.

55 The availability of alternative rules is one of the principal claims of theorists associated with Critical Legal Studies. For a discussion, *see* Chapter 5.

56 Kessler, *supra* note 45, at 637-39; Kennedy, *supra* note 1, at 1689.

57 *See* Slawson, *supra* note 47, at 561-63. *See also* Chapter 5.

58 Kennedy, *supra* note 1, at 1701.

59 *Id.* at 1697 (citing the parol evidence rule as an example).

60 *See* Spanogle, *supra* note 38, at 934. *See also* Lon L. Fuller, *American Legal Realism*, 82 U. PENN. L. REV. 429, 437 (1934).

ambiguous, even though the term actually seems clear on its face.[61] Alternatively, the court might look to the purpose of the clause and "find" that it required a reason tied to a real economic concern of MDM. Unconscionability, on the other hand, allows the judge to strike the offensive provision directly on the bases of Webb's superior bargaining power and sharp practices, Green's lack of opportunity to study the contract, and the sweep of the term.

Advocates of unconscionability also believe that honest, open use of a fairness standard helps establish minimum levels of commercial good faith[62] and, because of its *in terrorem* effect, discourages the use of offensive clauses or contracts.[63] A court's declaration that the salary provision in Problem 7 is unconscionable, for example, would deter other employers from using the term. A decision that the provision was ambiguous, on the other hand, would merely encourage lawyers to draft even clearer provisions.

Unconscionability proponents also assert that the standard deepens adherence to freedom of contract. The standard increases bargaining equality by enhancing the underdog's potential to make free choices: "There is still much to be gained by the further standardizing of the relations in which society has an interest, in order to remove them from the control of the accident of power in individual bargaining."[64]

---

[61] *See, e.g.*, Standard Ins. Co. of N.Y. v. Ashland Oil & Refining Co., 186 F.2d 44, 47 (10th Cir. 1950); McPeak v. Boker, 53 N.W.2d 130 (Minn. 1952).

[62] *See, e.g.*, Murphy v. McNamara, 416 A.2d 170, 177 (Conn. Super. Ct. 1979). *See also* Ellen A. Peters, *Remedies for Breach of Contracts Relating to the Sale of Goods Under the Uniform Commercial Code: A Roadmap for Article Two*, 73 YALE L.J. 199, 202 n.10 (1963).

[63] WILLIAM D. HAWKLAND, A TRANSACTIONAL GUIDE TO THE U.C.C. § 1.1603, at 46-47 (1964); Spanogle, *supra* note 38, at 934-36.

[64] Nathan Isaacs, *The Standardizing of Contracts*, 27 YALE L.J. 34, 47 (1917). *See also* Harry W. Jones, *The Jurisprudence of Contracts*, 44 U. CIN. L. REV. 43, 50 (1975) ("The incidence of genuine contractual bargaining has not been reduced necessarily; indeed, government interventions designed to establish equality of bargaining power may conceivably make contract a more vigorous institution in our day than in Sir Henry Maine's.").

Regulation may also foster norms of appropriate behavior of the contracting

Contextualists assert that a rule-based legal framework, on the other hand, favors parties repeatedly involved with the legal system, generally large companies that can most easily adapt to the rules.[65] Moreover, notwithstanding Fried's moral thesis for enforcing promises, discussed in Chapter 1, one can argue that regulation overturning one-sided contracts procured by a party with superior bargaining power does not violate a weaker promisor's "moral autonomy."[66]

Finally, contextualists find support in economic analysis. Judge Posner has suggested that judge-created law is more "efficiency-promoting" than legislative rules. Appellate judges, he asserts, view the parties as representing activities, such as "owning land [and] driving cars." These judges make their decisions based on which activity is more valuable economically.[67] Legislators, on the other hand, are influenced by interest groups and depend on the electoral process; they "sell" legislation to those parties that can enhance their prospects for reelection.[68] One may question Posner's premise that judges adhere to a model of economic efficiency and that efficiency is the appropriate basis upon which to make policy.[69] Nevertheless, his theory does indicate that, at least to the extent that judges are insulated from lobbying groups and politics, judicial decisions may be more objective than decisions made by legislators.

---

participants. *See* Bernard S. Black, *Is Corporate Law Trivial?: A Political and Economic Analysis*, 84 NW. U. L. REV. 542, 573 (1990) ("Legal rules, such as the duty of loyalty owed by managers to shareholders, can affect corporate norms.").

65 Kennedy, *supra* note 1, at 1699-1700.

66 *See* Atiyah, *supra* note 46, at 527.

67 RICHARD A. POSNER, ECONOMIC ANALYSIS OF LAW § 19.2, at 523-24 (4th ed. 1992).

68 *Id.* at 525.

69 For a critique of Posner's position that common law adjudication is more efficient than legislative decisionmaking, *see* Arthur A. Leff, *Economic Analysis of Law: Some Realism About Nominalism,* 60 VA. L. REV. 451, 470-73 (1974).

b. Frameworks for analysis

Proponents of unconscionability must deflect criticism that the standard is just too amorphous. Contextualists therefore have introduced "frameworks" for analyzing the cases. Ironically, Arthur Leff, a scholar critical of unconscionability, set forth the most widely adopted model in his classic article on the subject. Despite his view that U.C.C. Section 2-302 was "amorphous[ly] unintelligib[le]," his effort to determine whether the focus of inquiry is on the bargaining process or the substance of the agreement, or both, suggested a framework widely followed and expanded by courts and commentators.[70]

Professor Leff's paradigmatic case for finding unconscionability involved both "bargaining naughtiness" diminishing the quality of a party's assent (also called "procedural unconscionability") and grossly unfair terms (known as "substantive unconscionability").[71] To illustrate, in Problem 7 Webb, enjoying a quasi-monopoly position, took advantage of Green's economic need to induce her to sign the contract without studying it when he showed impatience at her request to consult a lawyer.[72] Webb's conduct arguably would be procedurally unconscionable under Leff's model.[73] Moreover, the term of the contract permitting Webb to decrease Green's salary for reasons unconnected to her performance, the success of the show, or MDM's financial state,

---

70 *See* Leff, *supra* note 25, at 488. *See also* Murray, *supra* note 53, at 12-13; Melvin A. Eisenberg, *The Bargain Principle and Its Limits*, 95 HARV. L. REV. 741, 748-85 (1982); Hillman, *supra* note 44.

71 Leff, *supra* note 25, at 488, 539-40.

72 In Allen v. Michigan Bell Telephone Co., 171 N.W.2d 689 (Mich. Ct. App. 1969), *rev'd on other grounds*, 232 N.W.2d 302 (Mich. Ct. App. 1975), the court invalidated as unconscionable a contract provision exculpating Bell Telephone from liability to yellow page advertisers for failure to include their advertisements in its directories. The court reasoned that the advertising could be obtained only from Bell, that advertising in the yellow pages was an economic necessity, and that the exculpatory clause was unreasonable. 171 N.W.2d at 693-94. *See also* Ryan v. Weiner, 610 A.2d 1377 (Del. Ch. 1992).

73 *See also* Ryan v. Weiner, 610 A.2d 1377 (Del. Ch. 1992).

arguably was unfair. The term is therefore substantively unconscionable as well. Overall, a court therefore should strike the term on the grounds of unconscionability.

Courts and theorists have broken down procedural and substantive unconscionability into still smaller components to illuminate the standard. In fact, Professor Leff's "procedural unconscionability," as interpreted by the courts, may take many forms beyond the quasi-duress present in Problem 7. A party may unduly influence her counterpart,[74] such as when a sophisticated seller knowingly induces an uneducated buyer to make a purchase beyond the buyer's means.[75] A party may misrepresent the facts.[76] Procedural unconscionability also encompasses sneaky drafting techniques such as hiding controversial terms in fine print, creating a "linguistic maze" of contradictory provisions,[77] or drafting incomprehensible terms.

Consider the venerable *Williams v. Walker-Thomas Furniture Co,*[78] which illustrates the latter. The case involved a contract clause that

---

[74] Undue influence consists of conduct that overpowers the will of another and induces her to do something that she otherwise would not have done. *See, e.g.*, Waters v. Min Ltd., 587 N.E.2d 231 (Mass. 1992).

[75] *See, e.g.*, Frostifresh Corp. v. Reynoso, 274 N.Y.S.2d 757, 758 (Dist. Ct. 1966), *rev'd on other grounds*, 281 N.Y.S.2d 964 (App. Term 1967) (contract unconscionable in part because of salesman's awareness of buyer's imminent termination of employment). *See also* Ellinghaus, *supra* note 10, at 771.

[76] *See, e.g.*, Davis v. Kolb, 563 S.W.2d 438 (Ark. 1978).

[77] Gladden v. Cadillac Motor Car Div., 416 A.2d 394 (N.J. 1980). The court, applying contract interpretation principles to a tire manufacturer's guarantee, concluded that a contract term limiting the buyer's remedy was unenforceable because the guarantee presented the tire owner with a "linguistic maze" of contradictory provisions; the court indicated that the conflicting terms of the guarantee had induced the purchaser into believing "that he was obtaining a guarantee of performance." The court called the contract "a melange of overlapping, variant, misleading, and contradictory provisions." *Id.* at 401. A concurring judge would have held that the remedy limitation was unconscionable. *Id.* at 404 (Pashman, J., concurring).

[78] 350 F.2d 445 (D.C. Cir. 1965).

permitted the seller to reclaim all goods previously sold to the customer upon a single default by the customer. The clause was sufficiently incomprehensible to a reasonable person that the court could have determined under the rules of contract interpretation that the clause should not be enforced.[79] The court, however, remanded the case for a determination on the broader ground of unconscionability.[80]

A party's failure to disclose information about the circumstances or even the legal effect of an agreement may also be procedurally unconscionable. Courts have found a duty to disclose when a party with superior knowledge of facts "resulting in an inequality of condition or knowledge between the parties" fails to disclose to the other party important facts regarding the circumstances of a bargain.[81] Courts have also found a duty to disclose information about contract terms in contracts containing fine print[82] or other hidden terms.[83]

---

79 The provision, which the court referred to as being "rather obscure," provided:

> [T]he amount of each periodical installment payment to be made by (purchaser) to the Company under this present lease shall be inclusive of and not in addition to the amount of each installment payment to be made by (purchaser) under such prior leases, bills or accounts; and all payments now and hereafter made by (purchaser) shall be credited pro rata on all outstanding leases, bills and accounts due the Company by (purchaser) at the time each such payment is made.

350 F.2d at 447 (emphasis omitted).

80 350 F.2d at 450.

81 Smith v. Peterson, 282 N.W.2d 761, 767 (Iowa Ct. App. 1979). *See also* Vom Lehn v. Astor Art Galleries, Ltd., 380 N.Y.S.2d 532 (Sup. Ct. 1976) (seller knew buyer was unfamiliar with value of carvings and charged more than twice their value without disclosing true worth).

82 *See, e.g.*, Egan v. Kollsman Instrument Corp. 234 N.E.2d 199, 202-03 (N.Y. 1967).

83 *See, e.g.*, Kergald v. Armstrong Transfer Express Co., 113 N.E.2d 53, 54 (Mass. 1953); Willard Van Dyke Prods., Inc. v. Eastman Kodak Co., 189 N.E.2d 693 (N.Y. 1963); David v. Manufacturers Hanover Trust Co., 287 N.Y.S.2d 503 (Civ. Ct. 1968). An example of a hidden term is a liability disclaimer on the back of a claim check.

To protect parties from unexplained terms that contradict their reasonable expectations,[84] courts have found a duty to disclose contract terms even in the absence of fine print or obfuscation when the party seeking to enforce the contract had superior knowledge or had the trust and confidence of the other party.[85] In *Weaver v. American Oil Co.*,[86] for example, the court held unenforceable a clause in a lease agreement between American and station-owner Weaver requiring Weaver to indemnify American for American's own negligence.[87] Weaver, who did not have a high school education, had never read the lease.[88] The court stated that "the party seeking to enforce such a contract has the burden of showing that the provisions were explained to the other party and *came to his knowledge* and there was in fact *a real and voluntary meeting of the minds and not merely an objective meeting.*"[89]

---

84 In Johnson v. Mobil Oil Corp., 415 F. Supp. 264, 269 (E.D. Mich. 1976), the court argued:

> [B]efore a contracting party with the immense bargaining power of the Mobil Oil Corporation may limit its liability vis-a-vis an uncounseled layman . . . it has an affirmative duty to obtain the voluntary, knowing assent of the other party. This could easily have been done in this case by explaining to plaintiff in laymen's terms the meaning and possible consequences of the disputed clause.

Professor Llewellyn recognized these realities and suggested that onerous terms, not expressly agreed upon, should be unenforceable. *See* KARL N. LLEWELLYN, THE COMMON LAW TRADITION 370-71 (1960).

85 The idea of a special relationship between consumers and merchants may explain the relatively common use of unconscionability in consumer cases and the relatively light use of unconscionability in cases involving agreements between merchants.

86 276 N.E.2d 144 (Ind. 1971).

87 *Id.* at 147-48.

88 In addition, the clause was in fine print. *Id.* at 147.

89 *Id.* at 148 (emphasis in original). Although the clause at issue in *Weaver* seems manifestly unreasonable, the court intimated that it would have upheld the clause if American had explained it to Weaver: "We do not mean to say or infer that

Procedural unconscionability thus protects parties from contracts or terms to which they have not assented because of breakdowns or deficiencies in the bargaining process. The subject of substantive unconscionability, on the other hand, is egregious terms. Some terms are substantively unconscionable because they are immoral or conflict with public policy ("I can cut off your head if you do not pay on time"). Even short of such obvious constraints, a term may be substantively unconscionable if it denies a party substantially what she bargained for and performs no reasonable function in the trade.[90]

Courts are not unfamiliar with analyzing what constitutes a bargain's substantive core. For example, problems involving materiality of breach, mistake affecting the root of the contract, frustration of the foundation of the contract, and adequacy of consideration all require courts to determine whether a contracting party will gain substantially what was bargained for in the contract.[91]

Courts also consider whether a term serves the legitimate needs of the party accused of unconscionability or simply takes unfair advantage of the other party. To determine whether a suspect term satisfies a reasonable need,[92] courts evaluate the term in the context of the commercial setting and in light of other contracts designed for similar purposes.[93] Under this approach, a court would not determine if a price

---

parties may not make contracts exculpating one of his negligence and providing for indemnification, but it must be done *knowingly and willingly* as in insurance contracts made for that very purpose." *Id.* (emphasis in original). *See also* Sho-Pro of Indiana, Inc. v. Brown, 585 N.E.2d 1357 (Ind. Ct. App. 1992).

When confronted with adhesion contracts, some courts, particularly in insurance cases, have enforced the reasonable expectations of the weaker party in part on unconscionability grounds even though specific contract terms contradict those expectations. C & J Fertilizer, Inc. v. Allied Mutual Ins. Co. 227 N.W.2d 169 (Iowa 1975).

90 Hillman *supra* note 44, at 32-33.

91 *See, e.g.*, Murray, *supra* note 53, at 74-79.

92 *See* Leff, *supra* note 25, at 543.

93 *See* U.C.C. § 2-302(2); Ellinghaus, *supra* note 10, at 785.

is excessive, for example, without considering the seller's credit risks, the financing terms, the costs of selling and collection, and the retail prices of comparable goods.[94] Contract terms drafted heavily in favor of one party actually may be fair in light of the risks involved.

Although the best case for finding unconscionability will include both procedural and substantive unconscionability, some contextualists assert that courts should intervene solely on the basis of the substantive fairness of the contested terms.[95] In fact, some courts do not ignore the plight of parties who cannot act with economic rationality, even when the bargaining process seems procedurally fair. Although controversy surrounds whether poverty alone should qualify a party for this special protection, its usual incidents, such as the absence of education, the lack of resources to gather information,[96] the inability to obtain reasonable credit, and possibly even special psychological needs,[97] may entitle a party to avoid certain terms.[98] If a consumer could not obtain market information, could not comprehend the subject of disclosure, or could not resist sophisticated marketing techniques because of her special situation, then the consumer did not actually assent to the terms at issue, no matter how clearly stated or how explicitly disclosed. The term challenged in

---

94 *See* Leff, *supra* note 25, at 549-51.

95 *See, e.g.,* Slawson, *supra* note 47.

96 *See, e.g.*, Leff, *supra* note 18, at 351.

97 For a reaction to the use of psychological weaknesses as defenses to the enforcement of contract terms, *see infra* Chapter 5 at notes 59-61, and accompanying text.

Ellinghouse argued that society's focus on consumption and sellers' persuasive marketing techniques diminished a consumer's real assent to contracts or terms even when a consumer purchased a luxury item instead of a necessity. Ellinghaus, *supra* note 10, at 768.

98 *Id.* at 772.

Weaver v. American Oil Co.[99] is a good example of a clause that should be unenforceable under this type of reasoning.[100]

In sum, contextualists maintain that unconscionability ensures fairness in individual cases, avoids manipulation of rules, establishes a modicum of commercial decency, and achieves structure through the procedural-substantive unconscionability framework. Moreover, the practice of determining whether an agreement or term is unconscionable, contextualists assert, helps fill out the meaning of assent within the relevant community.[101] We shall see shortly that neo-formalists take issue with all of these assertions.[102]

2. Good Faith

Unconscionability is not the only important twentieth-century contract-law standard. In the early and mid-twentieth century, courts imposed an obligation of good faith performance and enforcement of contracts in many cases and in various settings.[103] In an important 1968 article,[104] Robert S. Summers found that such decisions ruled out various types of bad faith performance, "including: evasion of the spirit of the

---

99 276 N.E.2d 144 (Ind. 1971); *see supra* notes 86-89, and accompanying text.

100 A termination-for-any-reason clause in an employment contract, when interpreted to permit termination because of personal animosity, also may be substantively unconscionable.

101 Braucher, *supra* note 45, at 701. *See also* Chapter 5.

102 *See infra* notes 182-223, and accompanying text. Even during the prominence of freedom of contract in eighteenth century England, courts barred agreements that were illegal or contrary to public policy. Samuel Williston, *Freedom of Contract*, 6 CORNELL L. Q. 365, 373 (1921).

103 Robert S. Summers, *The General Duty of Good Faith--Its Recognition and Conceptualization*, 67 CORNELL L. REV. 810, 812 (1982) [hereinafter Summers, *General Duty*]).

104 Robert S. Summers, *"Good Faith" in General Contract Law and the Sales Provisions of the Uniform Commercial Code,* 54 VA. L. REV. 195 (1968) [hereinafter Summers, *Good Faith*].

deal; lack of diligence and slacking off; . . . and interference with, or failure to cooperate in, the other party's performance."[105] Courts also excluded inappropriate conduct involving "the assertion, settlement, and litigation of contract claims and defenses."[106] Such conduct included "asserting an overreaching or 'weaseling' interpretation or construction of contract language; taking advantage of another's necessitous circumstances to secure a favorable modification; . . . and abusing a power to determine compliance or to terminate a contract."[107]

In light of the breadth of contexts in which courts employed good faith and the variety of conduct it ruled out, Professor Summers concluded that the principle has no general meaning of its own. Good faith simply excludes various forms of inappropriate conduct depending on the context.[108] As such, good faith is a "safety valve" employed by judges to ensure a minimum level of fairness in contracting.[109]

Professor Summers saw that the "excluder" approach to good faith conferred on judges considerable (although not unbounded[110]) discretion to determine the conduct to be ruled out and therefore would not appeal to those who prefer certainty in contract law. Yet, Summers observed that no distinct definition of good faith was possible because the concept did not lend itself to that kind of conceptualization:[111] The good faith obligation "is an unusually 'circumstance-bound' requirement, and excludes highly varied forms of bad faith, many of which become identifiable only in the context of circumstantial detail of a kind that

---

105 Summers, *General Duty*, *supra* note 103, at 813.

106 *Id.*

107 *Id.*

108 *See* Summers, *Good Faith*, *supra* note 104, at 199-207.

109 Summers, *General Duty*, *supra* note 103, at 811-812.

110 *See generally id.*

111 *Id.* at 817-821.

defies comprehensive formulation in a single rule."[112] As with unconscionability's "organic development by the courts,"[113] the task for judges applying good faith is to generate criteria for determining bad faith in particularized contexts and to formulate rules barring specific kinds of bad faith.[114]

In 1979, the American Law Institute promulgated Section 205 of the *Restatement (Second) of Contracts*, which set forth an obligation of good faith performance in every contract.[115] Influenced by Summers' analysis, Robert Braucher, the section's principal drafter,[116] did not attempt to define good faith. Instead Braucher acknowledged that

> [t]he phrase 'good faith' is used in a variety of contexts, and its meaning varies somewhat with the context. Good faith performance or enforcement of a contract . . . excludes a variety of types of conduct characterized as involving 'bad faith' because they violate community standards of decency, fairness or reasonableness.[117]

Not only has the excluder analysis influenced the *Restatement (Second)* approach to good faith, courts expressly follow it as well.[118]

---

[112] *Id.* at 821.

[113] Ellinghaus, *supra* note 10, at 795.

[114] Summers, *General Duty, supra* note 103, at 822.

[115] RESTATEMENT (SECOND) OF CONTRACTS § 205 (1979) provides: "Every contract imposes upon each party a duty of good faith and fair dealing in its performance and its enforcement."

[116] Summers, *General Duty*, *supra* note 103, at 810.

[117] RESTATEMENT (SECOND) OF CONTRACTS § 205 cmt. a.

[118] A sample of recent cases bears out this observation. *See, e.g.*, Tymshare, Inc. v. Covell, 727 F.2d 1145 (D.C. Cir. 1984) (then Judge Scalia agreeing with the "excluder" analysis); Carma Developers (Cal.), Inc. v. Marathon Dev. Cal., Inc., 826 P.2d 710, 727, (Cal. 1992) ("Instead of defining what is consistent with good faith and fair dealing, it is more meaningful to concentrate on what is prohibited."); Price v. Wells Fargo Bank, 261 Cal. Rptr. 735, 741 (Ct. App. 1989) ("The term `good faith' has been described as an 'excluder' phrase which is 'without general

Courts characterize good faith as an excluder with no general meaning of its own and isolate criteria for determining bad faith in the situation before them.[119]

For purposes of discussion, I now consider a few important recent good faith cases arising in two of the contexts isolated by Professor Summers. What conduct should be excluded as bad faith when a party allegedly asserts an overreaching interpretation of a contract clause or fails to cooperate in another's performance? To answer these questions courts must distinguish the laudable exercise of one's contract rights on the one hand and the engagement in "sharp" practices on the other. Contextualists assert that the doctrine of good faith, as developed in particular contexts, enables courts to draw this line with sufficient precision.

a. Asserting an overreaching interpretation of a contract term

In Problem 7, Webb will argue that he exercised a clear contract right to decrease Green's salary "for any reason." Can Webb withstand a claim of bad faith?

Several recent cases have involved claims of bad faith when a party exercised what appeared to be an express contract right. In two cases involving remarkably similar facts (somewhat simplified here for discussion), a written employment contract entitled an employee-sales representative to commissions on sales in excess of certain quotas.

---

meaning (or meanings) of its own . . . .'"); Centronics Corp. v. Genicom Corp., 562 A.2d 187, 191 (N.H. 1989) (Souter, J.) ("The differences between the obligations of good faith . . . are enough to explain why the commentators despair of articulating any single concept of contractual good faith, even after the more than fifty years of litigation following in the wake of the American common law's first explicit recognition of an implied good faith contractual obligation. . . ."); Nolan v. Control Data Corp., 579 A.2d 1252, 1258-60 (N.J. Super. Ct. App. Div. 1990) (quoting favorably from Tymshare, Inc. v. Covell's discussion of Summers); Best v. U.S. Nat'l Bank of Or., 739 P.2d 554, 557 (Or. 1987) ("Because [good faith] must be applied to the entire range of contracts, definitions of good faith tend to be either too abstract or applicable only to specific contexts."); Garrett v. Bankwest, Inc., 459 N.W.2d 833, 841 (S.D. 1990) (good faith's meaning "varies with the context").

[119] *See* cases cited *supra* note 118.

Nevertheless, the contract also expressly permitted the employer to raise the sales quotas retroactively without notice or justification and thereby to slash an employee's compensation. Not surprisingly, in both cases, the employee claimed the employer exercised the power in bad faith to deprive the employee of accrued compensation.[120] In another case, depositors' account agreements permitted their banks to set fees for checks written on insufficient funds. The depositors brought a class action against the banks alleging the banks acted in bad faith by setting the fees too high.[121]

Can the doctrine of good faith apply when a party exercises what appears to be an unfettered contract right? Under the excluder analysis, the question is whether such conduct can ever be ruled out as bad faith. Professor Summers observed that asserting an "overreaching" interpretation of a contract term could be bad faith. But how could an employer's or bank's interpretation "overreach" if the contract expressly authorized the party's actions?[122]

Because of the elasticity of language, courts have largely abandoned the "plain meaning" rule of contract interpretation, which bars the use of extrinsic evidence to determine a contract's meaning.[123] Mainly to support reasonable reliance on contracts, courts also interpret contract language according to a reasonable person's understanding. Thus, a

---

[120] *See* Tymshare, Inc. v. Covell, 727 F.2d 1145, 1148 (D.C. Cir. 1984) (employer had unlimited discretion to modify or terminate employee's compensation plan in its "sole discretion"); Nolan v. Control Data Corp., 579 A.2d 1252, 1254 (N.J. Super Ct. App. Div. 1990) (employer reserved the right to "make any retroactive, current and/or prospective adjustments or revisions to salaries, bonuses, [or] incentive compensation levels").

[121] Best v. U.S. Nat'l. Bank of Or., 739 P.2d 554 (Or. 1987).

[122] "We are aware of no reported case in which a court has held the covenant of good faith may be read to prohibit a party from doing that which is expressly permitted by an agreement." Carma Developers (Cal.), Inc. v. Marathon Dev. Cal., Inc., 826 P.2d 710, 728 (Cal. 1992). *But see* Wieder v. Skala, 609 N.E.2d 105, 109 (N.Y. 1992) (courts can enforce implied terms that seem to contradict express ones).

[123] *See, e.g.*, Edwin W. Patterson, *The Interpretation and Construction of Contracts*, 64 COLUM. L. REV. 833, 838-842 (1964); RESTATEMENT (SECOND) OF CONTRACTS § 212(1) and cmt. b (1979).

party's actual intentions do not control.[124] Applying these principles to the sales-quota cases, the question becomes whether an employer's retroactive alteration of its employee's sales quotas and compensation contradicted the employee's reasonable expectations, as determined in light of all admissible extrinsic evidence.[125] If so, the employer had asserted an "overreaching" interpretation by claiming the contract authorized its actions, and therefore acted in bad faith.

Courts confronting such questions have recognized that even a clause purporting to grant sole power to a party does not necessarily permit the party to exercise the power "for any reason whatsoever, no matter how arbitrary or unreasonable."[126] Such an interpretation would likely contradict the other party's reasonable expectations because it would deprive that party of the fruits of the contract. In the case of a provision affording an employer "sole discretion" to alter sales quotas, for example, then Judge Scalia,[127] speaking for the court in *Tymshare, Inc. v. Covell,*[128] stated:

> [A]greeing to such a provision would require a degree of folly on the part of these sales representatives we are not inclined to posit where another plausible interpretation of the language is available. It seems to us that the 'sole discretion' intended was discretion to determine the existence or nonexistence of the various factors that would

---

124 *See* Chapter 1; Hotchkiss v. Nat'l City Bank of N.Y., 200 F. 287, 293 (S.D.N.Y. 1911) (Learned Hand, J.). "We ask judges or juries to discover that 'objective viewpoint'--through their own subjective processes." Zell v. American Seating Co., 138 F. 2d 641, 647 (2d Cir. 1943) (Frank, J.), *rev'd,* 322 U. S. 709 (1944) (per curiam). *See also* CHARLES FRIED, CONTRACT AS PROMISE: A THEORY OF CONTRACTUAL OBLIGATION 82 (1981).

125 "[T]he mere recitation of an express power is not always the test" of whether the parties left the decision to alter quotas to the absolute and "uncontrolled discretion" of the employer. Tymshare, Inc. v. Covell, 727 F.2d 1145, 1153 (D.C. Cir. 1984).

126 *Id.* at 1154; Nolan v. Control Data Corp., 579 A.2d 1252, 1259 (N.J. Super. Ct. App. Div. 1990).

127 Judge Scalia is now Justice Scalia of the United States Supreme Court.

128 727 F.2d 1145 (D.C. Cir. 1984).

> reasonably justify alteration of the sales quota. Those factors would include . . . an unanticipated volume of business from a particular customer unconnected with the extra sales efforts of the employee assigned to that account; and . . . a poor overall sales year for the company, leaving less gross income to be expended on commissions. . . . But the language need not (and therefore can not reasonably) be read to confer discretion to [increase] the quota for any reason whatever--including . . . a simple desire to deprive an employee of the fairly agreed benefit of his labors.[129]

Not surprisingly, many courts appear to agree with the above reasoning.[130] The approach appeals to a sense of justice, and by invoking the parties' intentions, it also shows respect for contractual freedom. But some believe that determining the parties' expectations objectively "expand[s] the scope of `consent' far beyond anything remotely close to what the parties had in mind."[131] Instead of supporting the parties' intentions, the reasonable expectations test licenses courts to import interventionist principles such as fairness and justice. Did Judge Scalia decide what good faith ruled out not on the basis of the parties' view of the meaning of the sales-quota adjustment clause, but according to the dictates of fairness? More generally, does good faith rule out conduct based on the parties' intentions or according to general societal values?

---

129 *Id.* at 1154. The reasoning is similar when the issue is a bank's right to set NSF fees: "[D]iscretion had to be exercised within the confines of the reasonable expectations of the depositors." Best v. U.S. Nat'l Bank of Or., 739 P.2d 554, 558 (Or. 1987).

130 *See, e.g.*, *Best*, 739 P.2d 554 (Or. 1987). *But see* Corenswet, Inc. v. Amana Refrigeration, Inc., 594 F.2d 129 (5th Cir. 1979), *cert. denied*, 444 U.S. 938 (1979) ("for any reason" termination clause means any reason a franchisor deemed sufficient). *See also* Wieder v. Skala, 609 N.E.2d 105, 109 (N.Y. 1992) (courts can enforce implied terms that seem to contradict express ones).

131 Ian R. Macneil, *Contracts: Adjustment of Long-Term Economic Relations Under Classical, Neoclassical, and Relational Contract Law*, 72 NW. U. L. REV. 854, 883 (1978).

One response is that the issue is relatively unimportant-- generally courts reach the same result under either approach.[132] In a nutshell, Judge Scalia reasoned that the parties probably did not intend to permit the employer to reduce the employee's compensation retroactively and arbitrarily because a reasonable employee would not agree to such an onerous provision.[133] Reasonable parties, in other words, intend to incorporate the meaning of terms society would find fair and just.

Even assuming reasonable parties generally have such intentions, however, whether good faith is based on the parties' intentions or on general societal values matters because the parties do not always have good faith intentions. Suppose the contract in *Tymshare* had expressly permitted management to change the sales quotas at any time "for the sole purpose of reducing or eliminating the employee's earned commissions." Suppose further that the employer had pointed out and explained the legal effect of the clause before the employee signed the contract. Suppose later the employer had sought to exercise the clause for the purpose expressed. Although we may be repulsed by such conduct, it is not in bad faith if the good faith doctrine only excludes conduct outside of the parties' reasonable expectations, because the employee should have reasonably expected the employer's actions. Of course, such a clause may be unenforceable on other grounds, such as unconscionability.[134] But that doctrine may not always apply, for example, because of the absence of procedural unconscionability[135]--the employee may have been educated

---

132 *See, e.g.*, Market St. Assocs. Ltd. Partnership v. Frey, 941 F.2d 588, 596 (7th. Cir. 1991) ("[W]hether we say that a contract shall be deemed to contain such implied conditions as are necessary to make sense of the contract, or that a contract obligates the parties to cooperate in its performance in `good faith' to the extent necessary to carry out the purposes of the contract, comes to much the same thing.").

133 Tymshare, Inc. v. Covell, 727 F.2d 1145, 1154 (D.C. Cir. 1984).

134 *Id.* at 1152 n.5. *See supra* notes 43-102, and accompanying text. *See generally* Robert A. Hillman, *An Analysis of the Cessation of Contractual Relations*, 68 CORNELL L. REV. 617, 648-650 (1983).

135 *See supra* notes 72-73, and accompanying text.

and fully cognizant of the clause's import. Good faith may be determinative.

Many courts faced with such harsh facts would probably find bad faith. If so, good faith is not always tied to the parties' intentions. Instead, it can rule out conduct based on considerations of fairness and justice. Some courts may openly import such interventionist principles.[136] Others may engage in impressive judicial acrobatics to fit good faith within an assent framework, and then find bad faith.[137] In fact, some might claim that Judge Scalia's reasoning in *Tymshare* is itself an example of the latter approach.[138] After all, the contract appeared to authorize the employer's nasty behavior (recall that it permitted the employer to alter the quota plan "within [its] sole discretion"). Nevertheless, the judge reasoned that the employer could not in good faith reduce the sales quota arbitrarily because the parties had not intended to give the employer that power. By stretching assent beyond its obvious applications in hard cases, courts may do more harm to the rule of law than by acknowledging the interventionist nature of good faith.[139]

This is not to say that good faith invariably utilizes outside principles. Freedom of contract remains an important goal, and courts do not lose sight of it even in good-faith cases. Nevertheless, fairness in the contracting process is also an important contract aim. The good faith doctrine reflects this dichotomy. It sometimes rules out conduct based on the parties' expectations, either express or implied. It also excludes conduct abhorrent to society.

---

[136] *See, e.g.*, Best v. U.S. Nat'l Bank of Or., 739 P.2d 554, 559 (Or. 1987). ("When a party has the contractual right to specify a price term, the term specified may be so high or low that the party will be deemed to have acted in bad faith regardless of the reasonable expectations of the other party.").

[137] Market St. Assocs. Ltd. Partnership v. Frey, 941 F.2d 588 (7th. Cir. 1991).

[138] Compare the court's reasoning in Corenswet, Inc. v. Amana Refrigeration, Inc., 594 F.2d 129 (5th Cir. 1979), *cert. denied*, 444 U.S. 938 (1979) ("for any reason" termination clause means any reason a franchisor deemed sufficient).

[139] *See* Summers, *Good Faith*, *supra* note 104, at 226 n.288.

From what has been said, we can now identify criteria for determining what behavior is to be ruled out when a party allegedly asserts an overreaching interpretation of an express contract clause. Does the conduct deprive the other party of the fruits of the contract? Does the party engaging in the conduct mean to deprive the other party of those fruits? Does the contract language, interpreted objectively and in light of all the circumstances, bar the conduct? Is the conduct unfair? If the answer to the first two questions and either the third or fourth question is "yes," good faith rules out the conduct.

Let us apply these criteria to Problem 7. Webb's reduction of Green's salary deprived her of her contract fruits, namely fair compensation based on her work on "Journey." Webb sought to deprive her of fair compensation without justification. An objective interpretation of the "for any reason" clause would require Webb to have a justifiable "reason" for depriving Green of compensation, such as one tied to a real economic concern. Moreover, Webb's conduct was unfair because it deprived Green of her contract fruits for reasons unrelated to the quality of her performance. Webb therefore acted in bad faith.

b. Failing to cooperate

A good deal of modern contracting involves multiple interactions between familiar parties over an extended time period.[140] Given the likelihood of changed circumstances, the parties to such contracts rarely draft complete agreements and, instead, rely on norms such as cooperation, flexibility, and trust to govern their relations.[141] The principle of good faith supports such arrangements by ruling out behavior that conflicts with these norms even if the contract does not expressly forbid the behavior or if the conduct would not constitute fraud.[142] At the same time, parties to long-term contracts generally do not owe each other

---

140 *See* Chapter 7. *See also* Robert A. Hillman, *Court Adjustment of Long-Term Contracts: An Analysis Under Modern Contract Law*, 1987 DUKE L.J. 1, 4-6.

141 *See generally* Ian R. Macneil, *Values in Contract: Internal and External*, 78 NW. U. L. REV. 340 (1983).

142 Market St. Assocs. Ltd. Partnership v. Frey, 941 F.2d 588 (7th. Cir. 1991).

a fiduciary duty--a duty to put the other's interests first.[143] The challenge for courts is to determine when a party's conduct, although between the extremes of fraud on the one hand and the violation of a fiduciary duty on the other, demonstrates bad faith.

Consider the following problem based on a major recent case.[144] Seeking to develop its property, a landowner enters a sale and leaseback arrangement with a large finance company. The agreement entitles the lessee (the former landowner) to ask the lessor (the finance company) to finance improvements on the land and calls for good-faith negotiations toward that end. If the negotiations fail, the lessee can repurchase the property from the lessor at a price based on a computation set forth in the agreement. Later, the lessee decides to seek financing, but not from the lessor. The lessee is unable to secure financing, however, because it does not own the land. The lessee therefore seeks to repurchase the property from the lessor but the latter's price is too high. The lessee then realizes the formula for establishing the repurchase price under the sale-leaseback agreement is very favorable, about one-third of the lessor's current asking price and below market value. The lessee also understands that it must request financing from the lessor before the repurchase option matures. The lessee realizes that the lessor does not remember the agreement's repurchase option. The lessee therefore requests financing "pursuant to the lease," but never reminds the lessor about the repurchase provision.[145] In fact, the lessee hopes the lessor will reject the request. Does the lessee's conduct show bad faith?

The lessee does not have a fiduciary duty to call the repurchase option to the lessor's attention[146] and nothing in the contract requires the lessee to remind the lessor of this key term. Nevertheless, the question is whether a court should read such a requirement into the agreement on

---

143 *Id.* at 593.

144 *Id.*

145 *Id.* at 591. The lessee wrote to the lessor-finance company "to ask again that you advise us immediately if you are willing to provide the financing pursuant to the lease." *Id.*

146 *Id.*

the basis of good faith. Judge Posner responded affirmatively in *Market Street Associates v. Frey.*[147] Far from acknowledging the expansiveness of good faith, however, Posner went out of his way to convince that the parties' "constructive" intentions controlled. Recognizing the realities of long-term contracting, Judge Posner theorized that contracting parties impliedly condition their performance on each other's cooperation because express provisions become "progressively less apt" as time passes.[148] The duty to cooperate thus "give[s] the parties what they would have stipulated for expressly if at the time of making the contract they had had complete knowledge of the future" and encountered no transaction costs.[149] Judge Posner concluded that tricking the lessor into selling the land to the lessee at the favorable repurchase price runs afoul of the duty to cooperate because it "would be the type of opportunistic behavior in an ongoing contractual relationship" that the parties would never have authorized.[150]

Judge Posner located the good faith obligation to cooperate "halfway between a fiduciary duty . . . and the duty merely to refrain from active fraud."[151] But Posner refused to acknowledge that good faith injects moral or ethical principles into the law. Instead, he argued that the duty to cooperate "is a stab at approximating the terms the parties would have negotiated had they foreseen the circumstances that have given rise to their dispute."[152]

The parties very likely never considered whether their lease imposed a duty on the lessee to cooperate by reminding the lessor of its

---

147 941 F.2d 588 (7th. Cir. 1991). In the actual case, the court reversed a summary judgment in favor of the lessor. Judge Posner, for the court, remanded for a determination of the facts. In *dicta*, he suggested that, if the facts were as set forth here, he would find bad faith.

148 *Id.* at 595-596.

149 *Id.* at 596.

150 *Id.*

151 *Id.* at 595.

152 *Id.*

rights. Nevertheless, by tying the duty to the parties' presumed preferences, Judge Posner's conceptualization attracts admirers of contractual freedom. The problem with the analysis is that one suspects the parties likely would *not* have included a duty to remind if they had considered the matter. After all, the lessor was a large, experienced finance company, quite familiar with sale-leaseback arrangements. The lessor, "an immensely sophisticated enterprise,"[153] surely would have assumed the responsibility for understanding its rights and obligations under the lease.

Despite his protestations, Judge Posner's main goal may have been to advance his economic theory of the law.[154] He noted that good faith does not require "altruistic" behavior when the other party "gets into trouble in performing."[155] Otherwise, a party would be excused whenever a difficulty arose. On the other hand, a contracting party cannot "take deliberate advantage of an oversight by [a] contract partner concerning his rights under the contract. Such taking advantage "[is] sharp dealing."[156] The latter should not be condoned because "it has no social product, and also like theft it induces costly defensive expenditures, in the form of overelaborate disclaimers or investigations into the trustworthiness of a prospective contracting partner."[157] In a nutshell, condoning the lessee's conduct would increase unnecessary "defensive expenditures."[158]

We therefore must add to reasonable expectations and fairness an additional source of good faith as it is applied by courts: instrumental policies such as economic efficiency. As with cases involving an "overreaching" interpretation of a contract term, good faith here reflects

---

153 *Id.* at 597.

154 *See* RICHARD A. POSNER, ECONOMIC ANALYSIS OF LAW (4th ed. 1992).

155 Market St. Assocs. v. Frey, 941 F.2d at 594.

156 *Id.*

157 *Id.*

158 *Id.*

contract law's complexity and richness, even as the courts attempt to limit the standard.

Again, let us conclude by suggesting criteria for determining the behavior to be ruled out in failure-to-cooperate cases such as *Market Street Associates.* Several factors control. Was the lessee aware of the repurchase provision and its effect? Was the lessee aware that the lessor had overlooked the term and would have acted differently otherwise? Is the effect of the lessor's oversight a material windfall for the lessee? Does the lessee's conduct therefore conflict with the lessor's reasonable expectations? Is the conduct unfair? Is it inefficient? If the answer to each of the first three questions and any of the last three questions is "yes," good faith excludes the lessee's strategy.

In conclusion, Professor Summers' excluder analysis of good faith has withstood the test of time. Courts continue to utilize his approach almost twenty-five years after he published it. His conceptualization underscores the expansiveness of good faith.[159] Recent cases reinforce this truth. Courts invoke fairness and social policy, even as they insist that the doctrine reflects the parties' expectations. Yet the excluder analysis also tames good faith. As courts continue to face highly contextual issues, they will continue to develop the meaning of good faith (and the meaning of unconscionability, for that matter) in specific settings, forming over time criteria to guide them.

3. Feminist contract law

---

[159] For an effort to conceptualize good faith with greater particularity, *see* Steven J. Burton, *Breach of Contract and the Common Law Duty to Perform in Good Faith*, 94 HARV. L. REV. 369 (1980) (bad faith consists of "exercising discretion" to recapture forgone opportunities).

Feminist legal theorists offer many perspectives.[160] I have already investigated the feminist approach to marriage contracts in Chapter 3. Another developing point of view decries the "male frame of reference" underlying much of contract law.[161] The mainstream's treatment of principles supporting women (such as reliance and restitution) as "exceptions" or "deviations from the normal rules of contract," these theorists assert, evidences this male orientation.[162] Perhaps the most prominent school of feminist contract theorists, whose work is particularly relevant to the discussion in this chapter, reacts to what it perceives as the law's excessive abstraction, rigidity, and objectivity. The feminist method this school champions is subjective, contextual, and case-specific.[163] These feminist theorists stress the connection between

---

160 Overgeneralizing about women's views diminishes the female perspective and the contribution of feminism. Kathryn Abrams, *Feminist Lawyering and Legal Method*, 16 LAW & SOC. INQUIRY 373, 383 (1991). Professor Abrams is "not fully convinced that one's socialization 'as a woman' produces a particular orientation toward moral decision making." *Id.* at 375 n.5. But some suggest "feminist solidarity" to achieve change. Leslie Bender, *From Gender Difference to Feminist Solidarity: Using Carol Gilligan and an Ethic of Care in Law*, 15 VT. L. REV. 1 (1990).

161 *See, e.g.*, Lucinda Finley, *Breaking Women's Silence in Law: The Dilemma of the Gendered Nature of Legal Reasoning,* 64 NOTRE DAME L. REV. 886, 898 (1989).

162 *Id. See also* Carrie Menkel-Meadow, *Mainstreaming Feminist Legal Theory,* 23 PAC. L. J. 1493 (1992).

163 CAROL GILLIGAN, IN A DIFFERENT VOICE: PSYCHOLOGICAL THEORY AND WOMEN'S DEVELOPMENT (1982).

people,[164] the importance of compromise,[165] and the relevance of perspectives and values outside of the mainstream.[166] They advocate legal norms which explicitly reflect these truths.

Within contract law, Professor Mary Joe Frug's analysis of contract excuse best reflects this perspective.[167] Contract excuse cases involve a promisor's attempt to cease performance on the grounds of "unanticipated" or "disruptive" circumstances.[168] Frug compared Posner and Rosenfield's "masculine" analysis of the problem with my own treatment of the subject.[169] Judge Posner and Rosenfield asserted that courts should and do permit promisors to cease performance because of disruptive circumstances only when the promisee is the superior bearer

---

164 "[T]he feminine perspective views individuals primarily as interconnected members of a community .... [It] is ... more other-directed .... The essential difference between the male and female perspectives [is that] ... `[t]he basic feminine sense of self is connected to the world, the basic masculine sense of self is separate.'" Suzanna Sherry, *Civic Virtue and the Feminine Voice in Constitutional Adjudication*, 72 VA. L. REV. 543, 584-85 (1986) (quoting NANCY CHODOROW, THE REPRODUCTION OF MOTHERING: PSYCHOANALYSIS AND THE SOCIOLOGY OF GENDER 169 (1978).

165 Peter Linzer, *Uncontracts: Context, Contorts and the Relational Approach*, 1988 ANN. SURV. AM. L. 139, 162.

166 Peter Linzer & Patricia A. Tidwell, *Reply: Letter to David Dow-Friendly Critic and Critical Friend*, 28 HOUS. L. REV. 861, 862 (1991).

167 *See* Mary J. Frug, *Rescuing Impossibility Doctrine: A Postmodern Feminist Analysis of Contract Law*, 140 U. PENN. L. REV. 1029 (1992) [hereinafter *Rescuing Impossibility]*. *See also* Mary J. Frug, *Re-Reading Contracts: A Feminist Analysis of a Contracts Casebook*, 34 AM. U. L. REV. 1065 (1985). Professor Frug was tragically murdered on April 4, 1991. Her *Impossibility* article was in draft form at that time.

168 Frug, *supra* note 167, *Rescuing Impossibility*, at 1034.

169 *Id.* at 1031. *See* Richard A. Posner & Andrew M. Rosenfield, *Impossibility and Related Doctrines in Contract Law: An Economic Analysis*, 6 J. LEGAL STUD. 83 (1977); Hillman, *supra* note 134; Hillman, *supra* note 140.

(or avoider) of the risk.[170] We shall see more fully in Chapter 6 that the superior risk bearer is the party best able to bear the expense of an event, such as by purchasing insurance.[171] The superior-risk-bearer approach appeals to Posner and Rosenfield because in theory parties would prefer to place the risk on the superior risk bearer. The approach therefore decreases the overall cost of contract planning because it saves future parties the expense ("transaction costs") of bargaining to supplant a different gap-filling rule.[172]

Frug characterized Posner and Rosenfield's effort as masculine in nature. She argued that their work presents one "singular legitimate decisional objective . . . to facilitate efficient contract planning."[173] The authors "treat all contracts as if they fit a particular, abstract model of contractual relations . . . ."[174] Moreover, "the authors rely on and defend a sharply and cleanly dichotomized system of contractual remedies, according to which contractual obligations must either be performed in full or discharged."[175]

On the other hand, my own effort to analyze cessation, according to Frug, "presents a sharply contrasting approach to impossibility doctrine."[176] I argued that courts strive to enforce the parties' risk allocation, but often neither the contract nor the context helps identify the parties' intentions. Courts therefore turn to outside norms, such as favoring the party with the greater overall equities, requiring the parties to avoid harming each other without justification, favoring the party that acts reasonably to avoid loss, and, when possible, protecting the parties'

---

170 Posner & Rosenfield, *supra* note 169, at 90.

171 *See* Chapter 6.

172 *See, e.g.*, POSNER, *supra* note 68, § 4.1, at 92-93. Transatlantic Fin. Corp. v. United States, 363 F.2d 312, 316-19 (D.C. Cir. 1966), is a representative case.

173 *Rescuing Impossibility*, supra note 167, at 1035.

174 *Id.*

175 *Id.*

176 *Id.* at 1036.

expected fruits of the exchange.[177] According to Frug, this approach is a "pluralistic, context-sensitive model . . . emphasizing that in the real world many contracts are based on long-term relationships in which the parties rely on good faith, forbearance, and sharing, rather than insisting on a literal interpretation of their contract texts."[178] Frug concluded that my approach "neatly fits the popular interpretation of . . . virtuous feminine attitudes toward justice" because it "is characterized by a concern for multiple objectives, by an appreciation of contextualized relationships, and by a desire to achieve flexibility and sharing in the administration of contract remedies."[179] Moreover, my analysis "offer[s] a critique of the male model which is both powerful and also reminiscent of typical feminine criticisms of masculinity."[180]

Frug's work divided the standards-rule debate along a gendered axis. Its validity depends on whether women, on the whole, prefer discretionary standards and men rules. If so, this line of demarcation contributes to a better understanding of contract law rules and standards. Some feminists, however, decry the "jurisprudence of difference," asserting that it preserves harmful stereotypes of women's "roles" in society.[181] They would therefore contest any vision of contract law that creates dichotomous visions along gendered lines. Moreover, as we saw in the discussion of marriage theorists in Chapter 3 (and as we will see more fully in the next section), some feminists remain wary of the application of discretionary standards in a male-oriented society.

B. Neo-Formalist Contract Law

Neo-formalists contend that contract standards such as unconscionability and good faith decrease the law's predictability and

---

[177] Hillman, *supra* note 134, at 629-640.

[178] *Rescuing Impossibility*, supra note 167, at 1036.

[179] *Id.*

[180] *Id.* at 1037.

[181] Joan M. Shaughnessy, *Gilligan's Travels*, 7 LAW & INEQ. J. 1, 9 (1988).

increase the costs of contract planning and adjudication of disputes.[182] Indeed, standards tempt judges to decrease their "analytical rigor"[183] or worse, to venture into the legislature's or the parties' domain.[184] Moreover, neo-formalists have little faith that courts can and will successfully develop specific criteria and, ultimately, rules to fill out the meaning of these standards in various contexts.

Standards decrease the certainty of the law because they enlarge the factors judges can employ in deciding a case. A court considering Green's claim that the salary provision in Problem 7 is unconscionable, for example, can merely recite a list of factors influencing its decision--*e.g.*, the sweep of the salary term, the lack of an adequate opportunity to study the contract, Green's unemployment, the fine print, and Webb's status, business sophistication, bargaining power and inflexibility--and then simply conclude that the contract is or is not unconscionable. The court need not make any effort to show which factors are essential, which are sufficient, and which are superfluous. Critics of standards also argue that standards decrease the predictability of previously developed doctrines. Factors previously subsumed under appropriate common law categories simply may be lumped together without consideration of their weight and effect.[185]

Neo-formalists assert that standards increase the costs of contract planning because parties cannot predict the factors a court may take into account in resolving a dispute.[186] Webb therefore may have difficulty differentiating permissible from impermissible negotiating pressure and

---

182 As to the latter, *see* Kaplow, *supra* note 3.

183 Even Ellinghaus, a strong supporter of unconscionability, makes the point. Ellinghaus, *supra* note 10, at 761.

184 *See* Kennedy, *supra* note 1, at 1753 (describing the argument).

185 Hillman, *supra* note 44, at 19-23.

186 On the other hand, if most contracting parties pay little attention to contract law, the importance of clear rules may be overplayed. *See, e.g.*, Kennedy, *supra* note 1, at 1699; Chapter 7.

contract terms.[187] Webb may also have problems distinguishing permissible from impermissible manners of performing the contract. For example, can Webb require Green to sign the contract immediately? Can he utilize a "for any reason" salary reduction clause? Under what circumstances can he reduce Green's salary?[188] Can Webb base a reduction only on the lack of success of "Journey"? On his dissatisfaction with Green's work? On something else? Conversely, neo-formalists worry less about the costs of over- or underinclusive rules, such as the costs of inapposite rule-application. They simply claim that the parties can avoid litigation through careful contract planning or that the rule will be changed.[189]

Neo-formalists claim that judges will have no better insight than Webb when the parties' deal breaks down. The costs of adjudicating standards will therefore be high and will be incurred often. In fact, although the costs of promulgating a detailed and comprehensive rule may be higher than adopting a more general standard, neo-formalists believe that the savings realized by applying the rule more than make up for these potential greater costs.[190]

Neo-formalists also often criticize standards on the theory that courts are ill-equipped to evaluate social policy issues and to "legislate."[191] Judges, they assert, do not have sufficient resources or time

---

[187] *See* Richard A. Epstein, *Unconscionability: A Critical Reappraisal*, 18 J.L. & ECON. 293, 306 (1975): "It is difficult to know what principles identify the `just term,' and for the same reasons that make it so difficult to determine the 'just price.'"

[188] "Where . . . good faith conduct assertedly consists of preventing harm due to circumstances not created by the obligor, the absence of a direct causal relationship increases the likelihood of disagreement over whether the obligor must act and what he must do to fulfill the expanded obligation." Clayton P. Gillette, *Limitations on the Obligation of Good Faith*, 1981 DUKE L.J. 619, 643 (1981).

[189] Kennedy, *supra* note 1, at 1739 (describing the neo-formalist response).

[190] Kaplow, *supra* note 3, at 621.

[191] *See* Hale, *supra* note 18, at 625; Leff, *supra* note 18, at 356-57; Alan Schwartz, *Seller Unequal Bargaining Power and the Judicial Process,* 49 IND. L.J. 367, 368-70, 390-92 (1974).

to evaluate the effects of their decisions on society,[192] whereas legislators have vast resources available to investigate such matters.[193] At best, courts can make broad and often inaccurate generalizations about the responsibility of various social groups (e.g.,"the poor should be discouraged from frill buying"[194]) and about the need for particular contract clauses (e.g., cross-collateral clauses overstep a lender's right to security[195]). Courts can also compare the conduct of similarly situated commercial parties to determine whether particular behavior fits a community standard. This approach to fairness questions, however, presents many opportunities for error in evaluating individual behavior and assessing community standards.[196] Moreover, it ensures adherence to the "predominant morals of the marketplace"[197] and precludes a serious focus on potentially superior alternatives.[198]

At worst, standards may lull judges into feeling little need to engage in deep analysis of the issue at hand and the ramifications of a decision. Standards may "allow courts to act as roving commissions to

---

192 Leff, *supra* note 18, at 356-57.

193 There have been numerous legislative responses to the question of fairness in contracting. *See, e.g.*, UNIFORM CONSUMER CREDIT CODE §§ 6.104, 6.110-.111; Federal Trade Commission Act, 15 U.S.C. §§ 41-58 (1988).

194 Leff, *supra* note 25, at 558: "[W]ith respect to the . . . concept that the poor should be discouraged from frill-buying, no legislature in America could be persuaded openly to pass such a statute, nor should any be permitted to do so sneakily."

195 For example, Professor Epstein makes an argument in favor of cross-collateral clauses such as the term utilized in Williams v. Walker-Thomas Furniture Co., 350 F.2d 445 (D.C. Cir. 1965), based on the the seller's risk of depreciating security. Epstein, *supra* note 187, at 306-08.

196 Some believe that there is "no way to make a distributional judgment fairly." Alan Schwartz, *Comments on Professor Harrison's Paper*, 1988 ANN. SURV. AM. L. 115, 120.

197 Richard Danzig, *A Comment on the Jurisprudence of the Uniform Commercial Code*, 27 STAN. L. REV. 621, 629 (1975).

198 *Id.* at 629-30.

set aside those agreements whose substantive terms they find objectionable."[199] In so doing, courts may indiscriminately alter established contract rules or the parties' risk allocations in quest of the elusive, perhaps unachievable, goal of fairness. Such judicial activity decreases the law's certainty and stability. It also interferes with the parties' freedom of contract[200] and, concomitantly, their opportunity to maximize their welfare.[201] Ironically, such judicial activity may also deprive a protected party's class of future choices. For example, if a court finds certain types of warranty disclaimers unconscionable, sellers will have to increase their prices to cover the additional liability. Consumers will be unable to choose between a warranty disclaimer and a lower price.[202]

Some neo-formalists also worry that judicial decisionmaking under a regime of standards will be unfair. For example, unlike Professor Frug, some feminists fear that the application of standards ultimately may harm women because judges, typically male and insensitive to women's issues, will apply standards in a manner unfavorable to women. These theorists point to child custody cases to illustrate.[203] They point out that women make more economic sacrifices for and invest more time in their children than men. When a marriage breaks up, women are overly cautious about the prospect of losing custody. Standards for awarding custody such as "the best interest of the child," according to the argument, leave women subject to the discretion of typically male judges. These judges tend to enforce the "trades" made by the parties, which, because

---

199 Epstein, *supra* note 187, at 294.

200 *Id.* at 315.

201 Gillette, *supra* note 188, at 650-651.

202 Schwartz, *supra* note 196, at 120-21. *See also* Epstein, *supra* note 187, at 305: "[I]t will be more expensive for members of the 'protected' class to contract on their own behalf within a complex web of legal rules."

203 Mary E. Becker, Comments at the Association of American Law Schools Annual Meeting, Section on Women in Legal Education, Panel on *The Influence of Feminist Theory and Gender Bias in Contracts* (Jan. 1989) [hereinafter "Comments"].

of superior male bargaining power, inevitably favor that party.[204] For this reason a set of rules such as "the primary caretaker rule" may work better in custody cases.[205]

Some feminists go even further, asserting that women would actually be better off in their family affairs without legal intervention at all. For example, as we saw in Chapter 3, Professor Schultz decries the "barrier of familyness," which impedes private contracting within families.[206] Private ordering, with its respect for diversity and individual rights, Schultz argues, can help women improve their plight.[207] By contrast, courts may disfavor various groups by presuming their inability to take care of themselves.[208] Presumably, Schultz would therefore prefer rules over standards, which would give judges less liberty to exercise such views.

Seeking to refute the contextualists' view that courts can develop effective criteria for the application of standards, some neo-formalists assert that "the vagueness problem is not suited to temporal solutions."[209] They argue that standards such as unconscionability and good faith cannot be defined clearly and consistently:[210] "[I]t is probable that different judges will mean different things when using [good faith], thereby undermining any attempt to derive a single meaning or single principle from the combined usages."[211]

Even if the judiciary is equipped to explore issues of social policy, and even if, over time, courts can fill in the meaning of standards in

---

204 *Id.*

205 *Id.*

206 Marjorie Schultz, Comments, *supra* note 203.

207 *Id.*

208 Epstein, *supra* note 187, at 304-05.

209 Gillette, *supra* note 188, at 645.

210 *Id.* at 645.

211 *Id.*

specific contexts, neo-formalists argue that the common law process may be an inferior method for achieving the social policy goals ultimately identified. Professor Leff, for example, maintained that common law development is costly, time-consuming, and ineffective: "One cannot think of a more expensive and frustrating course than to seek to regulate goods or 'contract' quality through repeated lawsuits against inventive 'wrongdoers.'"[212] For one thing, contracting parties will encounter the significant costs of uncertainty waiting for the courts to do their job.[213] For another, Professor Leff contended that after cases such as *Williams v. Walker-Thomas Furniture Co.*,[214] sellers affected by unconscionability findings will only tinker with their form contracts and that the adjustments will not resolve the fundamental problems of the sellers' practices.[215] Nor will the decisions curb similar abuses that are not addressed specifically by the cases.[216] In sum, instead of discouraging employers like Webb from including "for-any-reason" salary adjustment clauses in cases such as Problem 7, a court's finding of unconscionability will simply cause drafters to "recur to the attack."[217] A rule that employers cannot alter employees' salaries for non-job related reasons is more likely to deter Webb.[218]

---

212 Leff, *supra* note 18, at 356. Professor Leff advocated a more direct approach--permit the legislature to declare illegal the kinds of clauses found offensive in *Williams v. Walker-Thomas Furniture Co.* and create an administrative agency to enforce the law. *Id.* at 357.

213 Kaplow, *supra* note 3, at 622-23.

214 350 F.2d 445 (D.C. Cir. 1965). *See* notes 78-80 and accompanying text *supra.*

215 Theorists point out the futitility of pursuing "distributional concerns in bargaining contexts when all of the rules can be altered or avoided" by the parties. Schwartz, *supra* note 196, at 120.

216 Leff, *supra* note 18, at 354-56.

217 Karl N. Llewellyn, Book Review, 52 HARV. L. REV. 700, 702-03 (1939).

218 *See* Kaplow, *supra* note 3, at 622: "[R]ules, announced in advance, are more likely to influence actual behavior . . . . "

For all of the foregoing reasons, neo-formalists prefer that legislators take responsibility for fleshing out the law in the form of specific rules. Professor Leff, for example, criticized the drafters of Section 2-302 of the U.C.C. for failing to offer sufficient guidance in the section.[219] Leff believed that the drafters should have defined specifically and clearly the bargaining ills that would render a contract procedurally unconscionable.[220] In fact, he thought the drafters had abdicated their responsibility by substituting unconscionability "for the possibility of more concrete and particularized thinking about particular problems of social policy" such as whether the law should permit sellers to disclaim warranties[221] and whether a price is fair in light of the seller's risk and other factors.[222] The drafters' wrongheadedness was all the more disappointing, Leff thought, because they demonstrated they could do better in provisions such as Sections 2-719 and 2-316, which set forth extensive criteria for determining the enforceability of remedy limitations and warranty disclaimers, respectively.[223]

The neo-formalists of contract law not only lash out at the use of standards, they also present an affirmative case for the value of rules. Specifically, they are convinced of the relative determinacy and objectivity of contract rules. Because the argument has been made most forcefully in response to the Critical Legal Studies criticism of contract law, I reserve the discussion for the next chapter.

---

219 Leff, *supra* note 25, at 501. "[W]hat may permissibly make the judges' pulses race or their cheeks redden, so as to justify the destruction of a particular provision, is, one would suppose, what the judge ought to have been told by the statute." *Id.* at 516.

220 *Id.* at 504.

221 *Id.* at 515-516.

222 *Id.* at 550-51.

223 *Id.* at 516-28.

Conclusion

Contextualists and neo-formalists disagree about the importance of flexibility and predictability in contract law. Contextualists believe that flexible contract law ensures fairness and avoids arbitrariness.[224] They consider judicial discretion necessary and beneficial. Contextualists therefore support contractual standards such as good faith and unconscionability, "paradigmatic concept[s] that can never be exhaustively described."[225] Neo-formalists, on the other hand, bemoan the loss of certainty and predictability in a regime of standards, which they believe increase the costs of contract planning and judicial decisionmaking.

A host of value judgments about law's goals and assumptions about the costs and benefits of rules versus standards comprise a large portion of each side's argument. Should the power to effect social change reside in the courts or in the legislature? Should we strive for more stability or adaptability in our legal system? Do the costs of some suboptimal decisions under a regime of rules outweigh the benefits of predictability? On the other hand, do the costs of poor decisions by some judges ill-equipped to exercise discretion under a regime of standards outweigh the benefits of flexibility?[226] Bereft of "hard" evidence, I suspect few arguments are likely to persuade anyone already aligned. Nevertheless, even committed partisans probably understand in their heart of hearts that the truth lies between any polar position. Lawmakers must and will continue to strive to make the law clear, certain, and efficient even as they enact or create safety valves such as unconscionability and

---

224 *See* Kennedy, *supra* note 1, at 1688.

225 Eisenberg, *supra* note 70, at 754.

226 For elaboration, *see* SCHAUER, *supra* note 3, at 135-166. For my taste, the current mix of contract law rules and standards, including relatively concise rules of formation, performance, and remedy and increasingly influential policing standards, probably represents the most sensible compromise. *See also* Ian Ayres, *Preliminary Thoughts on Optimal Tailoring of Contractual Rules,* 3 S.CAL. INTER. L. REV. 1, 18 (1993): "In areas of contract performance, contract law might specify per se rules of performance and non-performance, but specify a "reasonableness" standard to govern conduct falling outside the rule-governed conduct."

good faith and must and will continue to make the law flexible even as they select and apply particular rules. In short, the judicial process of developing criteria for applying standards on the one hand and for determining which rule to apply and how to apply it on the other decreases the distance between standards and rules.

I have already spent considerable time illustrating how judges make standards more rule-like.[227] The opposite is nicely illuminated by the judicial treatment of the parol evidence rule. The parol evidence rule bars contradictory evidence of the meaning of a written agreement when the writing is "integrated" (i.e. intended to be complete) and clear on its face.[228] The purpose of the rule is to protect the sanctity of a written contract. But in applying this "rule," courts generally admit extrinsic evidence of the parties' intentions on integration and even of the meaning of the writing, at least preliminarily, to determine whether the parol evidence rule should apply and extrinsic evidence ultimately should be excluded. Moreover, in deciding the meaning of a writing, courts often turn to reasons apart from formal contract rules of interpretation, such as fairness or morality (presuming, for example, that the parties would not have intended an overreaching term).[229] The parol evidence rule is therefore far less certain a shield for a written contract than might first be perceived.

Despite the absence of hard barriers separating rules and standards, a central disagreement between contextualists and neo-formalists involves the question of judicial competence. Do judges applying standards have the requisite skill, sophistication, and perspective to avoid hopelessly subjective or arbitrary decisionmaking, to consider and incorporate factors such as changed and extenuating circumstances, and to make good social policy decisions? Perhaps even more important, can judges successfully establish criteria for deciding cases in particular

---

227 *See supra* notes 74-159, and accompanying text.

228 *See, e.g.*, Pacific Gas & Electric Co. v. G.W. Thomas Drayage & Rigging Co., 68 Cal.2d 33, 442 P.2d 641 (1968).

229 *See, e.g.*, Stanley Fish, *The Law Wishes to Have a Formal Existence*, *in* THE FATE OF LAW at 178. (Austin Sarat & Thomas R. Kearns eds. 1991).

contexts, thereby conferring meaning on standards and limiting judicial discretion?[230] Contextualists argue that judges can succeed. Neo-formalists, on the other hand, doubt the effectiveness of the common-law process.[231] Thus, a crucial issue in the debate between the schools in large measure reduces to the factual question of judicial competence to establish criteria for deciding cases over the long term.[232]

We already have some evidence on this question. At least until the Chancery system began to decay under the weight of cases and financial problems, courts of equity maintained their allegiance to ethical standards and preserved their discretion to fashion flexible remedies[233] even as they began to establish and follow precedent.[234] We can observe a similar phenomenon in almost three decades of decisions applying the Uniform Commercial Code's versions of unconscionability and good faith.[235] As contextualists predicted, courts and scholars have begun to

---

230 *See supra* notes 74-159, and accompanying text. "[Unconscionability] must be articulated and extended through the develpment of more specific norms to guide the resolution of specific cases, provide affirmative relief to exploited parties, and channel the discretion of administrators and legislators." Eisenberg, *supra* note 70, at 800.

231 *See supra* notes 209-18, and accompanying text.

232 *See generally* Gillian K. Hadfield, *Judicial Competence and the Interpretation of Incomplete Contracts*, 23 J. LEGAL STUD. 159 (1994).

233 Baker, *supra* note 30, at 128-30; William F. Walsh, *Is Equity Decadent?*, 22 MINN. L. REV. 479, 482-83 (1938). *See also* BENJAMIN N. CARDOZO, THE NATURE OF THE JUDICIAL PROCESS 137 (1921). According to Cardozo, the Chancellors, "without sacrificing uniformity and certainty, built up the system of equity with constant appeal to the teachings of right reason and conscience." *Id.*

234 *See supra* notes 34-36, and accompanying text. Professor Leff thought the equity cases failed to shed light on modern unconscionability because, unlike the equity cases, unconscionability focuses on standard-form contracts. Moreover, the equity cases involved "overall imbalance," whereas most modern cases deal with the possible unconscionability of particular terms. Leff, *supra* note 25, at 533. For a partial rebuttal, *see* Hillman, *supra* note 44, at 35-41.

235 Theorists published much of their work on unconscionability and good faith in the 1960s and 1970s, about the time when states considered and adopted the Uniform

isolate criteria and establish precedent for applying modern contract standards. We now know much more about the application of unconscionability and good faith in distinct arenas. We understand that unconscionability involves the bargaining process and the resulting terms and that the best case for a finding of unconscionability involves unfairness in both. We know that problems such as duress, undue influence, misrepresentation, the failure to disclose, and the like comprise the bulk of bargaining unfairness problems. We grasp that terms that deny a party the fruits of the contract may be substantively unconscionable. We also recognize that a party acts in bad faith when he deprives the other party of her reasonable expectations. This occurs in diverse situations, such as when a party purposely asserts an overreaching interpretation of a contract term or when a party fails to point out a provision that the other party overlooks.

Still, perhaps we should ask more of the courts. Some courts considering unconscionability continue simply to list a variety of ills; other courts, aware of the difference between procedural and substantive unconscionability, fail to isolate those criteria critical to each. Some courts employ good faith without identifying what constitutes bad faith. Courts should strive to further the important goals emphasized by the neo-formalists and to achieve the appropriate mix of flexibility and certainty in contract law. After all, although contract law should not become stagnant, it must be sufficiently certain and predictable to support private arrangements.

Commercial Code, which, we have seen, includes both standards.

CHAPTER 5

"MAINSTREAM" CONTRACT THEORIES AND CRITICAL LEGAL STUDIES

I now consider two schools of contract thought that, because of their breadth and internal conflicts and inconsistencies, are unitary and distinct "theories" only in a very broad sense. Nevertheless, a focus on the essence of "mainstream," also called "liberal," contract theory on the one hand and Critical Legal Studies (CLS) on the other, helps establish the wide range of views on modern contract law's nature and roles. More important, because CLS theorists often invoke mainstream theory to serve as a counterpoint to their own views, the focus in this chapter helps clarify the principal tenets of CLS.

To flesh out the CLS perspective, I shall adopt the admittedly very broad CLS definition of mainstream or liberal contract theory. According to CLS, mainstream writers hold the dominant view of contract law and comprise everyone except "the left and right fringes of the political spectrum."[1] They therefore include, for example, both the promise theorists and interventionists described in Chapter 1 and most of the legal economists to be discussed in Chapter 6. Mainstream writers generally acknowledge, but downplay, the conflicts in contract law, and believe that courts can bridge the contradictions to reach decisions possessing "objective moral force."[2] Mainstream writers therefore assert the ultimate coherence and importance of contract law.[3] In addition, the mainstream believes that contract law neither favors any particular class nor impedes

---

1 Mark Kelman, A Guide to Critical Legal Studies 2 (1987).

2 *See* Allan C. Hutchinson & Patrick J. Monahan, *Law, Politics, and the Critical Legal Scholars: The Unfolding Drama of American Legal Thought*, 36 STAN. L. REV. 199, 208-209 (1984). According to Professor Unger, "objectivism is the belief that the authoritative legal materials . . . embody and sustain a defensible scheme of human association." ROBERTO M. UNGER, THE CRITICAL LEGAL STUDIES MOVEMENT 2 (1986).

3 For a more complete discussion of the contradictions in liberal thought, *see generally* KELMAN, *supra* note 1.

social change. In fact, contract law includes adequate methods for assuring fairness and real consent in "private" exchange.

CLS, a loosely affiliated group of scholars most vocal in the late 1970s and 1980s, often contrasts its views with mainstream contract scholars. According to CLS, the mainstream's enthusiasm over the contributions of contract (and other) law is misplaced. What unites the mainstream is the internal inconsistency of their views, their attempt to repress the conflicts, and their tendency to "privilege" one norm or another in deciding disputes.[4] Influenced by the legal realists, many CLS theorists assert that contract law is largely unscientific and indeterminate. Contract rules, they insist, consist of contradictory norms and doctrines that fail to dictate a result in a case or at least in an important case. CLS nonetheless posits that legal decisions are often predictable because the legal establishment masks contract law's indeterminacy and favors results that reinforce and legitimize the existing social status quo.[5] Critical of this approach, CLS contract writers would prefer to utilize contract law to achieve their view of progressive social change.

A. "Mainstream" Contract Theories

Problem 8: MDM Enterprises licenses its television series, "Why Spy?" to XYZ Television Network for one year and gives XYZ a series of options for up to seven additional years. The licensing fee is $650,000 per episode for twenty-two episodes the first season. The licensing fee escalates ten percent over the seven-year period and also increases in case of an industry-wide escalation of basic production costs. The agreement does not provide for fee escalation based on the success of "Why Spy?" or the increased salary demands of its stars, even though XYZ's advertising rates and the stars' salary demands will rise if the show is a success.

---

4 *Id.* at 3-4.

5 "CLS scholars . . . criticize as theoretically incoherent and ideologically deceptive the present system of neoclassical rules and standards." G. Richard Shell, *Contracts in the Modern Supreme Court*, 81 CAL. L. REV. 431, 503 (1993).

"Why Spy?" is a huge success its first year. Based on the show's ratings, XYZ is able to charge advertisers over $1 million more per episode during the second year. Before production begins for the second year, the show's star, Tom Slack, bargains for and receives a raise from MDM of $18,000 per episode. Slack had been under contract to MDM for the full seven years at a salary of $20,000 per episode, with a ten percent increase over the course of the seven years. MDM now seeks an increase in the licensing fee from XYZ Network. MDM points to an informal practice in the industry whereby parties renegotiate licensing fees to take into account actors' demands and a program's success. Attempting to avoid the possibility of losing the series during protracted negotiations or even litigation, and wishing to maintain industry good will and a profitable relationship with MDM, XYZ agrees to an increase without consulting its lawyers. Later, when the popularity of "Why Spy?" diminishes somewhat, XYZ refuses to pay the increased licensing fee.

1. The relative determinacy of contract doctrine

A brief discussion of two preceding schools of legal thought sets the stage for our consideration of the mainstream (and, for that matter, CLS) view of the nature of contract rules and how they apply to Problem 8. The nineteenth-century legal formalists were highly influenced by the period's analytic method.[6] They sought to generalize from judicial behavior, just as their colleagues in science observed phenomena and predicted actions.[7] The formalists concluded that one could understand the law by classifying cases according to previously constructed legal

---

[6] Girardeau A. Spann, *A Critical Legal Studies Perspective on Contract Law and Practice*, 1988 ANN. SURV. AM. L. 223, 226.

[7] *Id.* at 226.

categories[8] and by mechanically deducing the appropriate decision from these categories.[9]

According to the formalists, a judge would characterize Problem 8 as a "pre-existing duty" problem. The pre-existing duty doctrine holds that a promise of additional consideration or a promise to accept partial performance in exchange for consideration the other party already owes is unenforceable for lack of fresh consideration.[10] The judge would therefore hold XYZ's promise to increase MDM's licensing fee unenforceable for lack of fresh consideration. MDM had a pre-existing duty to produce "Why Spy?" for $650,000, plus the agreed escalation rate, therefore XYZ's promise to pay more for the series lacked consideration from MDM to support it.

The legal realists of the 1930s and 1940s sought to free judges from the intellectual handcuffs of legal formalism. Although varying in their degree of skepticism, the realists generally posited the lack of objectivity and impartiality of our legal system. They asserted that the legal rules and principles applied to a problem at best only modestly influenced decisionmakers and could lead to various results.[11] The realists perceived that courts based their decisions, not on abstract legal rules, but on the pragmatic evaluation of the particular facts and equities.[12] Law could therefore rarely "serve as a neutral, nonpolitical force."[13]

---

[8] *Id.*

[9] *See, e.g.*, Lawrence B. Solum, *On the Indeterminacy Crisis: Critiquing Critical Dogma*, 54 U. CHI. L. REV. 462, 496 (1987).

[10] Robert A. Hillman, *Policing Contract Modifications Under the UCC: Good Faith and the Doctrine of Economic Duress*, 64 IOWA L. REV. 849, 851-852 (1979).

[11] Hutchinson & Monahan, *supra* note 2, at 204. For a discussion of various views of the realists, *see* James J. White, *Promise Fulfilled and Principle Betrayed*, 1988 ANN. SURV. AM. L. 7, 9.

[12] Spann, *supra* note 6, at 226-27.

[13] G. Edward White, *Transforming History in the Postmodern Era,* 91 MICH. L. REV. 1315, 1342 (1993) (reviewing MORTON J. HORWITZ, THE TRANSFORMATION OF AMERICAN LAW, 1870-1960: THE CRISIS OF LEGAL ORTHODOXY (1992)); *see also* FREDERICK SCHAUER, PLAYING BY THE RULES: A PHILOSOPHICAL EXAMINATION

Reacting to what they believed was formalism's excessive rigidity, the realists applauded the judicial focus on a problem's context and policy objectives,[14] at a time when legal science was losing appeal.[15] In their methodology, then, legal realists "(were) empirical and sociological where formalism had been theoretical and conceptual."[16] In Problem 8, for example, instead of inquiring under the pre-existing duty doctrine whether consideration supported XYZ's promise to MDM to increase the fee, a judge reflecting the realist vision would want to know, among other things, the nature of the bargaining between the parties, the custom in the industry on renegotiating contract provisions, and any course of dealing between the parties with regard to the adjustment of contract terms.[17] The

---

OF RULE-BASED DECISIONMAKING IN LAW AND IN LIFE 192-95 (1991); Hutchinson & Monahan, *supra* note 2, at 204; White, *supra* note 11, at 15.

[14] *See, e.g.*, Karl N. Llewellyn, *What Price Contract? -- An Essay in Perspective*, 40 YALE L.J. 704, 705-707 (1931) (discussing theorists who have explored the social and historical foundation of contract doctrine). One commentator has noted that:

> Granted the dangers of generalizing about 'the realists', if there is one thread that runs consistently through the work of American jurists . . . it is this: that there is more to the study of law than the study of a system of rules; that for most purposes legal doctrine should be seen in the context of legal processes and legal processes should be seen in the context of the totality of social processes.

WILLIAM TWINING, KARL LLEWELLYN AND THE REALIST MOVEMENT 382 (1973).

[15] Spann, *supra* note 6, at 226. *See also* MORTON J. HORWITZ, THE TRANSFORMATION OF AMERICAN LAW, 1870-1960: THE CRISIS OF LEGAL ORTHODOXY 5-6 (1992) [hereinafter HORWITZ, LEGAL ORTHODOXY] ("Progressive legal thinkers sought to undermine the claim . . . that law was a 'science' that could be separate from politics and that legal reasoning could be sharply distinguished from moral or political reasoning.").

[16] Spann, *supra* note 6, at 227.

[17] *See generally* Duncan Kennedy, *Form and Substance in Private Law Adjudication*, 89 HARV. L. REV. 1685 (1976) [hereinafter Kennedy, *Form and Substance*]. Or, to cite another example, in determining whether an offeror can revoke an offer for a unilateral contract before acceptance, a realist judge would investigate the nature

judge would also consider the incentives created by a decision one way or the other. Finally, the judge would also investigate the social norms implicated by her decision. The judge would then "blend and compromise" these factors, add a touch of her own intuition, and decide the case.[18]

Mainstream contract writers generally agree with the realist criticism of formalism's adherence to "classical" contract rules and judicial methods, but they resist the implication that contract law is largely indeterminate.[19] Mainstream writers would argue, for example, that courts can harmonize the conflicting rules illustrated in Problem 8, can rationally locate the problem on one side of the line separating valid from coerced contract modifications,[20] and, therefore, can reach a moral,

---

of the parties, the context of the dispute, and the policy objectives. *See* Lawrence M. Friedman, *Contract Law and Contract Research (Part I)*, 20 J. LEGAL EDUC. 452, 454 (1968).

One criticism of the realists is that they accepted without question the objectivity and validity of social science. *See* Donald H. Gjerdingen, *The Future of Legal Scholarship and the Search for a Modern Theory of Law*, 35 BUFF. L. REV. 381, 396 (1986). *See also* ROBERT S. SUMMERS, INSTRUMENTALISM AND AMERICAN LEGAL THEORY 112-15 (1982). For example, economists have not proven the commitment of judges to the value of efficiency. *See* George P. Fletcher, *Two Modes of Legal Thought*, 90 YALE L.J. 970, 995-96 (1981).

18 Spann, *supra* note 6, at 228. For a discussion of judicial intuition, *see* Richard H. Weisberg, *Law, Literature and Cardozo's Judicial Poetics*, 1 CARDOZO L. REV. 283, 295-97 (1979).

19 For a CLS critique of the mainstream approach, *see* Jay M. Feinman, *Promissory Estoppel and Judicial Method*, 97 HARV. L. REV. 678, 679, 716-18 (1984) [hereinafter Feinman, *Promissory Estoppel*]; *see also* Clare Dalton, *An Essay in the Deconstruction of Contract Doctrine*, 94 YALE L.J. 997, 1006 (1985) ("Liberalism's obsession with, and inability to resolve, the tension between self and other suggests that our stories about politics, policy, and law will be organized along dualities reflecting this basic tension.").

20 *See* William C. Whitford, *Lowered Horizons: Implementation Research in a Post-CLS World*, 1986 WIS. L. REV. 755, 762 (discussing the CLS view); *see also* TWINING, *supra* note 14, at 255 ("[M]ost rules have 'a central core of habitually established content surrounded by a penumbra of doubtful border-line cases.'") (quoting John Dickinson, *Legal Rules: Their Application and Elaboration*, 79 U.

objective decision.[21] Moreover, the mainstream believes that acknowledging that in some disputes contract law prescribes a range of possible results, *i.e.*, that contract law is not completely predictable, does not lend judges unbridled discretion, because most cases fall within one principle or another.

Although some courts would cling to the terminology of the pre-existing duty doctrine in deciding Problem 8, mainstream writers point out the influence on courts of the legal realists' rule skepticism. The doctrine's formalistic, cumbersome, and manipulable rules are generally giving way to a more direct investigation of the voluntariness of XYZ's promise through the vehicle of duress.[22]

Duress occurs when a party employs improper means to exact a promise from another who has little choice but to make the promise.[23]

PA. L. REV. 1052, 1085 (1931)); Solum, *supra* note 9, at 483 (noting that CLS "simply provides another coherent explanation of why *some* legal rules are underdetermined over the set of all cases").

21 *See* Hutchinson & Monahan, *supra* note 2, at 208-209.

22 *See, e.g.*, Austin Instrument, Inc. v. Loral Corp., 272 N.E.2d 533, 535, (N.Y 1971) ("A contract is voidable on the ground of duress when it is established that the party making the claim was forced to agree to it by means of a wrongful threat precluding the exercise of his free will."); JOHN P. DAWSON, GIFTS AND PROMISES: CONTINENTAL AND AMERICAN LAW COMPARED 210-11 (1980) (suggesting that one of the real problems underlying contract modifications is whether there is economic duress); Hillman, *supra* note 10, at 854 (noting that the "real issue" under the pre-existing duty doctrine, according to some courts and scholars, "is whether the promisor entered into the modification voluntarily or whether the promisor was coerced into making the new promise").

"In general, contract law in the twentieth century has undergone a transformation from formal, rule-like doctrine to purposive, standard-based doctrine." Feinman, *Promissory Estoppel, supra* note 19, at 697.

23 *See* RESTATEMENT (SECOND) OF CONTRACTS §§ 175-176 (1979) (outlining instances when contracts are voidable because of improper threats at the formation stage). *See generally* John Dalzell, *Duress By Economic Pressure I*, 20 N.C. L. REV. 237 (1942) (discussing the use of economic pressure to achieve "agreements" and the need for legal intervention); John P. Dawson, *Economic Duress--An Essay in Perspective*, 45 MICH. L. REV. 253 (1947) (surveying the historical role of duress in private contract law).

For example, a court can overturn the deal in Problem 8 if MDM wrongfully applied pressure *and* XYZ had no viable choice but to agree to increase the fee.[24] Obviously, concepts such as improper conduct and lack of choice raise many questions. According to many in the mainstream, however, even this imprecise approach may be sufficient to decide many, if not most, cases. In fact, some cases would be easy. Suppose XYZ offered to increase the licensing fee, even though MDM had not sought an increase. Alternatively, suppose the parties' initial agreement included an express provision requiring adjustment of the licensing fee upon MDM's renegotiation of an actor's salary, and the increase requested by MDM merely reflected the actor's raise. In either case, XYZ would be hard pressed to claim duress.

Mainstream analysts argue that the rules of duress restrict a decision even in "hard cases."[25] Doctrines such as duress inform a decision by isolating various factual inquiries that together often suggest the appropriate result in a particular case: "[L]egal doctrines . . . . represent . . . time-tested approaches for determining what facts are relevant, why they are relevant, and the degree of strength of the relevance."[26] In Problem 8, a judge would consider a host of factors in investigating the "choice" and "means" questions of the duress doctrine: Did MDM refuse to perform without an increase or merely negotiate for one? What was the amount of the requested licensing fee increase? What do other similarly situated producers receive for comparable services? How common is adjustment in the industry? Does XYZ often adjust? Suppose MDM negotiated flexibly, sought an increase comparable to those negotiated by other producers in the same position, and pointed to

---

24 Hillman, *supra* note 10, at 883.

25 In a "hard" case, reasonable minds may differ as to the appropriate line drawing. Walter E. Oberer, *On Law, Lawyering and Law Professing: The Golden Sand*, 39 J. LEGAL EDUC. 203, 204 (1989). According to another definition, in a hard case a judge must choose among possible results that will "substantially affect" the litigants. Solum, *supra* note 9, at 474. *See also* UNGER, *supra* note 2, at 70-71 (noting that even though the economic duress doctrine may "serve as a roving commission to correct" economic disparity, it does not "[destroy] the vitality of decentralized decisionmaking through contract").

26 Oberer, *supra* note 25, at 205.

a fully ripened practice of adjustment in similar circumstances. Instead of conflicting, the rules of duress would coincide and support enforcement of the modification. After all, the parties bargained concerning an increase and XYZ agreed to one in a situation that called for compromise and cooperation.

The mainstream acknowledges that a thorough investigation may show that the facts and law dictate no clear result in a difficult case. Suppose, for example, that MDM refused to perform without an increase and that it was unclear whether industry practice would call for an adjustment. Our complex society is replete with conflicting and evolving ideas, policies, goals, and methods. It is hardly surprising that our law reflects these conflicts.[27] Many mainstream theorists therefore believe that we cannot achieve perfect certainty, predictability and uniformity, but it is sufficient if judges strive for these goals. Doctrinally isolated factual inquiries, along with constraints arising from a judicial culture of considering legal arguments carefully, pursuing justice reflectively, and deciding cases honestly, establish a range of possible choices and rationales that guide and restrict a court's decision, even in cases that do not dictate a particular result.[28] Thus, in a close case, a court could legitimately decide XYZ was not under duress because it had a duty to adjust, but a court could *not* legitimately decide that XYZ was not under duress simply because MDM made television comedies and not dramas.

---

27 According to one writer, the "reason to know" test of promissory estoppel is "an effort to collapse such norms as the protection of reasonable reliance, the preservation of freedom of action, and the promotion of transactional security into a readily administrable formulation." Feinman, *Promissory Estoppel, supra* note 19, at 713.

28 Llewellyn viewed the regularity of judicial behavior as ensuring the "reckonability" of result. KARL N. LLEWELLYN, THE COMMON LAW TRADITION: DECIDING APPEALS 17-18 (1960). He listed various factors promoting such regularity, including the dictates of doctrine, the judge's responsibility for justice, judicial honesty, and professionalism. *Id.* at 19. *See also* Solum, *supra* note 9, at 495 ("Even in the hardest hard case, legal doctrine limits the court's options. One of the parties will receive a judgment, not some unexpected stranger; the relief will be related to the dispute at hand . . . ."); Weisberg, *supra* note 18, at 301 (Cardozo "remind[ed] the judge of his duty to be sensitive to the values of his surrounding culture.").

In addition, as we shall see in the next subsection, some mainstream writers set forth theories to explain supplemental principles utilized by courts when doctrine gives out, such as theories of distributive justice and paternalism, which have the potential to further reign in judicial discretion.

Mainstream analysts also remind that many contract rules are less difficult than duress and indicate obvious solutions in most situations.[29] (Suppose, for example, XYZ refused to pay MDM even the original smaller fee without offering any reason for its actions.) This certainly seems to be the view of most judges:

> [L]egal doctrine is a real force, judges follow it, and they decide all but a small fraction of the cases that come before them in accordance with what they perceive to be the controlling legal rules. . . .
>
> . . .
>
> The cases in which [judges apply social or economic policy] may be the great cases, the texbook cases for the next edition of cases and materials. In any court, in any term, these are few. The rest, the cases society lives by almost all of the time, are decided by doctrine.[30]

In fact, many, or even most, instances of contract break down do not reach litigation at least in part because the results of litigation are predictable.[31] Furthermore, many litigated disputes may be quarrels about the facts, which do not involve doctrinal line-drawing at all. Mainstream writers therefore insist that on the whole contract rules are quite

---

29 *See* TWINING, *supra* note 14, at 249 (discussing Cardozo's point that at least 90% of the cases that come before a court are "predetermined").

30 Alvin B. Rubin, *Judges and the Critical Legal Studies Movement*, SYLLABUS: ABA SECTION OF LEGAL EDUCATION AND ADMISSION TO BAR, June-Sept. 1987, at 6.

31 I discuss other reasons in Chapter 7. *But see* PETER H. SCHUCK, AGENT ORANGE ON TRIAL: MASS TOXIC DISASTERS IN THE COURTS 119 (1987) (describing district court judge's theory of a correlation between uncertainty of outcome and settlement).

Professor Dalton concedes that we can predict the results of some cases because of our awareness of "cultural values" that affect decisionmakers. Thus, "doctrine-in-application" may be determinate, but "doctrine-as-rule-system" is not. Dalton, *supra* note 19, at 1009.

predictable despite the existence of some counter examples.[32]

2. Contract law's role in society

Because the CLS definition of the mainstream is so broad, it encompasses writers with diverse views on what contract law's role in society is and should be. On the whole, it may be fair to say that mainstream writers acknowledge the existence of monopolies, bargaining power imbalances, other market failures, and inequities in the distribution of wealth, all of which may qualify a contracting party's assent to particular terms.[33] Nevertheless, with varying degrees of enthusiasm, mainstream writers assert that these problems are surmountable[34] and some, in fact, affirm contract law's potential to ameliorate inequities in society.[35]

Mainstream writers generally subscribe to the theory of the "subjectivity of value," meaning that the parties alone should and can determine the value of their exchange.[36] Many imply that contract rules authorizing intervention beyond clear cases of market failure in order to redistribute wealth or to further a party's self-interest would be essentially lawless because of the absence of standards to determine "the collective or individual good."[37] Courts therefore should refrain from investigating an agreement's adequacy and should abide by the parties' manifested

---

32 Solum, *supra* note 9, at 482-83.

33 *See* Chapter 4.

34 *See, e.g.*, Richard A. Epstein, *Unconscionability: A Critical Reappraisal*, 18 J. L. & ECON. 293, 315 (1975) (courts should overturn contracts only because of formation problems such as duress or because a party was incompetent).

35 *See infra* notes 51-65, and accompanying text. *But see* Spann, *supra* note 6, at 229 (mainstream contract law "perpetuat[es] economic inequality").

36 *See infra* notes 111-114, and accompanying text.

37 MICHAEL J. TREBILCOCK, THE LIMITS OF FREEDOM OF CONTRACT 150 (1993); Alan Schwartz, *The Default Rule Paradigm and the Limits of Contract Law*, 3 S. CAL. INTER. L. J. 389, 417 (1993).

preferences. In fact, on this basis, writers at one end of the spectrum of mainstream analysts seek to justify what appear to be relatively harsh terms. For example, in *Williams v. Walker-Thomas Furniture Co.*,[38] the court declined to enforce the infamous cross-collateral clause, a provision that kept a balance due on every item purchased by a consumer until the consumer paid off the entire debt. Some mainstream writers, however, criticize the result, emphasizing the seller's need for the clause because of the likelihood of the consumer's default and the rapid depreciation of the collateral.[39]

Mainstream writers of this ilk also doubt whether redistributive rules ultimately improve the fortunes of those targeted for assistance. For example, making cross-collateral clauses unlawful, these theorists assume, might dry up credit to those most in need of it or otherwise worsen the lot of poor buyers because sellers would increase prices, stop selling on credit, or go out of business.[40] Landlords confronted with non-disclaimable warranties, to cite another example, would simply increase the rent,[41] thereby eliminating the tenants' option to accept the disclaimer and pay lower rent.[42]

---

38 350 F.2d 445 (D.C. Cir. 1965).

39 *See, e.g.*, Epstein, *supra* note 34, at 307; CHARLES FRIED, CONTRACT AS PROMISE: A THEORY OF CONTRACTUAL OBLIGATION 104-05 (1981). *See also* Epstein, *supra* note 34, at 308 ("the add-on clause can do no harm at all, for it only makes it more certain that the seller will be able to collect that to which on any view he is entitled."). Writers such as Epstein "have blurred the distinctions between economic and libertarian theories of legal regulation . . . ." Shell, *supra* note 5, at 501. I include Epstein in CLS's conception of the mainstream because of his affiliation with the former school.

40 FRIED, *supra* note 39, at 105-06. *See also* Anthony T. Kronman, *Paternalism and the Law of Contracts,* 92 YALE L.J. 763, 772-73 (1983) [hereinafter Kronman, *Paternalism]* (discussing arguments against redistribution).

41 Kronman, *Paternalism, supra* note 40, at 772-73.

42 Duncan Kennedy, *Distributive and Paternalist Motives in Contract and Tort Law, With Special Reference to Compulsory Terms and Unequal Bargaining Power*, 41 MD. L. REV. 563, 613 (1982) [hereinafter Kennedy, *Motives*].

Mainstream writers dubious of redistributive contract rules utilize similar arguments to deflect proposed contract solutions to the problem of plant closings, the subject of considerable recent concern by contract analysts. For example, in *Local 1330, United Steel Workers v. United States Steel Corp.*,[43] the steelworkers sought to enjoin the steel company from closing two large steel mills operated since the turn of the century in Youngstown, Ohio. The company had asserted that it would not close the plants if they became profitable and if the steelworkers made extra efforts toward that goal. The Sixth Circuit declined to overturn the district court's finding that, despite the steelworkers' extra efforts, the plants remained unprofitable according to the "normal corporate profit accounting" measure of profitability and therefore denied the workers' promissory estoppel and other claims.[44]

Although we will see that several writers identified with CLS have offered solutions to this problem that would have given the steelworkers a contract or related remedy,[45] some mainstream writers point out that such an approach might have an unintended adverse impact on the steelworkers or others. For example, the steelworkers might be better off by relocating. Moreover, others, even in worse shape than the steelworkers, might reap greater benefits from the company's relocation. Although these are highly debatable issues, difficult to verify empirically, some conclude from them that "the solutions to social problems are deceptively simple [and wrong] if the affected community is defined too narrowly."[46]

---

[43] 631 F.2d 1264 (6th. Cir. 1980).

[44] 631 F.2d at 1278-79.

[45] *See infra* notes 155-162, and accompanying text.

[46] Daniel A. Farber and John H. Matheson, *Beyond Promissory Estoppel: Contract Law and the "Invisible Handshake"*, 52 U. CHI. L. REV. 903, 944 (1985). Nevertheless, the authors criticize the decision in *Steelworkers* because the plants became profitable under an alternative definition of profitability employed by the company to induce the steelworkers' extra efforts. The court found that the company should not have reasonably expected the steelworkers to rely on the alternative definition.

Some mainstream skeptics of the instrumental potential of contract law also believe that wealth redistribution can be accomplished more efficiently and fairly by utilizing other legal instrumentalities such as the taxation, welfare, or bankruptcy systems. For example, Charles Fried asks rhetorically: "Why should just . . . one representative of the more fortunate classes be made to bear the burden of our redistributive zeal?"[47] He responds: "[T]here is no reason why the retailer or employer should assume more of a burden . . . than, say, a Beverly Hills plastic surgeon with ten times their income, just because the surgeon never has occasion to deal with the poor and unemployed."[48] On the other hand, the tax and welfare system's requirement that each citizen of the same class contribute equally "to reduce . . . poverty" and the system's neutrality concerning how people become wealthy appeal to Fried.[49]

Writers who approve of judicial regulation of "private" exchange on fairness grounds, even beyond clear cases of market failure, occupy the opposite end of the mainstream spectrum. These analysts affirm contract policing doctrines such as unconscionability, which, in part, temper the principle of the subjectivity of value by empowering courts to strike clauses that "shock the conscience."[50] Some also approve of contract rules

---

47 FRIED, *supra* note 39, at 105.

48 *Id.* at 106.

49 *Id. See also* TREBILCOCK, *supra* note 37, at 99, discussing JOHN RAWLS, A THEORY OF JUSTICE (1971):

> In Rawls's view, the function of the basic structure, especially the tax and transfer system, is to establish and maintain a framework of entitlements that satisfies the principles of distributive justice, within which individuals remain free to pursue their own ends through voluntary transactions with others, secure in the knowledge that elsewhere in the social system the necessary corrections to preserve background justice are being made.

50 *See* Chapter 4. "One thing that happens when you create a 2-302 [the U.C.C. section on unconscionability] is that you create a change in the balance of power to some extent about what people think the courts ultimately will do, and therefore you vary, to some extent, the context in which settlement will be worked out." Richard Danzig, *Comments on Professor White's Paper*, 1988 ANN. SURV. AM. L. 56, 59

designed specifically to achieve distributional effects.[51] For example, Dean Kronman posits that nondisclaimable warranties, such as the warranty of habitability, "may be an essential part of a program of distributive justice."[52] Warranties may be nondisclaimable because otherwise landowners, who can generally dictate terms, would disclaim them. Moreover, the supply of housing without habitability protection would "offend [ ] our conception of distributive fairness,"[53] because most tenants would not ultimately be better off by allowing such disclaimers. Such warranties are therefore nondisclaimable "to shift control over housing from one group (landlords) to another (tenants) in a way that furthers the widely shared goal of insuring everyone shelter of at least a minimally decent sort."[54] Despite the apparent justice of the result, Kronman's approach, which substitutes an inquiry into whether a

---

(discussing James J. White, *Promise Fulfilled and Principle Betrayed,* 1988 ANN. SURV. AM. L. 7). *See also* Robert A. Hillman, *Debunking Some Myths About Unconscionability: A New Framework for U.C.C. Section 2-302*, 67 CORNELL L. REV. 1 (1981).

The law often utilizes flexible standards to enable judges to adapt to varied and changed circumstances and to achieve equity. *See* TWINING, *supra* note 14, at 335-37. "It seems to be forgotten that approximately half of our private law--the part that prevailed when any conflict arose--was ascribed by the Chancellors who created it to standards no more precise than 'equity and good conscience.'" John P. Dawson, *Unconscionable Coercion: The German Version*, 89 HARV. L. REV. 1041, 1043 (1976). *See also* Shell, *supra* note 5, at 497.

51 *See, e.g.*, HUGH COLLINS, THE LAW OF CONTRACT 137 (1986). Fairness "almost always means some appeal to an equitable division of the gains or losses among existing parties given that certain events have come to pass. Fairness arguments are ex post . . . ." Frank H. Easterbrook, *Foreword: The Court and the Economic System*, 98 HARV. L. REV. 4, 11 (1984). *But see* Richard Craswell, *Contract Remedies, Renegotiation, and the Theory of Efficient Breach,* 61 S. CAL. L. REV. 630, 641 (1988) (economic analysts unconcerned with redistributive effects).

52 Kronman, *Paternalism, supra* note 40, at 770.

53 *Id.* at 771.

54 *Id.* at 772. The nondisclaimable warranty also helps ensure that landlords cannot exert a monopoly over housing. *Id.* Rent-control legislation is another example. COLLINS, *supra* note 51, at 142-43.

particular group (here tenants) would benefit in the long run from the mandatory contract term for a focus on the voluntariness of the particular transaction, is not likely to mollify those who worry about the absence of clear standards when lawmakers utilize contract law to redistribute wealth. [55]

A few mainstream writers also approve of mandatory contract terms on paternalistic grounds, which allow "the collectivity through its legal instrumentalities . . . to substitute its judgements for those of the individuals involved."[56] For example, by precluding tenants from waiving their warranty of habitability protection in return for lower rents, nondisclaimable warranties tend to "change[ ] . . . rule[s] in order to improve [the tenants'] welfare by getting them to behave in their own real interests . . . ."[57] The support by some unconscionability analysts for judicial policing of terms agreed to by the poor, uneducated, or psychologically impaired, illustrates the at least partial mainstream acceptance of paternalism.[58]

Writers advocating a paternalistic approach must explain how to determine when a person is not acting in her own interests and why the value of self-determination should yield to self-interest (as determined by a third party).[59] Critics remain largely dissatisfied with some of the

---

[55] TREBILCOCK, *supra* note 37, at 83-84.

[56] *Id.* at 147.

[57] Kennedy, *Motives, supra* note 42, at 570 (defining paternalism). Kennedy points out, however, that a judge can resolve issues on grounds other than redistribution or paternalism, such as on moral grounds or on the basis of freedom of contract, even though the latter reasons have a redistributive or paternalistic effect. *Id.* at 583.

Redistributivists recognize the close connection between redistributive and paternalistic motives and effects: A court's decision to aid an incompetent party likely will have a redistributive effect. Still, "[f]or an intervention to be paternalist, the distributive effects have to be 'side effects' rather than the purpose of the initiative." *Id.* at 625. Of course it may be very difficult to determine whether a distributive effect is a "side effect." *Id.*

[58] *See* Chapter 4.

[59] *See* the discussion in TREBILCOCK, *supra* note 37, at 149-50.

explanations (beyond traditional ones such as mental incapacity and infancy). These new explanations require deep explorations of the psychology of people's preferences, including, for example, whether a person convinces herself of the validity of the status quo only because she believes it is unchangeable.[60] As stated by Professor Trebilcock:

> [T]he case for paternalistic legal interventions on grounds of contingent, adaptive, or bad preferences becomes much more problematic and the burden of justifying intervention correspondingly much stronger, simply because clearly definable individual preferences are being repudiated in the absence of readily identifiable forms of coercion or information failure.[61]

At any rate, some interventionist mainstream writers not only endorse legal regulation, some believe that policing of agreements is effective and, in some instances, superior to other methods of achieving redistributive goals. For example, Dean Kronman has asserted that regulation of private contract may often be superior to taxation for redistributing wealth. Kronman concludes that taxation is not inherently more neutral in effect because tax burdens sometimes fall on particular groups only. Moreover taxes such as the sales tax, which attaches to all "private" sales of goods, are not necessarily less restrictive of individual liberty than contract regulation. In addition, Kronman argues that taxation is not necessarily a more efficient and less costly instrument for redistributing wealth than contract law. It may be superior, Kronman points out, to enforce a minimum wage law than to impose "a tax on income (designed to benefit the working poor) which relies on self-reporting by individuals subject to the tax."[62]

---

60 *Id.* at 157-158. In addition, analysts would have to explain how to determine when people make flawed decisions as the result of "systematic biases in the way they receive, understand, and frame information . . . ." Shell, *supra* note 5, at 525.

61 TREBILOCK, *supra* note 37, at 163.

62 Anthony T. Kronman, *Contract Law and Distributive Justice,* 89 YALE L.J. 472, 509 (1980) [hereafter Kronman, *Distributive Justice*]. *See also* TREBILCOCK, *supra* note 37, at 100.

According to one commentator, the exceptions to freedom of contract "are now so numerous that it makes sense to treat them as the general principle."[63] Many mainstream writers, even those inclined toward intervention, would feel uncomfortable with this proclamation because it relegates freedom of contract to a secondary position. On the whole, most mainstream writers probably believe that freedom of contract remains the dominant principle of contract law and would urge sufficient judicial restraint to maintain that situation.[64] Nevertheless, to the extent that unfair bargaining and one-sided contract terms are more prevalent than commonly believed, mainstream analysts advocating greater policing of private arrangements may fail to recognize the full implications of their theory. These analysts may also find difficult the line drawing necessary to determine when freedom of contract or interventionists principles should control.[65] CLS pursues the latter two points, as we shall soon see.

B. CLS Contract Theory

1. The relative indeterminacy of contract law

---

63 COLLINS, *supra* note 51, at 143.

64 *Cf.* KELMAN, *supra* note 1, at 238 ("the liberal regime's nominal commitment to completely free contract has been limited" in part by "welfare state reforms" and in part by "public utility regulation.").

65 "The liberal (like Fried) who concedes that unconscionability doctrine may be justified in rare situations of random market failure or in conditions of virtual breakdown of the social order may not appreciate how large this concession may turn out to be." P.S. ATIYAH, ESSAYS ON CONTRACTS 134 (1986). Professor Atiyah goes on to point out that market failure is "almost totally ubiquitous." *Id.* *See also* Robert W. Gordon, *Maccaulay, Macneil, and the Discovery of Solidarity and Power in Contract Law*, 1985 WIS. L. REV. 565, 576 (1985) ("[Courts] celebrate the core values of freedom of contract in dicta while doing freehanded equitable redistribution in the case before them."); Kennedy, *Motives*, *supra* note 42, at 586 ("The demise of freedom of contract has been accompanied by a distinct increase in self-consciousness about the various kinds of consequences of choosing basic rules about agreements.").

CLS has taken up and expanded the themes of the legal realists.[66] Although some CLS theorists concede the potential of contract doctrine to confine some decisions,[67] they assert that the legal system falls far short of "strict rule-bound legalism."[68] Instead, formal contract rules are largely "indeterminate" because they rarely dictate a particular result in an important case.[69] It is not that the *results* of litigation are necessarily unpredictable, we shall see,[70] but that contract doctrine offers the *potential*

---

66 *See* Whitford, *supra* note 20, at 758-60 (discussing the CLS view). For an application of CLS reasoning to a contracts case, see Robert W. Gordon, *Unfreezing Legal Reality: Critical Approaches to Law*, 15 FLA. ST. U. L. REV. 195 (1987).

67 Of course, writers associated with CLS often disagree among themselves; it is as difficult to synthesize the CLS view as it is to capture one for any other school of thought.

68 KELMAN, *supra* note 1, at 19. Professor Kennedy acknowledges that a definite and distinct rule may apply in a given case. Duncan Kennedy, *Freedom and Constraint in Adjudication: A Critical Phenomenology*, 36 J. LEGAL EDUC. 518 (1986).

69 Professor Solum describes strong and weak versions of the indeterminacy thesis. The strong version asserts that legal doctrine can support any result in every case. Solum, *supra* note 9, at 470; *see also* Dalton, *supra* note 19, at 1007 (suggesting that "legal argumentation disguises its own inherent indeterminancy" and that "legal doctrine is unable to provide determinate answers to particular disputes while continuing to claim an authority based on its capacity to do so"). The weak version holds only that all "interesting or important cases are indeterminate." Solum, *supra* note 9, at 489; *see also* Phillip E. Johnson, *Do You Sincerely Want to Be Radical?* 36 STAN. L. REV. 247, 252 (1984) (suggesting that the CLS movement is a derivative of the legal realism movement, which "rejects the notion . . . that there is a method of legal reasoning that can generate outcomes in controversial disputes independent of the political or economic ideology of the judge"); Duncan Kennedy, *Legal Education as Training for Hierarchy, in* THE POLITICS OF LAW: A PROGRESSIVE CRITIQUE 38, 45 (David Kairys ed., rev. ed. 1990) ("There is never a 'correct legal solution' that is other than the correct ethical and political solution to that legal problem."). Professor Schwartz characterizes the CLS indeterminacy thesis as "old hat," stating that "the 'Realists' made the same discovery 50 years ago." Louis B. Schwartz, *With Gun and Camera Through Darkest CLS-Land*, 36 STAN. L. REV. 413, 432 (1984).

70 *See infra* note 95, and accompanying text, and *infra* Part B(2).

for deciding cases in multiple ways.[71] At best, then, according to CLS, contract rules have a minor effect in litigation and even less of one outside it.[72] Legal decisions are constrained only by the limits of the legal community's imagination in creating methods of legal argumentation.[73] Notwithstanding contract law's relative worthlessness, lawyers and judges do their best to maintain the facade of legal determinism. Lawyers make legal arguments to judges as if legal doctrine determines the result "even if they know perfectly well that it is consistent with a wide range of possible results--which is usually the case if the legal issues are seriously disputed."[74]

Among the reasons CLS scholars set forth explaining the relative impotence of legal doctrine are the breadth of legal rules, the invalidity of doctrinal distinctions, the inherent ambiguities of language, and the multitude of strategies of rule-interpretation.[75] Many of these issues were taken up earlier in this chapter or in Chapter 4. Perhaps the principal reason advanced for legal indeterminacy, to be discussed here, is that traditional contract law reflects the "fundamental contradiction" between freedom of the individual and the need for relations with others.[76]

---

71 KELMAN, *supra* note 1, at 258: "internal contradictions . . . do not render daily outcomes wholly unpredictable or random . . . ." Instead, "commitments to principles that undermine that practice are invariably available."

72 *See* Robert W. Gordon, *Lawyers, Scholars, and the "Middle Ground,"* 91 MICH. L. REV. 2075, 2078 (1993) [Hereinafter Gordon, *Lawyers*].

73 *Id.* at 2092.

74 *Id.* at 2089.

75 For example, among other methods, courts can construe statutes literally, dynamically, or historically. *Id.* at 2090-91. As a result, "the system has argumentative resources that present varying possibilities for the resolution of every legal issue." *Id.* at 2092. *See also id.* at 2093; Solum, *supra* note 9, at 465-66 (listing various techniques that CLS scholars use to demonstrate the indeterminacy of law).

76 *See* Jay M. Feinman, *Critical Approaches to Contract Law*, 30 UCLA L. REV. 829, 844-47 (1983) [hereinafter Feinman, *Critical Approaches*]; Whitford, *supra* note 20, at 761.

Individualism, according to CLS usage, entails the belief in people's competence and right to pursue their own interests and affairs without regard to others.[77] Collectivism or altruism views people as members of an interdependent society, who need and care about others as well as themselves.[78] For each individualist rule designed to ensure freedom of contract, contract law provides, and judges may select, a counterrule designed to further collective interests, such as altruism and reciprocity.[79]

Analysts subscribing to rule indeterminacy have no shortage of examples to substantiate their position:[80] Contract law requires an offer and acceptance, but once negotiations begin a party may be obligated on the basis of good faith or promissory estoppel. Courts will not look into the adequacy of consideration, but will strike unconscionable agreements.[81] Courts determine the intentions of the parties objectively or subjectively.[82] In fact, some CLS theorists would assert that a judge confronted with the XYZ-MDM dispute in Problem 8 could decide the

---

According to Professor Schwartz, what CLS refers to as the fundamental contradiction has been "chew[ed] on" by philosophers, lawyers and political scientists for "millennia". Schwartz, *supra* note 69, at 437.

77 *See* Feinman, *Critical Approaches*, *supra* note 76, at 839; *see also* KELMAN, *supra* note 1, at 54; Jay M. Feinman, *The Significance of Contract Theory*, 58 U. CIN. L. REV. 1283, 1311 (1990) [hereinafter Feinman, *Significance*].

78 Feinman, *Critical Approaches, supra* note 76, at 842-844; KELMAN, *supra* note 1, at 55.

79 See generally Kennedy, *Form and Substance, supra* note 17, at 1700 (discussing contract modification and noting that there are circumstances in which "a 'rule' that appears to dispose cleanly of a fact situation is nullified by a counterrule whose scope of application seems to be almost identical."); UNGER, *supra* note 2, at 60-85 (discussing various principles of contract law and illustrating how one may apply counter principles to reach nontraditional results).

80 For example, in his study of promissory estoppel, Professor Feinman asserts that courts apply different tests of promise and reliance to promissory estoppel cases. Feinman, *Promissory Estoppel*, *supra* note 19, at 690-95.

81 KELMAN, *supra* note 1, at 19.

82 Gordon, *supra* note 72, at 2091.

contract modification issue in favor of either party with relative impunity.[83] An "individualist" judge, who believed that MDM should honor its original agreement to perform without an increase in the licensing fee, could find that MDM failed to supply fresh consideration to support XYZ's promise. Alternatively, a "collectivist" judge, who believed that MDM was entitled to an increase in the fee because of XYZ's huge gains and MDM's increased costs, could "find" that XYZ had a good faith duty to renegotiate and to agree to some increase. A more rule oriented "collectivist" judge could hold that MDM and XYZ had mutually rescinded the original contract just prior to entering the modification agreement, thereby eliminating MDM's pre-existing duty.[84]

Contract law's indeterminacy results not only because of the *existence* of contract principle and counter-principle, CLS writers point out, but because of the absence of an objective method for determining when to apply one or the other. Contract law lacks such a method in part because of the absence of a coherent strategy for delineating the borders between free bargaining and unlawful coercion.[85] For example, CLS finds little solace in the choice and means questions of the duress doctrine. As to the question of choice, influenced by Robert Hale's earlier analysis, they observe that all choices are narrowed by the reality of scarcity.[86] For example, people must "choose" to work or to pay for property or to go without.[87] Realistically, however, the latter option is open only to the wealthy. The degree of voluntariness of an exchange therefore depends on the preexisting distribution of wealth: "In *every* contract . . . it is an open question . . . whether the contract would have been made had each

---

[83] *See* Dalton, *supra* note 19, at 1007; Feinman, *Critical Approaches, supra* note 76, at 847; Feinman, *Promissory Estoppel, supra* note 19, at 709.

[84] For more on the pre-existing duty doctrine, *see* Hillman, *supra* note 10.

[85] KELMAN, *supra* note 1, at 259. According to Kelman, "substantive public norms specif[y] what one is entitled to 'threaten' or 'withhold'." *Id.* at 106. *See also* ATIYAH, *supra* note 65, at 131, 136.

[86] TREBILCOCK, *supra* note 37, at 79 (discussing problem).

[87] Robert L. Hale, *Coercion and Distribution in a Supposedly Non-Coercive State*, 38 POL. SCI. Q. 470, 471-73 (1923).

party had other physically imaginable though socially unavailable options accessible to him (that is, a question of "duress" arises in every case)."[88]

Judges must also decide in each case where to draw the line between acceptable and unacceptable bargaining power and methods. Professor Kelman and others have pointed out, however, that "one simply cannot define duress independently of rights: if the [party accused of duress] . . . is *entitled* to determine the choice conditions, the choice is not a product of duress . . . . Moreover, if the unhappy chooser has a right to be free from unwanted background conditions . . . his choices are 'unfree'."[89] In other words, if framed in terms of lack of choice and improper conduct, duress doctrine is little help in distinguishing hard bargaining worthy of our admiration and unfair advantage-taking. A judge attempting to determine in Problem 8 whether to approve of MDM's conduct in seeking an increase in the licensing fee would receive little guidance from the choice and means analysis of duress.

A judge's choice of a principle or counter-principle is also incoherent, according to CLS, because of the lack of an objective standard for determinining the fairness of the terms of an exchange. As Morton Horwitz has pointed out, courts began to doubt whether they could determine a fair price objectively during the rise of speculative markets.[90] Instead of making the effort, judges simply concluded that the existence of an exchange proved that the parties valued what they received more than what they gave up.

---

88 KELMAN, *supra* note 1, at 21. *See also* HORWITZ, LEGAL ORTHODOXY, *supra* note 15, at 195; TREBILCOCK, *supra* note 37, at 19-20.

89 KELMAN, *supra* note 1, at 131. *See also id.* at 76-77; Kronman, *Distributive Justice, supra* note 62, at 480-483.

90 White, *supra* note 13, at 1321. Professor Horwitz once quoted from Seymour v. Delancy, 3 Cow. 445 (N.Y. 1824), *rev'g* 6 Johns. Ch. 222 (N.Y. Ch. 1822), to illustrate. The court noted "that purchases are constantly made upon speculation; that the value of real estate is fluctuating; and that there . . . exists an honest difference of opinion in regard to any bargain, as to its being a beneficial one, or not." 3 Cow. at 533, *quoted in* Morton J. Horwitz, *The Historical Foundations of Modern Contract Law*, 87 HARV. L. REV. 917, 944-45 (1974) [hereinafter Horwitz, *Historical Foundations]*.

CLS also addresses whether judges can reach principled contract decisions by utilizing policy analysis. On the one hand, some CLS theorists appear to dismiss this methodology as itself manipulable and indeterminate. These writers argue that policy analysis lacks an objective scale for measuring the various factors that constitute a policy decision,[91] that it depends on value judgments about the goals of social reform,[92] and that it is unlikely to succeed because it conflicts with the pursuit of individualism.[93] On the other hand, at least some CLS writers endorse utilizing policy analysis within specific contexts. I will investigate the latter CLS position shortly.[94]

According to CLS, without adequate guidance to evaluate the quality of assent, the fairness of an exchange, and the appropriateness of policy prescriptions, and with the predilection to avoid these issues, judges fall back on on their own normative beliefs and attitudes in deciding contract cases. These judicial values are generally consistent with either one of the two deeply conflicting "social visions" constituting the fundamental contradiction, and involve "divergent views of efficiency, distributive fairness, the obligation . . . to look out for one another, and the meaning of 'consent' under conditions of need or subordination."[95] In the next subsection I focus on the CLS claim that judges most often choose the individualist pole when confronted with this dichotomy.

2. Contract law's role in society--the CLS legitimation thesis

---

91 *See* Gordon, *supra* note 72, at 2092 (policy analysis involves balancing various policies); Feinman, *Significance, supra* note 77, at 1312.

92 *See* Girardeau A. Spann, *Pure Politics*, 88 MICH. L. REV. 1971, 1989 (1990).

93 *Cf.* Gregory S. Alexander, *The Dead Hand and the Law of Trusts in the Nineteenth Century*, 37 STAN. L. REV. 1189, 1263 (1985).

94 *See infra* notes 150-62, and accompanying text.

95 Gordon, *supra* note 72, at 2092. Professor Kennedy asserts that individualistic law most often takes the form of rules, whereas altruistic law most often takes the form of standards. *See* Kennedy, *Form and Substance, supra* note 17, at 1685-87, 1737-1751. Professor Kelman doubts the correlation. KELMAN, *supra* note 1, at 56-59.

CLS contract law analysts assert that the mainstream suppresses the indeterminacy of contract doctrine, reflexively prefers individualism over altruism, and, therefore, ultimately reinforces existing social inequities.[96] Discontent with contract law's role in society, these writers endorse the use of contract law to redistribute wealth.[97]

Although greeted with some skepticism both by scholars identified within[98] and without the CLS movement,[99] and the subject of his own recent amplification,[100] Professor Horwitz's historical account of the "transformation of American law" during the nineteenth century has influenced many CLS writers.[101] Horwitz acknowledged the "orthodox" view that the seeds of modern contract law were planted when English courts began to enforce executory exchanges as early as the end of the

---

96 *See infra* notes 126-37, and accompanying text.

97 Kronman, *Distributive Justice, supra* note 62, at 472 (citing, among others, Kennedy, *Form and Substance, supra* note 17, at 1778).

98 *See* KELMAN, *supra* note 1, at 238.

99 Some find Horwitz's recounting of history suspect. "The collective assessment of [book reviews of MORTON J. HORWITZ, THE TRANSFORMATION OF AMERICAN LAW, 1780-1860 (1977)] was that the book was a provocative thesis in search of evidence, resting more on rhetoric and passion than on fact." White, *supra* note 13, at 1318-19. Particularly, the book lacked evidence of a relationship between "legal and commercial elites." *Id.* at 1340.

100 Professor White points out that Horwitz's view has changed somewhat in his recently published companion volume, HORWITZ, LEGAL ORTHODOXY, *supra* note 15. Horwitz appears to accept the view that legal change can occur, not only because of political influences, but also because of the evolution in "American legal thought." White, *supra* note 13, at 1336-37. Horwitz thus embraces the "'multi-factored complexity'" of legal analysis. *Id.* at 1326. Still, in his new book he accounts for the systematization of legal rules into "abstract set[s] of legal categories," by an aspiration to separate law and politics so that law could be thought of as neutral and objective. *Id.* at 1329, quoting HORWITZ, LEGAL ORTHODOXY, *supra* note 15.

101 *See generally* MORTON J. HORWITZ, THE TRANSFORMATION OF AMERICAN LAW, 1780-1860 (1977) [hereinafter HORWITZ, TRANSFORMATION].

sixteenth century.[102] Nevertheless, he saw a more important transition in contract law in the nineteenth century from a focus on fairness and equity to a concern about how to support the growth of business.

Professor Horwitz reported that until nineteenth-century commercial expansion, "[t]he most important aspect of . . . exchange [was] an equitable limitation on contractual obligation."[103] For example, he pointed out that both equity and law courts focused on the adequacy of consideration.[104] As with the system of instantaneous exchange that preceded the recognition of executory contracts, the law required goods or services supplied by one party to an exchange to be matched by something of equal value given by the other.[105] Moreover, judges determined the value of what was given according to a "customary" or "just price."[106] This approach "was essentially antagonistic to the interests of commercial classes," who turned to other legal vehicles to avoid "the equalizing tendencies of courts and juries."[107] Horwitz asserted that the exclusive delegation by law courts to juries of the obligation to make damages awards also illustrated the equitable nature of pre-nineteenth century contract law.[108]

According to Horwitz, to facilitate commerce during nineteenth-century industrialization and market growth and in response to "[t]he absorption of commodities transactions into contract law,"[109] judges began

---

[102] Horwitz, *Historical Foundations, supra* note 90, at 919.

[103] *Id.* at 923.

[104] *Id.* at 923-24. *But see* KELMAN, *supra* note 1, at 238: "Critics of Horwitz's work . . . have argued, not unpersuasively, that few preliberal courts actually struck down unfair bargains.").

[105] Horwitz, *Historical Foundations*, *supra* note 90, at 919-25.

[106] *Id.* at 935-36.

[107] *Id.* at 927.

[108] *Id.* at 925-27.

[109] *Id.* at 941.

to transform contract law from its focus on the fairness of an exchange to the reenforcement of the "will" of the contracting parties.[110] Judges doubted whether they could elaborate a principled standard for determining a fair price in a speculative market economy,[111] and therefore abandoned their investigation of the adequacy of an exchange:[112] "[A] regime of markets and speculation was simply incompatible with a socially imposed standard of value."[113] Horwitz concluded that "[t]he rise of a modern law of contract . . . was an outgrowth of an essentially procommercial attack on the theory of objective value which lay at the foundation of the eighteenth century's equitable idea of contract."[114]

The demise of an adequacy standard for evaluating exchange and the rise of additional rules that facilitated business,[115] Horwitz asserted, enabled merchants to consolidate their gains despite the seeming neutrality and objectivity of contract law.[116] Although nineteenth-century lawmakers and analysts "did not succeed in entirely destroying the ancient connection between contracts and natural justice, they were able to elaborate a system that allowed judges to pick and choose among those

---

110 *Id.* at 946-52. Professor Simpson disagrees with this theory in A.W.B. Simpson, *The Horwitz Thesis and the History of Contracts*, 46 U. CHI. L. REV. 533 (1979).

111 White, *supra* note 13, at 1321.

112 Horwitz, *Historical Foundations, supra* note 90, at 946-49.

113 HORWITZ, TRANSFORMATION, *supra* note 101, at 181.

114 *Id.*

115 Horwitz, *Historical Foundations*, *supra* note 90, at 952.

116 Eben Moglen, *The Transformation of Morton Horwitz*, 93 COLUM. L. REV. 1042, 1046 (1993) (reviewing HORWITZ, LEGAL ORTHODOXY, *supra* note 15).

> 'Classical Legal Thought' . . . served both to strengthen the conformity of legal theory to the central dogma of an apolitical rule of law, and to cushion the legal system against the intellectual effort necessary to adjust to extraordinary changes in social reality.

Id. at 1047.

groups in the population that would be its beneficiaries."[117] In Horwitz's view, then, instead of independent, objective contract rules, "the core themes of the material world drove the legal system."[118]

In a recent companion work examining the path of American law through 1960,[119] Horwitz reports that early twentieth-century forces of reform, such as progressive legal realists, challenged the value of "[a] self-regulating, competitive market economy presided over by a neutral, impartial, and decentralized 'night watchman' state."[120] This movement was energized by increasing "social and economic inequality" resulting from the "centralization of economic power"[121] in the hands of "giant corporations capable of exercising enormously disproportionate market power,"[122] by the perceived unfairness of expanding conceptions of commercial property rights worthy of protection, and by an overall sense that the legal system favored the wealthy.[123] Just as this movement gained momentum, however, conservative thought coopted it, in part because of second thoughts during the Nazi period about whether the law was a dependent "social creation."[124] The turn to conservatism included, for example, the idea of judicial obeisance to other branches of government, which themselves showed little enthusiasm for reform.[125]

---

117 Horwitz, *Historical Foundations*, *supra* note 90, at 955-56.

118 White, *supra* note 13, at 1321. *See also* Simpson, *supra* note 110.

119 HORWITZ, LEGAL ORTHODOXY, *supra* note 15.

120 *Id.* at 4.

121 *Id.*

122 *Id.* at 33.

123 *See generally*, Robert W. Gordon, *The Elusive Transformation*, 6 Yale J. L. & Human. 137, 140-43 (Book Review of HORWITZ, LEGAL ORTHODOXY, *supra* note 15) [hereinafter Gordon, *Elusive Transformation*].

124 HORWITZ, LEGAL ORTHODOXY, *supra* note 15, at 247-48; Gordon, *Elusive Transformation*, *supra* note 123, at 143.

125 *Id.*

Many CLS theorists assert that modern contract law continues to be ideologically aligned with commercial interests. Notwithstanding contract law's "fundamental contradiction," these analysts assert that individualist norms occupy its "central arena"[126] with collective principles "assigned a strictly supplemental role."[127] By emphasizing its "liberal-individualist core premises,"[128] modern contract law supresses "understanding and imagination" capable of challenging the existing social system,[129] "justif[ies] the prevailing conditions of social life and erect[s] . . . barriers to social change."[130] Contract actors--lawyers, judges, even theorists--"become 'imbued' with the 'logic of the system' . . . . and

---

126 Dalton, *supra* note 19, at 1014.

127 *Id.* at 1010. *See also* KELMAN, *supra* note 1, at 20.

128 Gordon, *supra* note 65, at 576. Professor Feinman asserts that modern contract law accepts the application of social values by courts, but retains the parties' private agreement as the core principle. Feinman, *Critical Approaches*, *supra* note 76, at 834. "Because conventional analysis wants to avoid, if not the reality, at least the appearance of . . . an appeal ["to a larger vision"] it also systematically downplays the counterprinciples." UNGER, *supra* note 2, at 60.

129 Feinman, *Significance, supra* note 77, at 1313.

130 Hutchinson & Monahan, *supra* note 2, at 209 (discussing the CLS view); *see also* UNGER, *supra* note 2, at 121 (noting that CLS theory holds "that law and legal doctrine reflect, confirm, and reshape the social divisions and hierarchies inherent in a type or stage of social organization such as 'capitalism'"); Feinman, *Critical Approaches*, *supra* note 76, at 852-57. CLS deconstructionists, on the other hand, seek "to delegitimatize existing legal rules and existing consciousnesses by exposing their latent contradictions and ambiguities." Whitford, *supra* note 20, at 775 (discussing CLS). The connection between the view of contract as legitimating ideology and the indeterminacy thesis is discussed by many CLS writers. *See, e.g.*, Feinman, *Critical Approaches*, *supra* note 76, at 852-853; Joseph W. Singer, *The Player and the Cards: Nihilism and Legal Theory*, 94 YALE L.J. 1, 12 (1984); David Kairys, *Introduction to* THE POLITICS OF LAW, *supra* note 69, at 3-7.

. . . legitimize it,"[131] thereby concealing the exploitation of the underclasses.[132]

CLS writers believe that modern contract law emphasizes individualism in several ways. For example, confident that they can recognize coercion or fraud in the isolated case[133] and largely unconcerned about or unwilling to consider the fairness of preexisting wealth patterns and how people form their preferences (at least beyond traditional categories of inquiry such as mental incompetence and infancy),[134] courts continue to presume free assent to contract terms. Courts also remain hesitant to investigate the adequacy of an exchange, deferring instead to the parties' measure of value. Moreover, the dominance of individualist principles, CLS writers conclude, influences the legal community to perceive falsely the existence of free contracting in society: "Once we decide . . . that we *should* ordinarily bolster a private sphere of free action . . . we come to believe that we will find such a sphere out in the world."[135]

Many CLS theorists are concerned that the reality may be very different. Some CLS theorists concede the lack of bite of the individualist-collective rule dichotomy in some contract cases, such as

---

131 Hutchinson & Monahan, *supra* note 2, at 223 (quoting Peter Gabel and Jay M. Feinman, *Contract Law as Ideology*, *in* THE POLITICS OF LAW, *supra* note 69, at 175-76). *See also* Feinman, *Critical Approaches*, *supra* note 76, at 854 (noting that contract law "present[s] a system of belief which affirms the legitimacy of the existing social order while denying its true nature"). For an excellent discussion of the theory of legitimation, *see* John Stick, *Charting the Development of Critical Legal Studies*, 88 COLUM. L. REV. 407, 424-32 (1988) (reviewing KELMAN, *supra* note 1).

132 *See* Feinman, *Critical Approaches, supra* note 76, at 849, 852, 854; *see also* HORWITZ, TRANSFORMATION, *supra* note 101, at 201 (1977) (arguing that the objective theory of contract "destroyed most substantive grounds for evaluating the justice of exchange" and "disguise[d] gross disparities of bargaining power under a facade of neutral and formal rules of contract law").

133 *See* KELMAN, *supra* note 1, at 121, 237.

134 For a general discussion of these issues, *see* TREBILCOCK, *supra* note 37.

135 KELMAN, *supra* note 1, at 291.

those involving businesses of equal bargaining power. A "collective" rule such as excuse, for example, benefits one business party over the other and changes the risk allocation, but may be "perfectly compatible with liberal capitalist enterprise."[136] Nevertheless, various CLS writers focus on cases exhibiting "background conditions" adverse to one party, such as lack of resources, education, information, and market alternatives, which diminish free choice and culminate in one-sided exchanges.[137] Generalizing from these examples, these writers conclude that our contracting system's emphasis on individualism results in "gross inequality, selfishness, and the glorification of anticommunitarian exclusiveness,"[138] thereby demonstrating the hollowness of freedom of contract. In fact, viewed from the CLS perspective, freedom of contract ironically constitutes a form of state intervention in favor of the privileged classes because it preserves their freedom to coerce others.

Some CLS writers express pessimism over the prospect of effective reform even when courts utilize contract theories and principles reflecting a collective vision, such as promissory estoppel and unconscionability: "Just because the UCC has formally adopted a code section on unconscionability does not mean that substantive contractual relations have altered a great deal, that substantive fairness of exchange is guaranteed."[139] For example, influenced by Karl Llewellyn's analysis (discussed in Chapter 4), CLS analysts worry about the ease in which contracting parties can adopt strategies to override decisions based on fairness. Even though the *Williams v. Walker-Thomas*[140] court directly disapproves of the unfair bargaining between the parties and declines to enforce the cross-collateral clause,[141] some CLS adherents argue that the

---

136 *Id.* at 239.

137 *Id.* at 103. *See also* Hale, *supra* note 87.

138 KELMAN, *supra* note 1, at 184.

139 *Id.* at 225.

140 350 F.2d 445 (D.C. Cir. 1965).

141 The court stated:

decision preserves the free-contract construct because it concludes only that Ms. Williams probably did not consent to the confusing cross-collateral clause.[142] The case therefore invites the draftsperson to "recur [ ] to the attack" by drafting a clearer clause.[143]

In addition, some CLS proponents assert that equitable theories "divert [ ] resources available for the reform of the overall substantive structure into a dead end."[144] In other words, these principles defuse social problems, they do not resolve them.[145] For example, according to Professor Kennedy, "the doctrine of unequal bargaining power represents a partial acceptance of distributive motives into the domain of contract law, but an acceptance that is rhetorical rather than real--intended to disarm."[146] At best, Kennedy adds, the doctrine "may achieve . . . randomly good results" and therefore "is a weapon on the side of

---

> But when a party of little bargaining power, and hence little real choice, signs a commercially unreasonable contract with little or no knowledge of its terms, it is hardly likely that his consent, or even an objective manifestation of his consent, was ever given to all the terms. In such a case the usual rule that the terms of the agreement are not to be questioned should be abandoned and the court should consider whether the terms of the contract are so unfair that enforcement should be withheld.

350 F.2d at 449-50 (footnotes omitted).

142 The court remanded the case for a factual determination of this issue. *Id.* at 450.

143 Llewellyn, *supra* note 14, at 733; *see* Kennedy, *Form and Substance*, *supra* note 17, at 1747 (noting that if a term is not enforced, parties "will readjust the rest of the bargain, and the stronger will exact . . . the advantage" in another form). But Professor Kennedy has also stated that "there is value as well as an element of real nobility in the judicial decision to throw out, every time the opportunity arises, consumer contracts designed to perpetuate the exploitation of the poorest class of buyers on credit." *Id.* at 1777.

144 *Id.*

145 Spann, *supra* note 6, at 229.

146 Kennedy, *Motives*, *supra* note 42, at 622.

equality."[147] Similarly, in his discussion of "radical critics," Hugh Collins remarks that "by invalidating the outcomes of aberrational markets, the principle of fairness indirectly legitimates the ordinary market's distribution of wealth."[148]

As with the mainstream, Kennedy and others acknowledge the difficulties of achieving social reform through contract law, even if lawmakers were inclined toward collectivism. For example, Kennedy recognizes the difficulty of constructing standards for determining when to intervene on paternalistic grounds and the need for "a sophisticated economic analysis" of the advisability of compulsary terms such as non-disclaimable warranties to ensure "helping the purported beneficiaries . . . . If we get this analysis wrong, then it may well be that an initiative that is supposed to redistribute from rich sellers to poor buyers does exactly the opposite (or hurts both)."[149]

Despite all of these caveats about contract law's potential, Kennedy and others still enthusiastically endorse redistributive and paternalistic principles and believe that "[c]ontract law may be an ideal context for [creating an altruistic order]."[150] In fact, seemingly throwing caution to the wind, Kennedy urges courts to render decisions based on "intuitive assessments" of the relevant issues.[151] What accounts for this apparent about-face? CLS has incurred a great deal of criticism for lacking a positive agenda.[152] In attempting to respond to the criticism,

---

147 *Id.*

148 *See* COLLINS, *supra* note 51, at 148-49.

149 Kennedy, *Motives*, *supra* note 42, at 612. *See also id.* at 613 (instrumental decisions involve "an empirical question of great difficulty").

150 Kennedy, *Form and Substance, supra* note 17, at 1778.

151 Kennedy, *Motives*, *supra* note 42, at 614.

152 *See, e.g.*, Hugh Collins, *The Transformation Thesis and the Ascription of Contractual Responsibility*, in PERSPECTIVES OF CRITICAL CONTRACT LAW 295 (Thomas Wilhelmsson ed., 1992): "[T]he critical programme needs to become much clearer about the nature and content of the new values which are said to inform the modern law of contract."

CLS adherence to indeterminacy may mean that "ad hoc paternalism" is all that is left.[153]

Alternatively, some CLS analysts have offered reasonably specific solutions to problems, often utilizing a mode of analysis surprisingly similar to the mainstream's.[154] For example, unconvinced by the mainstream's concern about unintended impacts of plant closing decisions, Kennedy himself argues that the court in *Local 1330*[155] should have found a non-waivable implied term requiring the company to "convey the plant to the union in trust" for the workers based on their efforts to make the plant profitable. Moreover, the implied term would also bar the union from selling the plant to the detriment of the town.[156] Evidencing the influence of "mainstream" economic analysis of the law, Kennedy asserts that the parties would have preferred such terms and failed to agree only because of information deficiencies. For example, the workers may "have underestimated the long-term value of worker control, and . . . the risks of capital flight . . . ." Moreover, the company probably

---

This, of course, is not a weakness peculiar to CLS. Cornel West of Princeton recently wrote in a review: "But like most prophets of participatory democracy, including Dewey, Mr. Bellah and his colleagues are short on strategy. . . . [T]hey give us no clue as to how this coming together can take place, or what will hold such a movement together." Cornel West, *The Struggle for America's Soul,* N.Y. TIMES, Sept. 15, 1991, § 7 (Book Review), at 13 (reviewing ROBERT N. BELLAH ET AL., THE GOOD SOCIETY (1991)). But alas, writing about Cornel West, Robert Boynton recently stated: "To counter the crisis, West advocates nothing less than a 'politics of conversion.' . . . West has no concrete solution; he's making a plea for blacks to seize their own destiny through 'modes of valuation and resistance' that offer 'a chance for people to believe that there is hope for the future and a meaning to struggle.'" Robert S. Boynton, *Princeton's Public Intellectual,* N.Y. TIMES, Sept. 15, 1991, § 6 (Magazine), at 39, 45. Theorists without solutions are easy targets.

153 *See, e.g.*, TREBILCOCK, *supra* note 37, at 159 (discussing Kennedy): "[P]rincipled paternalism . . . collapses, according to Kennedy, once one recognizes the repugnant implications of pervasive authoritarianism. This leads Kennedy to endorse a form of ad hoc paternalism premised on moral intuition on a case-by-case basis . . . ."

154 *See* Gordon, *Lawyers*, *supra* note 72, at 2093-95.

155 631 F.2d 1264 (6th Cir. 1980). *See supra* notes 43-44, and accompanying text.

156 Kennedy, *Motives*, *supra* note 42, at 630.

would not have been able to pass along the cost of terms protecting the workers, which terms would therefore "work a redistributive benefit" in favor of the workers.[157]

Analyzing the same case, Professor Singer maintains that the steelworkers' reliance on the continued operation of their steel plant should have been protected because it is "analogous" to the kinds of reliance already recognized by the legal system.[158] .Moreover, according to Professor Gordon, Singer demonstrated that "the arguments used to distinguish plant closings rest upon unexamined and unsupported ideological and empirical premises about the natural justice and economic efficiency of a 'property right' in employers to close plants at will."[159]

Professor Kelman agrees that "the existing social world" is neither "inevitable" because of the "immutability of the power of the contracting parties" nor "beneficial."[160] As to the former point, Kelman asserts that

> depending on the shape of demand and supply curves for goods with desired traits or terms to which the law entitles a buyer, the buyer *class* may well be enriched at the expense of the seller class by even the most minimal entitlement shifts, ones establishing compulsory terms, even though particular buyers may be hurt by the imposition of undesired compulsory terms.[161]

Kelman points out, for example, that by denying one side monopoly power, the application of the duress doctrine can result in lower prices.[162]

---

[157] *Id.*

[158] Joseph Singer, *The Reliance Interest in Property,* 40 STAN. L. REV. 611, 621 (1988).

[159] Gordon, *Lawyers*, *supra* note 72, at 2094 (discussing Singer, *supra* note158).

[160] KELMAN, *supra* note 1, at 184.

[161] *Id.* at 178. Kelman adds: "shifts in rules explicitly or implicitly affecting the situations in which parties can void or alter a contract because they were inadequately 'free,' given the pressures others put on them, will lead to distinct distributions." *Id.* at 180.

[162] *Id.* at 180.

Conclusion

CLS theorists and their counterparts in the "mainstream" address crucial issues of contract law. Is contract doctrine too indeterminate? Do courts invoke freedom of contract and individualism at the expense of equity? Can courts successfully fashion a progressive reform program utilizing contract law? Although adherents within each movement often disagree among themselves, the two schools have come to symbolize very different propositions about the nature and functions of contract law. Nevertheless, the disagreements may be more a matter of emphasis than of kind, especially as the theories have evolved.

The dispute over rule-indeterminacy boils down to a quarrel over the magnitude of indeterminate cases to those readily decided by rules. Although mainstream writers "respect decisions . . . made by others," they reject the legal formalists' view of legal determinism and concede the role of judicial discretion in "hard" cases.[163] Many CLS analysts in turn acknowledge the efficacy of legal rules and downplay the "fundamental

---

[163] James B. White, *Law Teachers' Writing*, 91 MICH. L. REV. 1970, 1973 (1993). Professor White's entire thought bears repeating:

> Of course when a case is thought about more fully it often becomes increasingly open to decision either way, and the considerations of policy and prescription become increasingly relevant. Yet in the lawyer's life the question is almost never one of pure policy, pure choice; the heart of her experience is facing a choice where respect must be paid to decisions made by others. Which decisions, how much respect, and why? These are the central questions of legal thinking; they are essential to the maintenance of the law as a constituted system of authority. To erase them, by thinking of a question as one of pure policy, as if there were no authoritative context of judgments made by others, is to destroy the essence both of law and of legal education.

Id. See also HENRY HART, THE CONCEPT OF LAW 119 (1961) ("Nothing can eliminate [the] duality of a core of certainty and a penumbra of doubt when we are engaged in bringing particular situations under general rules.").

contradiction" in "easy" cases.[164] Despite the standoff on whether there are more easy or hard cases, CLS's indeterminacy thesis is quite persuasive when it focuses on cases involving challenging issues of assent in a multi-tiered society.[165] In fact, the CLS insight that judges possess discretion to decide those cases in conformity with either the individual or collective vision reinforces my view discussed in Chapter 1 of the prominence in contract law of both consensual and non-consensual principles. Notwithstanding this duality in difficult cases, however, the mainstream's admonition that the constraints of doctrine and common judicial norms limit the range of possible results even in "hard" cases also seems convincing. In the end, contract law is probably not as indeterminate as CLS wants to claim and not as objective as the mainstream would like.

The dialogue concerning the role of contract law in the legitimation of social hierarchies also reveals more agreement than first assumed.[166] Few in either school doubt the existence of at least some inequities in society or the lack of equal information, resources, and abilities in many exchanges. As with CLS, most mainstream theorists therefore believe that an account of contract law focusing only on private preferences is incomplete. In fact, perhaps influenced in part by CLS,

---

164 *See, e.g., supra* note 69, and accompanying text; Gordon, *Lawyers*, *supra* note 72, at 2091. *See also* SCHAUER, *supra* note 13, at 195 ("realist challenge" essentially empirical).

165 Stanley Fish applauds contract law's indeterminacy: "It is *because* it is a world made up of materials that pull in diverse directions that contract law can succeed in its endless project of making itself into a formal whole." Stanley Fish, *The Law Wishes to Have a Formal Existence*, *in* THE FATE OF LAW, 184 (Austin Sarat & Thomas R. Kearns eds., 1991). Consideration doctrine is therefore "upheld by the rhetorical structure it has generated." *Id.* at 187.

Fish's belief that the law's rhetorical content is a strength sets him apart from CLS. Law is legitimate not because it is a "determinate system of rules and distinctions" but because it specifies "the vocabulary and conceptual 'neighborhood' of decision making." *Id.* at 195. Moreover, the law's failure to acknowledge its indebtedness to "other discourses" is not unlike every other practice, which proceeds in "ignorance of its debts and complicities." *Id.* at 204.

166 *See* TREBILCOCK, *supra* note 37, at 163 (comparing Duncan Kennedy and Milton Friedman).

many mainstream writers advocate increased judicial surveilance on the basis of market failures, distributive justice, or paternalism even as they ultimately underscore the essential validity of contract law as a whole. CLS's primary goal seems to be to chide the contract law establishment for being too complacent and to urge even greater judicial activism.

The precise extent and nature of the inequities in contract law are obviously very controversial questions.[167] CLS could substantiate its case by adopting an empirical agenda.[168] For now, the claims that existing rules as administered by courts maintain an undesirable heirarchy remain subject to counterattack.[169] Moreover, although critics of CLS have not proved the conflicting position that contract law sufficiently reinforces collective values or that those values should not enter the equation, the burden of proof belongs on those who claim, contrary to conventional understanding and inconsistent with significant evidence of the importance of fairness theories and principles, contract doctrine's repressiveness.

A great deal of uncertainty also surrounds whether contract law is a desirable instrument of reform. CLS writers do not deny the issue's murkiness, but many support the use of contract law, for example, to find

---

167 For an effort to consider the relationship between efficiency and distributional goals in contract law, *see* Richard Craswell, *Passing On the Costs of Legal Rules: Efficiency and Distribution in Buyer-Seller Relationships*, 43 STAN. L. REV. 361 (1991).

168 *See* David M. Trubek, *Where the Action Is: Critical Legal Studies and Empiricism*, 36 STAN. L. REV. 575, 611-12 (1984) (discussing CLS reliance on cases rather than empirical evidence). *See also* SCHAUER, *supra* note 13, at 195. For a critique of empiricism, *see* Mark G. Kelman, *Trashing*, 36 STAN. L. REV. 293, 337-41 (1984) (arguing that inadequate data and simplistic modeling deter the production of reliable empirical studies of specific legal rules).

169 *See* Trubek, *supra* note 168 at 611-12. Moreover, even if a judge's conscious or unconscious hidden agenda were to maintain the status quo, existing empirical work suggests that there may be very little connection between contract doctrine and social behavior. *See* Feinman, *Critical Approaches*, *supra* note 76, at 851 (noting that "research suggests that contract law has little influence on the incentives, planning, or contract performance of business people"); Trubek, *supra* note 168, at 612 (noting that CLS fails to "provide[] evidence that legal consciousness does affect what goes on in society").

a remedy for the steelworkers in Youngstown. Some of these proposals are surprisingly mainstream in method. Many in the mainstream also approve of contract-law approaches to problems, although perhaps on the whole these analysts would be more cautious.

It is difficult to say whether the mainstream is too reticent or CLS too unrestrained. We probably can never know, for example, whether employing contract law to keep the steel mills open in Youngstown would have ultimately produced greater benefits to society than costs. Some evidence suggests that it would have: The demise of the steel mills in Homestead, another steel town, apparently reduced the lives of its workers:

> Homestead's demise would be less worrisome if its former residents had gone on to achieve better lives for themselves and their children. But available data suggest the opposite: most of them, after migrating west and south, got jobs in the service sector paying no more than one-half to two-thirds of what they had once earned in the mill. This is not so much the tragedy of an American steel town as it is the ragedy of modern America.[170]

Whether Homestead's tragedy is really the "tragedy of modern America," however, depends on many other factors, of course, such as the impact of the steel company's relocation elsewhere, and whether Homestead is able to rebuild and thrive with a more diversified economy.[171]

---

[170] Robert B. Reich, *On the Slag Heap of History*, N.Y. TIMES, Nov. 8, 1992, § 7 (Book Review), at 15, reviewing WILLIAM SERRIN, HOMESTEAD: THE GLORY AND TRAGEDY OF AN AMERICAN STEEL TOWN (1992).

[171] *See supra* note 46, and accompanying text.

CHAPTER 6

THEORIES OF ECONOMIC ANALYSTS OF CONTRACT LAW AND THEIR CRITICS

Economic analysis of law has increased in importance and influence at least since Ronald Coase published *The Problem of Social Cost* in 1960.[1] Legal economics fills a void resulting from the demise of other movements, such as formalism and realism.[2] By introducing a social science into legal analysis, legal economics also excites theorists dissatisfied with what they believe to be the tunnel vision of traditional legal inquiry.

Legal economics is also a useful counterweight to the indeterminacy thesis of Critical Legal Studies (CLS).[3] By testing the various rules and doctrines of contract law against the principles of economics,[4] legal economists present a more-or-less unified view of what promises courts should enforce and what sanctions courts should impose for non-performance.[5] Moreover, economic analysts claim that principles of economics also explain existing contract law,[6] which, when viewed

---

1 Ronald H. Coase, *The Problem of Social Cost*, 3 J.L. & ECON. 1 (1960). *See generally* William M. Landes & Richard A. Posner, *The Influence of Economics on Law: A Quantitative Study*, 36 J. L. & ECON. 385 (1993).

2 *See* Chapter 5.

3 *See* MARK KELMAN, A GUIDE TO CRITICAL LEGAL STUDIES 114 (1987) ("[r]elationship between CLS and Law and Economics is in fact quite intimate. . ."). Conversely, legal economics is a target of CLS: Law and economics "is the best worked-out, most consummated liberal legal ideology of the sort that CLS has tried both to understand and to critique." *Id.* For a discussion of CLS, *see* Chapter 5.

4 Jay M. Feinman, *The Significance of Contract Theory*, 58 U. CIN. L. REV. 1283, 1296 (1990).

5 Lewis A. Kornhauser, *An Introduction to the Economic Analysis of Contract Remedies*, 57 U. COLO. L. REV. 683, 685-86 (1986). *See also* Richard A. Posner, *A Reply to Some Recent Criticisms of the Efficiency Theory of the Common Law*, 9 HOFSTRA L. REV. 775, 775-89 (1981) (discussing and rebutting criticisms of the efficiency theory).

6 ANTHONY T. KRONMAN & RICHARD A. POSNER, THE ECONOMICS OF CONTRACT LAW 5 (1979).

through the economic lens, proves to be largely objective, determinate,[7] and generally divorced from politics.[8]

Perhaps the most prominent school of legal economics in the contract-law field, often called "neoclassical" law and economics, focuses on the efficiency of markets.[9] I have already introduced this approach in the specialized context of Chapter 3's corporation contractarians, and I touched upon it in the discussion of "conservative" mainstream scholars in Chapter 5. I shall broaden the inquiry here. Neoclassical legal economists observe that people allocate society's scarce resources through the exchange process. Voluntary exchange occurs in a free-market setting because the parties, seeking to maximize their economic welfare,[10] give up resources in return for more valuable resources.[11] Such exchange is socially desirable because it moves resources to "higher valued uses," thereby increasing "allocative efficiency."[12] By pursuing self-interest,

---

7 *See, e.g.*, Steven D. Smith, *The Pursuit of Pragmatism*, 100 YALE L.J. 409, 426 (1990). *See also* Mark M. Hager, *The Emperor's Clothes Are Not Efficient: Posner's Jurisprudence of Class*, 41 AM. U. L. REV. 7, 16 & nn.55 & 56 (1991).

8 KELMAN, *supra* note 3, at 125.

9 Another school of law and economics identified with Oliver Williamson focuses on "transaction costs and their effect on choice of contract governance structures." Ian R. Macneil, *Economic Analysis of Contractual Relations: Its Shortfalls and the Need for a "Rich Classificatory Apparatus,"* 75 Nw. U. L. Rev. 1018, 1022 (1981). Transaction costs hinder or block the performance of competitive markets. *See generally* Oliver E. Williamson, *Transaction-Cost Economics: The Governance of Contractual Relations*, 22 J. L. & ECON. 233 (1979). For a brief discussion, *see infra* notes 75-79, and accompanying text.

10 *See, e.g.*, Kornhauser, *supra* note 5, at 688 (pointing out that "[t]he assumption of rational choice implies that . . . obstacles and costs do not prevent the individual from choosing the alternative that maximizes her welfare."); *see also* E. ALLAN FARNSWORTH, CONTRACTS 846 (2d ed. 1990) (noting that traditional economic theory "presupposes people who are rational and who strive to maximize their own welfare.").

11 FARNSWORTH, *supra* note 10, at 846; RICHARD A. POSNER, ECONOMIC ANALYSIS OF LAW 10-11 (4th ed. 1992).

12 POSNER, *supra* note 11, at 10-11. Under the concept of "Pareto superiority" a transaction is efficient "if a movement from one allocative state to another leaves at least one person better off and no one worse off." Jeffrey L. Harrison, *Trends and Traces: A Preliminary Evaluation of Economic Analysis in Contract Law*, 1988

then, people promote the interests of society.[13] Skeptical of the capacity of lawmakers to improve on this "private" method of economic organization,[14] neoclassical legal economists believe that contract law appropriately enforces voluntary exchange.[15]

Critics of neoclassical legal economics point out the many assumptions underlying the efficiency model. For example, they claim that legal economists tend to minimize the problem of determining the voluntariness of an exchange.[16] As we saw in Chapter 5, however, this depends in part on the legal community's normative view of what constitutes fair bargaining.[17] By utilizing the preexisting wealth distribution as a starting point, the legal economists' "willingness to give up resources" measure of value[18] also favors the rich and does not address the critical issue of how wealth should be distributed in the first place.[19]

ANN. SURV. AM. L. 73, 93 (1988).

13 *See* ADAM SMITH, THE WEALTH OF NATIONS 423 (Modern Library 1937) (1791) (an "invisible hand" leads individuals to promote the interests of society). *See also* KRONMAN & POSNER, *supra* note 6, at 2. On the other hand, Cohen characterized as "classical economic optimism" the view that "there is a sort of preestablished harmony between the good of all and the pursuit by each of his own selfish economic gain." Morris R. Cohen, *The Basis of Contract*, 46 HARV. L. REV. 553, 558 (1933).

14 *See* MICHAEL J. TREBILCOCK, THE LIMITS OF FREEDOM OF CONTRACT 7, 15-16 (1993).

15 Legal economists "of the Chicago school" see "society as fundamentally successful when it *responds* to the will of individuals, and mediates the conflicts between individuals simply by making everyone pay his way." KELMAN, *supra* note 3, at 118. Judge Posner asserts that voluntary exchange would take place without contract law. However, the system would be inefficient because of advantage-taking and the costliness of security devices. POSNER, *supra* note 11, at 90-91.

16 *See* TREBILCOCK, *supra* note 14, at 19-20.

17 *See* Chapter 5.

18 KRONMAN & POSNER, *supra* note 6, at 2.

19 TREBILCOCK, *supra* note 14, at 57 (economics offers "limited insights" on "fashioning an appropriate set of background legal entitlements."). *See also* Richard Craswell, *Contract Remedies, Renegotiation, and the Theory of Efficient Breach,* 61 S. CAL. L. REV. 629, 641 (1988) (economic analysis not concerned with redistributive effects).

This gauge of value also downplays utilitarian measures such as happiness and satisfaction, which are supposed to be (but critics think are not) enveloped by the efficiency model.[20]

Critics also complain that many neoclassical legal economists assume the absence of market failures, such as imperfect information and monopolies, or that the efficiency formula can easily encompass these problems. Critics point out, however, that market failures require lawmakers to confront complex issues, such as the quantity and quality of information that one party must disclose to the other to ensure the latter's "autonomous choice."[21] Moreover, neoclassical legal economists generally suppose the economic rationality of parties and the lack of countervailing motives such as altruism, or at least assume the ability to factor altruism into the self-interest equation.[22] According to critics, these analysts have "no theory of how preferences are formed, whether they are good or bad in terms of the welfare of those holding them, or whether some ordering or hierarchy of individuals' preferences is possible or desirable."[23] As I will illustrate more fully shortly, critics also believe that neoclassical legal economists too often assume the absence of transaction costs.[24]

According to some critics, many neoclassical legal economists also minimize the problem of third-party effects--whether an exchange decreases the wealth of third parties more than it increases the wealth of the contracting parties. Analysts point out that the issue raises difficult questions such as what third-party effects to take into account and how to measure them. For example, should decisionmakers consider only an exchange's effect on third-party property or contract rights or should a

---

20 *See, e.g.*, Hager, *supra* note 7, at 21-22.

21 TREBILCOCK, *supra* note 14, at 103.

22 *Id.* at 147. *See also* Jay M. Feinman, *Relational Contract and Default Rules*, 3 S. CAL. INTER. L. J. 43, 52 (1993). "Individual preferences may neither be as fixed nor as informed by self-interest as economists might wish. People appear to vary widely in their power of self-control and may not dependably make wise, self interest decisions, as economists assume." G. Richard Shell, *Contracts in the Modern Supreme Court*, 81 CAL. L. REV. 431, 526 (1993).

23 TREBILCOCK, *supra* note 14, at 147.

24 *See* Daniel A. Farber, *Contract Law and Modern Economic Theory*, 78 NW. U. L. Rev. 303, 305 (1983); KELMAN, *supra* note 3, at 119, 123.

third party's personal offense (to, say, an exchange of pornography) be sufficient? Ultimately, of course, the problem requires decisionmakers to confront the "big picture" question of the boundaries between freedom of individuals and the rights of the collective.[25]

Because of all these problems, critics assert that neoclassical legal economics is divorced from reality and sometimes supports unfair or unwise results.[26] In response, "second generation" legal economists have increased the sophistication of their models.[27] As new economic theories begin to approach reality, they run the danger of losing much of their descriptive and predictive power. Nevertheless, they are likely to be more helpful and compelling than the models they replace.

The literature on the law and economics of contract law, both favorable and critical, is vast, and I cannot hope to analyze even much of it here. My strategy is to discuss the strengths and weaknesses of two important contributions by legal economists to contract-law theory. The first section analyzes the theory of efficient breach, which typifies how neoclassical legal economists sort out welfare enhancing and reducing exchanges. The second section, which focuses on economic theories of contract gap-filling, presents the neoclassical approach followed by more recent strategies for filling gaps, involving transaction-cost reduction and deterring unfair advantage-taking.

A. The Theory of Efficient Breach

---

25 On all of these third-party issues, *see, e.g.*, TREBILCOCK, *supra* note 14, at 58-77. *See also id.* at 243, 251.

26
> As Duncan Kennedy has pointed out with some force, our attraction to an efficiency analysis stems from its apparent value-neutral base. It offers us the opportunity to avoid much more uncomfortable discussions about values and politics that inhere in discussions about redistribution and paternalism. But, as Kennedy also demonstrates, the insulation from value judgments that economic analysis offers is illusory, providing only indeterminate solutions.

Elizabeth Warren, *Bankruptcy Policymaking in an Imperfect World*, 92 MICH. L. REV. 336, 340 (1993) (footnotes omitted).

27 *See, e.g.*, Ian Ayres & Robert Gertner, *Strategic Contractual Inefficiency and the Optimal Choice of Legal Rules*, 101 YALE L.J. 729, 734 (1992) [hereinafter Ayres & Gertner, *Strategic Contractual Inefficiency*]. *See generally Symposium, Law, Economics & Norms*, 144 U. PENN. L. REV. 1643 (1996); sources cited in note 75, *infra*.

Problem 9: During the second year of production of "Why Spy?," MDM Enterprises learns that a popular actress, Katherine Taft, is interested in performing on the program on a regular basis. MDM wishes to substitute Taft for a minor actress in the series, Michele Green. Green has signed a three-year contract with MDM for $2500 per episode, with a ten percent increase over the three years. MDM calculates that it can pay Green's damages for breach of contract and Taft's higher salary, and still come out ahead because of higher revenues resulting from Taft's participation in the series.

1. The theory described

Should contract law encourage MDM to break its contract with Green because MDM and Taft will be better off and Green will not be worse off? Proponents of the "efficient breach" theory[28] would argue that MDM should be encouraged to break its contract with Green in the name of allocative efficiency.[29] First, MDM is not considering breaking the contract with Green simply to extract salary concessions or otherwise improve its agreement with Green. Advocates of efficient breach condemn such "opportunistic" behavior because it does not result in a net gain, it merely increases MDM's wealth at Green's expense. These theorists therefore prescribe rules to discourage this kind of advantage-taking, such as awarding Green restitution of any gains made by MDM as a result of the strategy.[30]

Second, instead of attempting to coerce Green to make concessions, MDM wants to break the contract because its gains from doing so will exceed its liability to Green. After paying Green her damages, MDM would still come out ahead and Green would not be worse off because MDM would compensate her for her loss. The strategy

---

[28] Professor Birmingham presented the theory in 1970 and many law and economics articles and books address it. For a list of articles as of 1982, see Ian R. Macneil, *Efficient Breach of Contract: Circles in the Sky*, 68 VA. L. REV. 947, 947 n. 5 (1982).

[29] Theorists disagree on the appropriate remedy to ensure efficient breach. For a discussion and collection of sources, see Christopher T. Wonnell, *The Contractual Disempowerment of Employees*, 46 STAN. L. REV. 87, 101 & n. 85 (1993).

[30] *See* POSNER, *supra* note 11, at 117-18.

would therefore result in a net social gain.[31] Judge Posner would support encouraging MDM to break its promise in this context in the following terms:

> [I]n some cases a party is tempted to break his contract simply because his profit from breach would exceed his expected profit from completion of the contract. If it would also exceed the expected profit to the other party from completion of the contract, and if damages are limited to the loss of that profit, there will be an incentive to commit a breach. But there should be.[32]

Advocates of efficient breach point to other contract rules consistent with the strategy to demonstrate the close alignment of economic principles and existing contract law. For example, contract law generally denies specific performance. In a world free of transaction costs the remedial rule--damages or specific performance--would have no impact on efficiency (and would "only" affect the distribution of wealth) because under either remedy MDM would replace Green with Taft.[33] We have already discussed MDM's financial incentives to proceed in this fashion when the remedial rule is damages. If specific performance were generally granted, MDM would still break the contract with Green, but would share with her the surplus created by hiring Taft in order to convince Green to release MDM. In the real world, however, the relative transaction costs propogated by each remedy determine the efficient remedial rule.[34] If Green were entitled to specific performance, efficient breach analysts posit, MDM's strategy to "buy out" her right in order to

---

31 The result is "Pareto superior" because MDM is better off and Green is no worse off. *Id.* at 190. The result also satisfies the Kaldor-Hicks measure because of the net social gain. Daniel Friedmann, *The Efficient Breach Fallacy*, 18 J. LEGAL STUD. 1, 3 (1989).

32 POSNER, *supra* note 11, at 119. *See also* Kornhauser, *supra* note 5, at 686: "If the gain to the promisor from his breach outweighs the loss to the promisee, the promisor should not perform."

33 Macneil, *supra* note 28, at 951-952.

34 *Id.* at 952-53.

hire Taft would increase the transaction costs of moving resources to their highest valued use.[35]

Contract law also denies Green the right to restitution of MDM's additional gains by replacing her with Taft, which, if awarded to Green, would destroy MDM's incentive to break the contract with Green. Contract law awards the injured party lost expectancy and no more "to give the reluctant party an incentive to break the contract if, but only if, that party gains enough from the breach that it can compensate the injured party for its losses yet still retain some of the benefits from the breach."[36]

Notwithstanding their recognition of moral grounds for the enforcement of promises, efficient breach analysts insist that their approach is not immoral.[37] Inspired by Holmes's famous dictum ("The duty to keep a contract at common law means a prediction that you must pay damages if you do not keep it,--and nothing else."),[38] they assert that contract law offers a promisor the option to perform or to compensate the injured party for non-performance.[39]

2. Criticism of the theory of efficient breach

Critics claim that efficient breach advocates make too many assumptions about human behavior and downplay many economic and other consequences of the approach. For example, the assumption that parties seek only or predominantly to maximize their welfare, as measured by willingness to pay, is too facile.[40] Analysts employing this view must ignore people's preferences unrelated to wealth, the complexities of human psychology, and the irrational aspects of human

---

[35] POSNER, *supra* note 11, at 131. For a brief discussion of the effects of transaction costs, *see infra* notes 75-79, and accompanying text.

[36] FARNSWORTH, *supra* note 10, at 847.

[37] *See* Chapter 1.

[38] Oliver Wendell Holmes, *The Path of the Law*, 10 HARV. L. REV. 457, 462 (1897).

[39] POSNER, *supra* note 11, at 118.

[40] *See* Mark G. Kelman, *Trashing*, 36 STAN. L. REV. 293, 307 (1984).

behavior.[41] Although, as a purely economic matter, MDM may be tempted to break its contract with Green if it believes its monetary gains will exceed its liabilities, analysts should also consider "cultural processes that take the edge off [MDM's] selfishness."[42] MDM's managers may be willing to forgo pure financial gain for the positive feelings that would accompany a decision to honor appropriate contractual behavior.[43] The tendency of individuals to regard losses as more important than gains, to ignore information that conflicts with beliefs, to fail to process other information, to make short-term decisions inconsistent with long-term goals, and to accede to desires not in one's best interest, also belongs in any equation predicting human behavior.[44]

Even assuming that people are generally welfare maximizers, critics point out that the efficient breach paradigm fails to take into account many other ramifications of the theory. For example, efficient breach theorists assume unrealistically that contract damages actually would make Green whole. Numerous remedial doctrines qualify an injured party's recovery rights, however, such as foreseeability (discussed in the next subsection), avoidable consequences, certainty of proof of loss, and rules with respect to attorney's fees and interest. For example,

---

41 A good example of the lengths to which a writer may go to fit an existing doctrine into a unified theory is Judge Posner's economic analysis of past-consideration cases such as Webb v. McGowin, 27 Ala. App. 82, 168 So. 196 (1935). Posner asserts that, if McGowin's promise to pay Webb $15 every two weeks after Webb injured himself saving McGowin had not been enforceable, McGowin might have paid Webb all at once at a much lower present value. According to Posner, such a payment would have made both parties worse off. Richard A. Posner, *Gratuitous Promises in Economics and Law*, 6 J. LEGAL STUD. 411, 418-419 (1977).

For an interesting article on legal economics that takes into account the complexities of behavior, *see* Richard A. McAdams, *Relative Preferences*, 102 YALE L.J. 1 (1992).

42 Robert C. Ellickson, *Bringing Culture and Human Frailty to Rational Actors: A Critique of Classical Law and Economics*, 65 CHI.-KENT L. REV. 23, 45 (1989).

43 *Id.* at 48. "In one well-documented historical case, Standard Oil of California responded to a severe shortage of gas by rationing its product rather than by raising price when it could have." *Id.* at 49 (citing Alan L. Olmstead & Paul Rhode, *Rationing Without Government: The West Coast Gas Famine of 1920*, 75 AM. ECON. REV. 1044 (1985)).

44 *Id.* at 35-43; KELMAN, *supra* note 3, at 130; Shell, *supra* note 22, at 526 & n. 582.

some of Green's losses caused by the breach may be too speculative to recover, such as the impediment to her career.[45]

According to critics, efficient breach advocates also minimize the costs of post-breach negotiations between the parties and other strategies. Some costs may be economically irrational but still very real, such as expenses of litigation started in spite or strategically to induce a favorable settlement. The parties may incur other costs because of uncertainty as to the measurement of the injured party's damages. For example, MDM and Green may haggle over whether MDM should pay Green for the damage to her career. As Ian Macneil points out:

> The whole thrust of the [efficient breach] analysis is breach first, talk afterwards . . . . And this is so despite the fact that "talking after a breach" may be one of the more expensive forms of conversation to be found, involving, as it so often does, engaging high-priced lawyers, and gambits like starting litigation, engaging in discovery, and even trying and appealing cases.
>
> . . . Cooperative behavior postulates relations. A model assuming away relations slips with the greatest of ease at any stage into favoring uncooperative and--ironically enough--highly inefficient human behavior.[46]

Deficiencies in information also make the efficient-breach gamble unrealistic for the prospective breacher. For example, MDM may be unable to predict Green's damages accurately or the benefits of including Taft in the show's cast.[47] MDM may therefore break a contract and incur liability for damages well above its returns from the gambit.

Critics also rebut the view that contract rules generally support efficient breach. First, they point out that virtually all the rules that seemingly support it can be explained more persuasively on other grounds. For example, history may explain the limitations on the availability of specific performance. Chancellors in equity granted

---

[45] *See* Melvin A. Eisenberg, *The Principle of Hadley v. Baxendale*, 80 CAL. L. REV. 563, 587 (1992) (the rule that an injured party can recover only reasonably foreseeable damages is inconsistent with the theory of efficient breach).

[46] Macneil, *supra* note 28, at 968-69.

[47] Proponents of legal economics often assume the parties' ability to allocate all relevant risks. *See id.* at 951. Of course, many analysts do not make this or other assumptions. *E.g.*, Victor P. Goldberg, *Price Adjustment in Long-Term Contracts*, 1985 WIS. L. REV. 527 (1985).

specific performance only rarely, when the common law damages remedy was inadequate, to reassure common law judges that chancellors were not usurping the judges' power. Alternatively, the preference for damages may result from the need to ensure jury trial rights, guaranteed by the Constitution only in cases "at law." Or judges may be reluctant to grant specific performance because they wish to minimize the need to exercise their coercive authority. Finally, on fairness grounds courts may seek to protect inadvertent breachers from the pitfalls of specific performance and to create incentives for entering contracts. These and many other explanations for the primacy of damages remedies obviously are not conclusive, but they certainly show that more is at work than a preference for efficient breach.[48]

Critics also point out rules and trends in contract law that conflict with efficient breach. For example, courts increasingly grant specific performance and award restitutionary measures exceeding lost expectancy.[49]

Perhaps most worrisome to critics, admirers of efficient breach do not address the effects of contract breach on other values pertinent to the contracting process.[50] For example, what would be the effect of efficient breach on planning and on the general stability of contracts?[51] One critic predicts acceptance of the theory would increase costs: "If a party . . . cannot rely on the contract to guarantee performance, then he may turn to other more costly and less efficient means (for example, becoming a self-supplier or vertically integrating with his supplier) to gain greater assurance that he will get what he seeks."[52] As a related matter, how would such a strategy affect the parties' trust and cooperation? What are the distributional consequences of promoting efficient breach?

Moreover, critics contest efficient breach theorists' reliance on Holmes's dictum about the choice to perform or pay damages and claim

---

48 *See* Robert A. Hillman, *Contract Modification and "Self-Help Specific Perormance": A Reaction to Professor Narasimhan*, 75 CORNELL L. REV. 62, 73-74 (1989).

49 Friedmann, *supra* note 31, at 18-19.

50 *See* Harrison, *supra* note 12, at 99.

51 *See* LON L. FULLER, THE MORALITY OF LAW 28 (rev. ed. 1969).

52 Friedmann, *supra* note 31, at 7.

that the efficient breach paradigm creates a moral dilemma for prospective breachers.[53] One analyst posits that Holmes confused contract remedies with substantive rights, "when in truth the purpose of the remedy is to vindicate [a] right, not to replace it."[54] The logic of efficient breach of contract leads too far, the critic adds: "Why not generalize the proposition so that every person has an 'option' to transgress another's rights and to violate the law, so long as he is willing to suffer the consequences?"[55] For example, should A have the right to steal B's Porsche and sell it to C who values it more than B so long as A is willing to compensate B for all of her damages? The example requires the efficient breach proponent who frowns on theft to distinguish between property and contract rights, something the efficient breach proponents have failed to do satisfactorily.[56]

Efficient breach analysts need not exclude the foregoing values and issues from their calculus. They could recast them as potential costs of the strategy. But such an equation might then be too slippery to explain very much.[57] Notwithstanding all of the above caveats, however, the efficient breach paradigm contributes by focusing on the values at stake in enforcing promises and on the nature and role of contract remedies.

B. Economic Theories of Gap Filling

---

53 Harrison, *supra* note 12, at 102-103.

54 Friedmann, *supra* note 31, at 1.

55 *Id.*

56 *See generally id.*

57 *See generally* POSNER, *supra* note 11, at 17 (arguing that by bringing in too many variables the analyst may be left "with a model so rich that no empirical observation can refute it").

Perhaps in recognition of the limitations of paradigms such as efficient breach, law and economics is becoming more sophisticated about some contract-law issues.[58] By abandoning simplifying assumptions, these "second generation" theories may lose much of their clarity and simplicity. Nevertheless, they are far richer and ultimately more helpful than their predecessors.

Consider gap filling, another issue often addressed by legal economists. As we saw in Chapter 1, contracting parties leave gaps in their contracts for many reasons, even gaps pertaining to the allocation of the risk of onerous events. How should courts fill these gaps when a costly event occurs, the parties did not specify in advance how to allocate the risk of the event, and litigation follows? Until recently, most neoclassical legal economists urged courts to supply gap-filling terms the parties would have agreed to themselves if they had bargained over the matter costlessly and with perfect information.[59] How would the parties have agreed to fill a gap? According to the analysis, they would have placed the risk on the "superior risk bearer" or the "superior risk avoider," thereby maximizing the efficiency of the transaction.[60] Assuming the parties could not have prevented an event from occurring, the superior risk bearer is the party better able to bear the expense of the event, such as by purchasing insurance. If the parties could have prevented the occurrence, the superior risk avoider is the party better able to avert the contingency.[61]

The superior-risk-bearer (or avoider) approach appealed to economic efficiency enthusiasts because in theory the efficient gap-filling or "default" rule is what most parties would want. This methodology

---

58 For an example of a study recognizing the complexity of efficient breach problems, *see* Richard Craswell, *Contract Remedies, Renegotiation, and the Theory of Efficient Breach*, 61 S. CAL. L. REV. 629, 640 (1988) ("Even when ex post renegotiation is costless, contract remedies can still affect many other variables besides the decision to breach.").

59 Richard A. Posner & Andrew M. Rosenfield, *Impossibility and Related Doctrines in Contract Law: An Economic Analysis*, 6 J. LEGAL STUD. 83, 90 (1977). *See also* Frank H. Easterbrook & Daniel R. Fischel, *The Corporate Contract*, 89 COLUM. L. REV. 1416, 1428-1430 (1989).

60 Posner & Rosenfield, *supra* note 59, at 90.

61 POSNER, *supra* note 11, at 102-109. *See also* Posner & Rosenfield, *supra* note 59, at 90-91.

decreases the overall cost of contracting because it saves most future parties the expense ("transaction costs") of bargaining to supplant a different gap-filling rule.[62] By connecting gap filling to the parties' presumed preferences, the method is also more palatable to contract theorists who favor individualism.[63]

Let us depart from our format of utilizing the exploits of XYZ and MDM to illustrate and employ the venerable *Hadley v. Baxendale*[64] (as do many recent law and economics' analyses of contract gaps).[65] In *Hadley*, a carrier delayed the delivery of a miller's broken crankshaft to a repair shop, and the miller suffered lost profits. The court held that the miller could not recover its lost profits, but rather only damages "arising naturally" or "reasonably . . . to have been in the contemplation of both parties, at the time they made the contract, as the probable result of the breach of it."[66] The *Hadley* rule fills a gap in the parties' agreement because the agreement did not allocate the risk of the miller's lost profits should the carrier delay delivery. Is the rule consistent with superior-risk-bearer analysis? Perhaps not! Under *Hadley*, the miller bears the risk of its own reasonably unforseeable lost profits. Some law and economics work surmises, however, that the carrier may be the superior risk avoider because it could prevent the loss by taking precautions to ensure delivery on time at a lower cost than the miller would have encountered in averting the loss.[67]

As with the efficient breach theory, the superior-risk-bearer methodology raises numerous questions and assumes too much. First,

---

62 *See, e.g.*, POSNER, *supra* note 11, at 93. Transatlantic Fin. Corp. v. United States, 363 F.2d 312, 318 (D.C. Cir. 1966), is a representative case.

63 *See, e.g.*, Randy E. Barnett, *The Sound of Silence: Default Rules and Contractual Consent*, 78 VA. L. REV. 821, 881-882 (1992).

64 156 Eng. Rep. 145 (Ex. Ch. 1854).

65 *See, e.g.*, Ian Ayres & Robert Gertner, *Filling Gaps in Incomplete Contracts: An Economic Theory of Default Rules*, 99 YALE L.J. 87, 101-104 (1989) [hereinafter Ayres & Gertner, *Filling Gaps*]. *See also* Ayres & Gertner, *Strategic Contractual Inefficiency*, *supra* note 27, at 734-35; Jason Scott Johnston, *Strategic Bargaining and the Economic Theory of Contract Default Rules*, 100 YALE L.J. 615 (1990).

66 156 Eng. Rep. at 151.

67 Ayres & Gertner, *Filling Gaps*, *supra* note 65, at 101.

determining how the parties would have allocated an unanticipated risk may be more difficult than adherents believe, even with the benefit of hindsight.[68] For example, identifying the superior risk bearer or avoider may challenge the courts. A court must consider among other things the probability of the risk occurring,[69] the parties' "attitude [] toward risk,"[70] the likely amount of loss, each party's ability to prevent or minimize the loss, and each party's cost of insurance.[71] The conclusion that the carrier in *Hadley* is the superior risk avoider assumes, among other things, that the miller cannot reduce or avoid the loss more cheaply than the carrier, for example, by keeping a spare crank shaft.[72]

The superior-risk-bearer approach is also problematic because parties sometimes misanalyze or ignore information, dismiss remote risks, or otherwise mistakenly agree to allocate the risk to the inferior risk bearer. Ironically, if most parties make these errors, courts should fill gaps by allocating the risk to the inferior risk bearer, according to the logic of the traditional economic gap-filling approach.[73] Otherwise, these error-prone parties would engage in costly negotiations to contract around the efficient gap-filling rule. Businesses continually making such mistakes, of course, may be weeded out by competition so that courts may never have to take such a drastic step.

Mistakes aside, parties entering voluntary agreements still may not allocate the risks of a particular exchange to the superior risk bearer. For example, especially in long-term relationships, a party to a given exchange may willingly accept the risk of an event that her counterpart

---

68 *See, e.g.*, Jules L. Coleman et al., *A Bargaining Theory Approach to Default Provisions and Disclosure Rules in Contract Law*, 12 HARV. J. L. & PUB. POL'Y 639 (1989); Posner & Rosenfield, *supra* note 59, at 110-11.

69 Harrison, *supra* note 12, at 90.

70 Ayres & Gertner, *Filling Gaps, supra* note 65, at 101 n.64.

71 Harrison, *supra* note 12, at 90.

72 Ayres & Gertner, *Filling Gaps, supra* note 65, at 101 n.64.

73 Clayton P. Gillette, *Commercial Relationships and the Selection of Default Rules for Remote Risks*, 19 J. LEGAL STUD. 535, 544 (1990).

could bear less expensively, hoping to extract future concessions.[74] A court would therefore have to take into account the parties' entire relationship to uncover the terms the parties "would have wanted" in a particular transaction, a task possibly beyond the skills of a court.

In fact, many legal economists, seeking to identify the terms parties to long-term relations would prefer, have moved away from the superior-risk-bearer gap-filling analysis. Instead, they investigate possible cost-reduction strategies of the parties. For example, would the parties to a long-term contract craft complex formulae to allocate the risk of potential problems, such as a price escalation clause tied to inflation or production costs, or would they choose basic all-or-nothing terms and rely on non-legal factors to discourage advantage-taking, such as the value of a good reputation?[75] By focusing on the contracting parties in a relation as a "single maximizing unit"[76] and seeking to isolate suitable governance structures that minimize costs, this mode of analysis (often

---

[74] *See* Macneil, *supra* note 28, at 1023-1025. A party may agree to bear such a risk to establish trust and cooperation even though the particular exchange would be inefficient. *See also* Coleman, et al., *supra* note 68, at 707-709 (need to focus on context to determine efficient gap filler).

[75] *See, e.g.*, Gillette, *supra* note 73; Robert E. Scott, *A Relational Theory of Default Rules for Commercial Contracts*, 19 J. LEGAL STUD. 597, 613-15 (1990); Lisa Bernstein, *Social Norms and Default Rules Analysis*, 3 S. CAL. INTER. L. J. 59, 76 (1993). According to Professor Trebilcock, Scott "persuasively argues that generalized default or interpretative rules and individualized contractual alternatives together reduce the costs and errors of contracting." TREBILCOCK, *supra* note 14, at 136. For additional approaches to gap filling, *see, e.g.*, David Charny, *Hypothetical Bargains: The Normative Structure of Contract Interpretation*, 89 MICH. L. REV. 1815 (1991); Lawrence A. Cunningham, *Hermeneutics and Contract Default Rules: An Essay on Lieber and Corbin*, 16 CARDOZO L. REV. 2225 (1995); Charles J. Goetz & Robert E. Scott, *The Limits of Expanded Choice: An Analysis of the Interactions Between Express and Implied Contract Terms*, 73 CAL. L. REV. 261 (1985); Gillian K. Hadfield, *Judicial Competence and the Interpretation of Incomplete Contracts*, 23 J. LEGAL STUD. 159 (1994); Gillian K. Hadfield, *Problematic Relations: Franchising and the Law of Incomplete Contracts*, 42 STAN. L. REV. 927 (1990) [hereinafter Hadfield, *Problematic Relations*]; Alan Schwartz, *Relational Contracts in the Courts: An Analysis of Incomplete Agreements and Judicial Strategies*, 21 J. LEGAL STUD. 271 (1992).

[76] Macneil, *supra* note 28, at 1022.

called "transaction-cost economics"[77]) obviously increases the sophistication and helpfulness of the neoclassical model.

Professor Farber's discussion of the potential strategies of a property owner seeking to build a new house helpfully illustrates the transaction-cost approach.[78] Assuming the prospective owner has perfect information and will incur no transaction costs, she might ask contractors to separately bid for each hour of construction and award each hour of work to the lowest bidder. The contract for that hour would specify in detail what was to be accomplished. This process would not succeed, of course, because the owner does not have perfect information about what is required each hour and would incur transaction costs, including the cost of writing separate, detailed contracts for each hour, of conducting the competitive bidding, and of moving workers to and from the site. Transaction-cost economists would analyze the potential of different kinds of owner-builder contracts based on cost reduction and the need for information. Such an analysis would explain why owners typically hire general contractors who in turn contract with subcontractors. Professor Farber points out that firms make long-term contracts for similar reasons.[79]

Recently some legal economists have broadened the focus of the gap-filling puzzle to include the problem of unfair advantage-taking and have concluded that in some circumstances the efficient gap filler may be based not on what the parties would have wanted, but on deterring "opportunism."[80] These writers introduce the idea of a "penalty default,"

---

[77] *See* Edward L. Rubin, *The New Legal Process, The Synthesis of Discourse, and the Microanalysis of Institutions*, 109 HARV. L. REV. 1393, 1413 (1996) (discussing "new institutional economics").

[78] Farber, *supra* note 24, at 325-26.

[79] *Id.* at 325. For an application of relational analysis and legal economics to gap filling in franchising contracts, *see* Hadfield, *Problematic Relations, supra* note 75. Professor Hadfield points out, for example, that "[t]he use of franchisor control to overcome free-riding improves efficiency as franchisees are forced to provide a level of quality that takes account of the effect of their actions on other franchisees and the franchisor." *Id.* at 954. *See generally* RICHARD A. POSNER, OVERCOMING LAW 433-437 (discussing the "new institutional economics").

[80] Ayres & Gertner, *Filling Gaps, supra* note 65. *See also* Lucien A. Bebchuck & Steven Shavell, *Information and the Scope of Liability for Breach of Contract: The Rule of Hadley v. Baxendale*, 7 J. L. ECON. & ORG. 284 (1991).

which penalizes a party with superior information for failing to reveal it. The rule in *Hadley*, for example, is a penalty default according to this approach (and possibly not what the parties would have wanted) because it places the risk of unforeseeable lost profits on the miller who did not reveal its potential losses to the carrier at the time of contracting.[81]

Penalty-default theorists posit that the *Hadley* limitation on consequential damages creates an incentive for shippers such as the miller to reveal to the carrier any special losses from delay.[82] Were it not for this rule--if the shipper could recover all of its losses even if not reasonably foreseeable--the shipper might fail to reveal its special circumstances. Because the carrier bases its price on the average shipper's potential loss, the shipper might fail to disclose to avoid paying the carrier an increased price.[83] Penalty-default enthusiasts believe that *Hadley* is efficient because it will influence parties such as the carrier to elect the appropriate level of precaution: "*Hadley* penalizes high-damage millers for withholding information that would allow carriers to take efficient precautions."[84] In sum, the penalty-default model increases the sophistication of the economic approach to gap filling by including in the equation gaps caused by calculated failures to disclose, which are motivated by the opportunity to increase one's gains at the expense of the other party.[85]

By recognizing that a unitary approach may be inadequate to resolve the mysteries of gap filling, the penalty-default paradigm greatly increases the usefulness of the law and economics' insight into gap filling. But we will see that the questions raised and the assumptions made by this approach are also numerous and perplexing. In fact, penalty-default theory ultimately may detract from the allure of economic analysis of law because it helps burst the law-as-science bubble.[86]

---

81 Recall that the superior risk avoider is arguably the carrier. *See supra* note 67, and accompanying text.

82 Ayres & Gertner, *Filling Gaps, supra* note 65, at 101-104.

83 *See* Johnston, *supra* note 65, at 622.

84 Ayres & Gertner, *Filling Gaps, supra* note 65, at 104.

85 *See* TREBILCOCK, *supra* note 14, at 122.

86 "When the parties' knowledge is not symmetric . . . choosing the efficient contract rule can entail an extraordinarily complex analysis--which depends on subtle pieces

Let us consider some of the issues raised by penalty defaults.[87]

1. The incentives created by penalty defaults

Do penalty defaults create the incentives predicted by their advocates? Some analysts are not convinced. As a general matter, penalty-default theorists may oversimplify the dynamics of bargaining:

> In the carrier-shipper example, we might more naturally think of bargaining as involving a series of assertions, bluffs, offers, and counteroffers, as the carrier tries to figure out exactly how much he can charge the shipper without losing the deal, and the shipper attempts to get an idea of how reliable the carrier is and how much it really costs her to deliver on time.[88]

Specifically, critics point out that *Hadley* may not move high-value shippers to disclose and may not motivate carriers to take additional precautions even if shippers did disclose. High-value shippers may not disclose because the costs of disclosure may outweigh the gains of additional carrier liability. Shippers may have to invest significant resources gathering information, predicting potential gains and losses, and communicating with carriers.[89] Shippers would also have to run the risk that the carrier would exploit the information.[90] As to the latter, suppose the carrier can dictate the terms because of superior bargaining power. The shipper might fail to reveal its large potential consequential damages even under a penalty-default rule because the carrier might then

---

of information that lawmakers are unlikely to know." Ayres & Gertner, *Strategic Contractual Inefficiency, supra* note 27, at 765. For an interesting discussion of whether default rules should be drafted as rules or standards, an issue which obviously adds to the conceptual complexity, *see* Ian Ayres, *Preliminary Thoughts on Optimal Tailoring of Contractual Rules*, 3 S. CAL. INTER. L. J. 1 (1993).

87 *See generally* Eisenberg, *supra* note 45, Johnston, *supra* note 65, and Ayres & Gertner, *Strategic Contractual Inefficiency, supra* note 27, for a more complete discussion.

88 Johnston, *supra* note 65, at 626.

89 Eisenberg, *supra* note 45, at 594-95.

90 *Id.* at 595-96.

charge a "supracompetitive price,"[91] a price determined "not by the carrier's costs, but by his beliefs about how much the shipper will be willing to pay."[92]

Even if shippers disclosed their high-value status, Melvin Eisenberg points out that carriers would not necessarily take additional precautions because the costs of using the information might outweigh the gains.[93] Costs would include processing the information, such as "train[ing] . . . employees to recognize relevant information, creat[ing] and maintain[ing] protocols for utilizing such information, and expend[ing] employee time in applying the protocols."[94] Costs would also include segregating shippers into groups based on their potential damages, with different safeguards for each group. "A high-volume [carrier] with a low rate of breach will normally find it cheaper not to stratify precaution, and simply to pay high damages in some cases, than to reduce its damage exposure by paying the costs of segregating transactions along a number of different tracks, with different precautions for each track."[95]

Even if carriers geared their level of precaution to shippers' potential damages under *Hadley*, the same might happen if the "default rule" were full carrier liability. In that case, the carrier's potential losses would be greater and it would charge a higher price. But low-damage shippers would then notify the carrier of their circumstances to avoid paying the inflated price. The *Hadley* rule would therefore be irrelevant from an efficiency standpoint. Under either a full- or limited-liability regime, carriers would elect the optimal level of precaution because they

---

91 Ayres & Gertner, *Strategic Contractual Inefficiency, supra* note 27, at 736.

92 Johnston, *supra* note 65, at 628. Consider also the carrier's bargaining dilemma: "[I]f [the carrier] persuades the shipper that the shipper will be better off with the high price, high liability alternative, then he may also persuade the shipper that the shipper in fact is better off not contracting with him at all, because the breach probability is too high, no matter what the extent of carrier liability." *Id.* at 633.

93 Eisenberg, *supra* note 45, at 592-594.

94 *Id.* at 592-93.

95 *Id.* at 593. Eisenberg supports with "casual empirical" evidence the assertion that airlines, express-mail carriers, and moving companies, do not take greater precautions when transporting high-value goods even when they agree to compensate the shipper for the entire loss. *Id.* at 593-94.

would be aware of each shipper's potential damages.[96] Penalty-default theorists must therefore restrict their theory to situations in which low-value shippers vastly outnumber high-value ones. In such contexts, in theory, low-value shippers would lose their incentive to contract out of the carrier's full liability because the savings in price would be very low, in fact less than the cost of contracting out of full liability.[97] (Remember that the carrier bases its price on the average shipper's potential loss.)

Even in a context where low-value shippers greatly outnumber high-value ones, however, a penalty default rule may not be necessary to make high-value shippers disclose. High-value shippers may disclose and pay a premium to convince the carrier to take the precautions. These shippers may want to avoid a loss from ever occurring and the potential quagmire of a lawsuit. After all, a shipper would have to prove the amount of consequential damages at trial, which may be difficult and costly.[98] In other words, the cost of fighting in court, discounted by the probability of having to do so, may outweigh the gains of a lower price for carriage.

High-value shippers may also disclose and pay more in a full-liability state if they intend to do business with the carrier in the future. Strategic failure to disclose high-value status may fly in the face of general business norms of sharing and cooperation designed to keep the the parties' relation from falling apart, with all the costs that would entail.[99] Some penalty-default analysts acknowledge this limitation of their model and generally limit it to one-shot deals.[100]

In summary, penalty defaults may not create the incentives predicted. Moreover, to the extent that they do create appropriate incentives, high-value shippers may reveal their status even under a full-

---

96 This is an example of the Coase theorem. *See* Coase, *supra* note 1.

97 Ayres & Gertner, *Filling Gaps, supra* note 65, at 102.

98 The consequential damages would have to be certain and unavoidable. *See, e.g.*, ROBERT A. HILLMAN ET AL., COMMON LAW AND EQUITY UNDER THE UCC §§ 9-13, 9-14 (1985).

99 "Norms of sharing and cooperation that some advance on moral grounds turn out to make good economic sense." Mark P. Gergen, *The Use of Open Terms in Contract*, 92 COLUM. L. REV. 997, 1080 (1992).

100 Johnston, *supra* note 65, at 625 n.36.

liability regime. We shall now see that the costs of penalty defaults may also be high.[101]

2. Penalty defaults and other economic theories

Even if penalty defaults create appropriate incentives, they still may be inefficient because they may conflict with other efficiency goals. For one thing, requiring parties to disclose information may deter them from seeking "socially useful information" in the first place.[102] Although not particularly the case in *Hadley*, as a general matter gathering information is costly. Parties who invest in information expect to "sell" the information, not to give it away.[103] Penalty defaults, which require the latter, may discourage the investment.

Information production may not be the only efficiency goal adversely affected by penalty defaults. Consider again the theory of efficient breach and assume its validity.[104] The penalty-default rule of *Hadley* may be inefficient because a carrier may break an agreement when the shipper has not disclosed its special circumstances, the carrier is therefore not liable for the shipper's unforeseen consequential damages, but those damages exceed the carrier's gains in breaching.[105] If the costs of such broken agreements exceed the gains resulting from shipper disclosures, then *Hadley* is not efficient. Professor Eisenberg comes to just that conclusion: "[T]he principle of *Hadley v. Baxendale* gives greater weight to the efficient rate of precaution than to the efficient rate of performance. This strikes the wrong balance. . . . [T]he loss of efficiency that the principle causes in the rate of performance outweighs the gain of efficiency that the principle causes in the rate of precaution."[106]

---

101 *See infra* notes 102-112, and accompanying text.

102 Ayres & Gertner, *Filling Gaps, supra* note 65, at 107.

103 Anthony T. Kronman, *Mistake, Disclosure, Information and the Law of Contracts*, 7 J. LEGAL STUD. 16 (1978).

104 *See supra* notes 28-39, and accompanying text.

105 Eisenberg, *supra* note 45, at 596-597.

106 *Id.* at 597.

3. Problems of implementation

Even if we assume away all of the above problems and conclude that penalty defaults create the correct incentives and are efficient, implementation issues arise. For example, a court would have to determine whether a gap resulted from a party's selfish failure to reveal information or from both parties' decision that the costs of filling the gap were too high.[107] The penalty-default approach, we have seen, should apply only in the former situation.[108] Determining the motives of the parties, however, would be no easy task. The court would have to consider the length of the contract, the amount and quality of the bargaining, and the custom concerning completeness of terms, among other things, to discern whether a party engaged in a strategic failure to disclose.[109]

The wisdom of implementing penalty defaults would still be uncertain even if a party had hidden important information. Some argue that business parties involved in long-term relations rarely pay much attention to contract law.[110] Instead, extralegal factors, such as the need to maintain a good reputation and to avoid contract breakdown, often determine the parties' conduct.[111] Penalty defaults may therefore have little effect on the future behavior of the parties[112] and may not result in more information and optimal precaution. In this light, perhaps legal rules should be certain, simple, and inexpensive to apply. The added costs of considering penalty defaults may not be worth the potential, but remote, gains.

---

[107] Ayres & Gertner, *Filling Gaps, supra* note 65, at 127.

[108] *Id.*

[109] *Id.* at 128 n. 177.

[110] *See* Chapter 7. *See also* James J. White, *Contract Law in Modern Commercial Transactions: An Artifact of Twentieth Century Business Life?* LAW QUADRANGLE NOTES, SPRING 1983, at 23.

[111] *See* Robert A. Hillman, *Court Adjustment of Long-Term Contracts: An Analysis Under Modern Contract Law*, 1987 DUKE L.J. 1, 30 (1987).

[112] *See* William C. Whitford, *Ian Macneil's Contribution to Contracts Scholarship*, 1985 WIS. L. REV. 545, 551-52 (1985).

In sum, the superior-risk-bearer analysis offered only the illusion of certainty. The penalty-default model sacrifices even that. The model demonstrates that once legal economists increase the level of abstraction by taking into account transaction costs, by acknowledging the existence of multiple goals, and by considering contextual realities such as the cost of information, their "science" loses some of its appeal because it loses much of its predictability.[113] Nevertheless, by emphasizing that efficient default rules sometimes will "reflect what most people want while at other times [will] encourage the revelation of information,"[114] the approach is richer and moves closer to reality. In fact, traditional legal scholars have long understood that one role of *Hadley* was to encourage disclosure. The court makes the point itself: "[H]ad the special circumstances been known, the parties might have specially provided for the breach of contract by special terms as to the damages in that case; and of this advantage it would be very unjust to deprive them."[115]

Conclusion

By emphasizing the general importance of social science in legal analysis and by illustrating the use of the principles of one social science, economic analysis has had a profound impact on legal theory.[116]

---

[113] "Clearly, if there is to be a *social* basis for the efficiency norm . . . indirect effects must be considered. Any attempt, however, to incorporate such factors into the analysis raises the information requirements of the system to such an extent as to make the whole enterprise unmanageable." Mario J. Rizzo, *The Mirage of Efficiency*, 8 HOFSTRA L. REV. 641, 642 (1980). *See also* Gergen, *supra* note 99, at 1079 n.270: "[M]inor changes in assumptions about market power and transaction costs may significantly change the optimal background rule, a point that makes the design of optimal rules daunting."

[114] Ayres & Gertner, *Filling Gaps, supra* note 65, at 107. For an analysis combining approaches, *see* George M. Cohen, *The Negligence-Opportunism Tradeoff in Contract Law*, 20 HOFSTRA L. REV. 941 (1992). Additional types of default rules are catalogued and discussed in Alan Schwartz, *The Default Rule Paradigm and the Limits of Contract Law,* 3 S. CAL. INTER. L. J. 389 (1993).

[115] 156 Eng. Rep. at 151.

[116] Even scholars closely aligned with other movements, such as CLS, grudgingly give law and economics its due:

> [E]fficiency" in some sense--if only that of reducing "transaction costs" or

Moreover, the discipline has successfully weathered the storm of criticism surrounding some of its early formulations by increasing its sophistication and complexity. This positive evolution of legal economics as applied to contract law is nicely illustrated by examining and comparing the early formulations of efficient breach of contract and contract gap filling according to the superior-risk-bearer standard on the one hand and the more recent penalty-default approach to gap filling on the other.

Even the more advanced theses of legal economics in the contract law field nonetheless are incomplete. Once legal economists recognize the abundance of values and goals beyond efficiency that are pertinent to the exchange process, they should also admit that their notion of utility is too narrow. People may derive utility from rules that create "a more just world"[117] or that result in more stable contract relations:

> In a sense, then, the smaller pie that is more evenly divided may not be smaller at all. Thus, if I am absolutely stuck on efficiency, I cannot rule out the possibility that once in a while it is efficient to adopt a so-called inefficient rule that turns out to have the types of distributive consequences that a number of people find pleasing.[118]

> "deadweight losses"--is usually at least one of the norms of functions that almost any legal rule might be thought to serve, even if it must be balanced or traded off against some other norms. *If* the notion of "efficiency" were coherent, *if* "efficient outcomes" were determinate, and *if* the methods of law and economics could really identify those outcomes--three admittedly rather large and improbable *ifs*--surely knowing what such outcomes were would be very useful information for judges and administrators, even if applicable law told them to consider other values as well.

Robert W. Gordon, *Lawyers, Scholars, and the "Middle Ground,"* 91 MICH. L. REV. 2075, 2083-2084 (1993) (emphasis in original).

According to Gordon, law and economics "is really nothing more than an extended version of [the] familiar postrealist method of policy analysis." It "provides a somewhat more elegant and elaborate method for doing what law teachers were doing already--digging out the latent functions of legal rules and asking whether the rules in force effectively serve them." *Id.*

117 Harrison, *supra* note 12, at 103.

118 *Id.*

This criticism, of course, raises questions of its own. For example, lawmakers obviously cannot successfully frame legal rules based on a standard that "a number of people" find the rule "pleasing." What objective standards can lawmakers apply beyond the parties' preferences? For that matter, can lawmakers adopt policies apart from their own self-interest? Can they avoid abusing their powers? These issues, considered in earlier chapters, help explain the wide appeal of legal economics, which at least provides the aura of objectivity: "A preference for markets . . . reveals a scepticism with respect to any claim to know best how social relations should be organized, and perhaps a fear that any such institutionalized power will be abused and used to destroy individuality."[119]

Even assuming legal economists persuade us of the importance and relevance of the efficiency norm, they should not lose sight of the difficulty of applying it:

> [A]ny serious pursuit of efficiency . . . will often require complex rules. After all, the goals and constraints relevant to a given policy are likely to be numerous, and the legal rules, in order to be efficient, must take account of, and be tailored to, each of them. Accomplishing this may necessitate a system of multi-factored rules, multiple defenses, complex party structures, sequential burden-shifting, and so on.[120]

---

119 Hugh Collins, *The Transformation Thesis and the Ascription of Contractual Responsibility*, *in* PERSPECTIVES ON CRITICAL CONTRACT LAW 309 (Thomas Wilhelmsson ed., 1992).

120 Peter H. Schuck, *Legal Complexity: Some Causes, Consequences, and Cures*, 42 DUKE L.J. 1, 37 (1992). *See also* Jason S. Johnston, *Default Rules/Mandatory Principles: A Game Theoretic Analysis of Good Faith and the Contract Modification Problem*, 3 S. CAL. INT'L. L. REV. 335, 344 (1993) ("The notion of contractual 'efficiency' is not unambiguous."); Mark J. Roe, *Chaos and Evolution in Law and Economics*, 109 HARV. L. REV. 641, 667 (1996) (taking into account "path dependence analysis" defeats the "presumption of utility" of surviving systems).

For a rather caustic view of legal economics, *see* MORTON J. HORWITZ, THE TRANSFORMATION OF AMERICAN LAW 1870-1960: THE CRISIS OF LEGAL ORTHODOXY 271 (1992) (law and economics is "one more expression of the persistent yearning to find an olympian position from which to objectively cushion the terrors of social choice.").

The many issues raised by the prospect of implementing the penalty-default strategy, such as whether it creates the correct incentives, whether it conflicts with other policies, and whether the costs of implementation would outweigh the gains, illustrate the problem.

In conclusion, although not a complete descriptive or normative theory of contract law, legal economics advances the analysis by helping to isolate the many issues involved in effective contract lawmaking. This is true even of the early, less complete economic theories of contract law. By setting forth the theory of efficient breach, for example, legal economists have forced us to think about the reasons for enforcing promises, the appropriate remedies for breach, and the problem of transaction costs. Legal economists quite legitimately can boast of advancing contract analysis much further than any other group of social scientists. Moreover, although legal economics raises many questions, so do other approaches to normative contract law.[121]

---

[121] *See, e.g.*, Richard Craswell, *Contract Law, Default Rules, and the Philosophy of Promising*, 88 MICH. L. REV. 489 (1989) (Fried's "content neutral" moral theory cannot determine "background rules").

CHAPTER 7

THEORIES OF EMPIRICISTS AND RELATIONALISTS

Some analysts have concluded, on the basis of empirical studies, that business people often ignore contract law, which is largely irrelevant to the business world. In this chapter, I first consider this thesis. I then turn to the relational perspective, which helps explain the empirical findings. Relationalists posit that contract doctrine's focus on specific or "discrete" promises makes it unsuitable to govern most modern business arrangements, which are characterized by cooperation, flexibility, and willingness to adjust terms, not adherence to precise promises. Although the theories of empiricists and relationalists of contract law are thus compatible, they also contrast in important ways. For one thing, many empiricists, whose studies suggest the irrelevancy of contract law, ultimately acknowledge its importance. For another, recent empirical findings cast doubt on the irrelevancy and unsuitability theses. Building on these findings, I conclude that contract law continues to be important and adaptable to the needs of a relational world.

A. Is Contract Law Irrelevant?

Problem 10: MDM Enterprises licenses the television series "Why Spy?" to XYZ Television Network for one year and gives XYZ a series of options for up to seven additional years. The licensing fee is $650,000 per episode for twenty-two episodes the first season. The licensing fee escalates ten percent over the seven-year period. The agreement does not expressly provide for fee escalation based on the success of "Why Spy?" or the increased salary demands of its stars, even though XYZ's advertising rates and the stars' salary demands will increase if the show is a success.

"Why Spy?" is a huge success its first year. Based on the show's ratings, XYZ is able to charge advertisers more than $1 million more per episode the second year. Before production begins for the second year, the show's star, Tom Slack, bargains for and receives a raise from MDM of $18,000 per episode. MDM now seeks an increase in the licensing fee from XYZ Network. MDM points to an

informal practice in the industry whereby parties renegotiate licensing fees to take into account actors' demands and a program's success. XYZ agrees to a new licensing fee in order to maintain good will and a profitable relationship with MDM and does not renege later.

Stewart Macaulay and others[1] have reported that business people often fail to plan and draft their agreements carefully,[2] to consult lawyers,[3] to consider their legal rights, and to utilize courts when something goes awry.[4] Moreover, they frequently do not even understand the law that applies to their agreements or the legal ramifications of their conduct.[5] "Business cultures," not legal rules, influence commercial parties' conduct and govern their day-to-day relations.[6] Problem 10 helps illustrate this point: Even though MDM was not contractually entitled to an increase in the licensing fee, XYZ readily agreed to one.

Empiricists explain that the power of non-legal incentives and

---

1 *See infra* notes 17-18, and accompanying text.

2 Stewart Macaulay, *Contract Law and Contract Research (Part II)*, 20 J. LEGAL EDUC. 460, 461 (1968) [hereinafter Macaulay, *Contract Law*].

3 *Id.* at 461-62 (lawyers are frequently "not . . . invited to the party." For example, a purchasing agent may "dispense with the annoyance of legalistic advice.")

4 *Id.* at 462-64. Unlike Problem 10, which concerns the entertainment industry, Macaulay's principal study surveyed business people and lawyers representing manufacturing concerns. *See* Stewart Macaulay, *Non-Contractual Relations in Business: A Preliminary Study*, 28 AM. SOC. REV. 55, 55-56 (1963) [hereinafter Macaulay, *Preliminary Study*].

5 James J. White, *Contract Law in Modern Commercial Transactions, An Artifact of Twentieth Century Business Life?*, 22 WASHBURN L.J. 1, 18-19 (1982). *See also* Jay M. Feinman, *The Significance of Contract Theory*, 58 U. CIN. L. REV. 1283, 1305 (1990) [hereinafter Feinman, *Significance*.]

6 *See* Stewart Macaulay, *An Empirical View of Contract*, 1985 WIS. L. REV. 465, 467 [hereinafter Macaulay, *Empirical View*]; Macaulay, *Contract Law, supra* note 2, at 462-64.

customs explains business's inattention to law.[7] Business people are usually comfortable with their contracting partners, familiar with the subject matter of their deals, and eager to do additional business in the future. They believe that deals should be honored and that "legalese" symbolizes distrust and selfishness.[8] Business people also want to establish and maintain good reputations. They are therefore generally content with informal arrangements.[9] In addition, aware of the costs of finding and dealing with substitute partners after investing in an arrangement[10] and after forming understandings that decrease the costs of doing business,[11] business people prefer long-term relationships.

Business people are also interested in ensuring a supply or a market at a reasonable price, and not having to worry about shifts in price.[12] Although they expect disruptions during the course of their dealings, they do not attempt to allocate the costs of nebulous risks.

---

7 On non-legal sanctions generally, *see* David Charny, *Non-legal Sanctions in Commercial Relationships*, 104 HARV. L. REV. 373 (1990). They include "conscience, the displeasure of family and friends, a reputation in the business community as someone who cannot be trusted, and the censure of coworkers for impeding the marketing of the company's products." Russell J. Weintraub, *A Survey of Contract Practice and Policy*, 1992 WIS. L. REV. 1, 7.

8 Stewart Macaulay, *The Reliance Interest and the World Outside the Law Schools' Doors*, 1991 WIS. L. REV. 247, 260.

9 *See* Robert A. Hillman, *Court Adjustment of Long-Term Contracts: An Analysis Under Modern Contract Law,* 1987 DUKE L. REV. 1, 5 [hereinafter Hillman, *Long-Term Contracts]*.

10 *See* Thomas M. Palay, *A Contract Does Not a Contract Make*, 1985 WIS. L. REV. 561, 562-63; Oliver E. Williamson, *Transaction-Cost Economics: The Governance of Contractual Relations*, 22 J.L. & ECON. 233 (1979).

11 *See* William C. Whitford, *Ian Macneil's Contribution to Contracts Scholarship*, 1985 WIS. L. REV. 545, 550.

12 Professor Goldberg states that, with the exception of commodities sales, "[f]irms do not generally enter into multi-year contracts because of their concern for the future course of prices. Rather, they enter into the agreements to achieve the benefits of cooperation." Victor P. Goldberg, *Price Adjustment in Long-Term Contracts*, 1985 WIS. L. REV. 527, 531.

Business people often even decline to bargain over foreseeable, but remote risks because bargaining would cost too much[13] or might rock the boat.[14] Put another way, both parties can increase their gains from a contract by remaining flexible during performance, thereby eliminating the need for costly planning or bickering after a contract breakdown.[15]

In sum, business parties often believe that flexibility and compromise, not resort to the "letter of the law," will ensure success in a business relation.[16] Other empirical studies, although not compelling in

---

13 One incentive for price-adjustment features, according to Professor Goldberg, is to avoid the expense of investigating future costs. Price-adjustment terms decrease the value of information concerning the future and therefore discourage costly investigations. *See id.* at 532. Goldberg also asserts that price-adjustment features avoid costs resulting when the "loser" in a fixed-price contract engages in conduct such as insisting on "strict compliance with quality standards" or otherwise "reads the contract literally." *Id.*

14 *See* Hugh Beale & Tony Dugdale, *Contracts Between Businessmen: Planning and the Use of Contractual Remedies*, 2 BRIT. J.L. & SOC'Y 45, 47 (1975). Professor Palay has suggested that parties with "strong relational ties" are not concerned with a contract's initial terms. Instead, they assume they will adjust the contract based on changed circumstances. *See* Palay, *supra* note 10, at 562 ("Since the costs of drafting, monitoring, and enforcing a once-and-for-all agreement outweigh the benefits, it is far more efficient to cross bridges as they are reached.").

15 *See* Goldberg, *supra* note 12, at 532; *see also* Gidon Gottlieb, *Relationism: Legal Theory for a Relational Society*, 50 U. CHI. L. REV. 567, 572-73 (1983) ("*In sustained and inextricable relations a principal use of contracts is to provide a basis for renegotiations* once a defective performance occurs." (emphasis in original)); Palay, *supra* note 10, at 562. Parties also avoid lawsuits to avoid "a reputation for litigiousness." Weintraub, *supra* note 7, at 21.

16 *See* Macaulay, *Contract Law*, *supra* note 2, at 463 (noting that business is not interested in contract law because of the existence of less expensive private sanctions). *See generally* Hillman, *Long-Term Contracts*, *supra* note 9 (noting that such business realities may justify inferring an agreement to modify a contract). "[F]lexibility is a marked trend in marketing of goods . . . wherever long-range buyer-seller *relations* come to seem more important than exact definition of the risks to be shifted by the particular dicker in terms of quantity, quality, or price." Karl N. Llewellyn, *What Price Contract? - An Essay in Perspective*, 40 YALE L.J. 704, 727 (1931).

According to Professor White, the law has little power because rules are vague

number or scope,[17] substantiate Macaulay's views.[18] For example, a recent study confirms the frequency of contract adjustment on account of market changes, even by parties whose contracts did not contain provisions authorizing modification.[19] I suspect too that many analysts have confirmed Macaulay's findings, at least in their own minds, by engaging in casual conversations with practicing lawyers and business people. These conversations, along with the costs of empirical work[20] and

---

and nonlawyer corporate managers rather than in-house counsel make the ultimate decisions. White, *supra* note 5, at 14-17.

17 "Despite [the] need for data . . . to date there have been only a handful of empirical studies focusing on particular contract problems and relationships . . . ." Weintraub, *supra* note 7, at 4. For a list of additional empirical studies, *see id.* n.10.

A recent important study of new car dealers in Chicago found discrepancies in the amounts black and white men and women had to pay for cars. *See* Ian Ayres, *Fair Driving: Gender and Race Discrimination in Retail Car Negotiations*, 104 HARV. L. REV. 817 (1991).

An interesting body of empirical work investigates the efficiency of nonlegal sanctions and relational norms. *See* articles cited in Lisa Bernstein, *Social Norms and Default Rules Analysis*, 3 S. CAL. INTER. L. J. 59, 68 n.38 (1993).

18 *See, e.g.*, Beale & Dugdale, *supra* note 14, at 46 (noting that their study of the use of contract law yielded results "broadly similar" to Professor Macaulay's); Franklin M. Schultz, *The Firm Offer Puzzle: A Study of Business Practice in the Construction Industry*, 19 U. CHI. L. REV. 237, 283 (1952) ("One thing is clear: contractors in general are neither aware of nor significantly influenced by the law in this area."). *See also* Joe C. Creason, Jr., Note, *Another Look at Construction Bidding and Contracts at Formation*, 53 VA. L. REV. 1720 (1967); John H. Samuels, Note, *Business Practices and the Flexibility of Long-Term Contracts*, 36 VA. L. REV. 627 (1950). One study found, however, that business people typically favor the statute of frauds. Note, *Statute of Frauds and the Business Community: A Re-Appraisal in Light of Prevailing Practices*, 66 YALE L.J. 1038 (1957).

19 Weintraub, *supra* note 7, at 19 (75.6 percent of corporate counsel respondents would agree to modify a contract after an increase in the market price when the request to adjust was based on a trade custom). Moreover, a plurality of 46.2 percent thought that adjustment was appropriate after "an unprecedented OPEC oil embargo" caused a fuel supplier catastrophic losses. *Id.* at 41.

20 "[E]mpirical study . . . has not flourished to nearly the same degree as scholarship that can be done without ever leaving one's office." Paul Brest, *Plus Ca Change*,

lawyers' lack of training in conducting such studies, may help explain the dearth of new studies testing Macaulay's thesis.[21]

Some scholars may conclude too much based on existing empirical work, however. Despite Macaulay's acknowledgment in his original study that contract "often plays an important role in business,"[22] some analysts assert that business people *rarely* plan[23] and that they resort

---

91 MICH. L. REV. 1945, 1946 (1993).

21 *See* Nathan M. Crystal, *An Empirical View of Relational Contracts Under Article Two of the Uniform Commercial Code*, 1988 ANN. SURV. AM. LAW 293, 305 (pointing out that few lawyers are trained to conduct empirical research); Robert A. Hillman, *Empiricism in Bankruptcy*, 75 CORNELL L. REV. 1095 (1990) (reviewing TERESA A. SULLIVAN ET AL., AS WE FORGIVE OUR DEBTORS: BANKRUPTCY AND CONSUMER CREDIT IN AMERICA (1989)) (discussing the costs of empiricism).
Empirical study is an easy target, but is still important:

> Empirical social study . . . is never going to yield lawlike regularities that can make law practice into some sort of exact predictive science. Social science is a value-soaked, fuzzy, messy, dispute-riddled, political enterprise like any other interpretive activity--like law, for instance. But unless it is total hack work or ideological claptrap, the sketch maps it draws are better than nothing--and *nothing* about the actual workings of the legal system is what the traditional doctrinal education typically provides.

Robert W. Gordon, *Lawyers, Scholars, and The "Middle Ground,"* 91 MICH. L. REV. 2075, 2087 (1993).
Schultz, *supra* note 18, is a fine study of the practices of general and subcontractors in the construction industry. But see Jason Scott Johnston, *The Statute of Frauds and Business Norms: A Testable Game - Theoretic Model*, 144 U. PENN. L. REV. 1859, 1860-61 (1996) (criticizing Schultz and others).

22 Macaulay, *Preliminary Study, supra* note 4, at 67.

23 *See* David M. Trubeck, *Where the Action Is: Critical Legal Studies and Empiricism,* 36 STAN. L. REV. 575, 587 (1984); *see also* Robert W. Gordon, *Macaulay, Macneil, and the Discovery of Solidarity and Power in Contract Law,* 1985 WIS. L. REV. 565, 571 (noting that Macaulay's 1963 article described business people "who did not rely on legal norms"). Macaulay pointed out, however, that "many business exchanges reflect a high degree of planning" on certain points. Macaulay, *Preliminary Study, supra* note 4, at 60. "One can conclude that while detailed planning and legal sanctions play a significant role in some exchanges

to the courts only sparingly.[24] Others aver that contract law is largely irrelevant[25] or insist that it has a "very limited practical role." [26] Still others hint that the goal of current writers, who continue to analyze "residual" contract law, is to preserve the existing social hierarchy[27] or to accumulate financial gain.[28] Summing up, one writer insists that "contract law is not an important tool of commercial regulation."[29]

Why is contract law relevant and important? First, Macauley's observations do not apply in many contexts. Consumer form contracts, which may constitute the majority of modern-day contracts,[30] are typically very formal and involve considerable planning, at least by one side. Little

---

between businesses, in many business exchanges their role is small." *Id.* at 62.

24 Trubek, *supra* note 23, at 587. Macaulay's 1963 study of Wisconsin companies substantiated this point, *see* Macaulay, *Preliminary Study, supra* note 4, but even Macaulay called his work a "preliminary study," and he seems to have altered his position somewhat as of 1985. *See* Macaulay, *Empirical View, supra* note 6 at 471-477.

25 *See* Gordon, *supra* note 23, at 571, 573 (noting that Macaulay posits the "relative insignificance" of contract and assigns it a "relatively trivial status"). *See also* Macaulay, *Empirical View, supra* note 6, at 467-68 (stating that business persons are largely oblivious to contract law).

26 Macaulay, *Empirical View, supra* note 6, at 465. This apparently is Professor Macaulay's position, although he recognizes contract's importance as an institution. He concludes that parties often turn to contract law after a breakdown when significant money is at stake. *See id.* at 471. Furthermore, he notes the large volume of contract litigation in recent years and seems to concede the importance of contract law. *Id.* at 471-477.

27 Gordon, *supra* note 23, at 575. Macaulay also intimates this. *See* Macaulay, *Empirical View*, supra note 6, at 478.

28 *See* Macaulay, *Empirical View, supra* note 6, at 479. *See also* Feinman, *supra* note 5, at 1308 (contract law is "a self-serving exercise for law professors")

29 Feinman, *supra* note 5, at 1308.

30 Professor Slawson asserts that standard-form contracts constitute most contracts. W. David Slawson, *Standard Form Contracts and Democratic Control of Lawmaking Power*, 84 HARV. L. REV. 529, 530 (1971).

is left to adjust, and flexibility is not the norm. Although these contracts present difficult issues for courts involving the meaning of assent,[31] they are hardly irrelevant to the parties concerned. Many kinds of employment, construction, sales, and bailment contracts also exhibit great formality and inflexibility.[32]

Furthermore, empiricists concede that contract planning plays an important role in many circumstances, even in industries that generally value flexibility.[33] Negotiating parties will plan extensively if they do not know each other, they do not intend to deal with each other in the future, or the subject matter of their negotiations is unusual, important, or risky.[34] In addition, parties may negotiate important elements of their agreements even if they ignore others.[35] There is even some evidence of a greater reliance on contract planning simply because of the growing "professionalism among young managers, many of whom have studied contract."[36] Contract law also comes into play when adverse economic conditions convince parties to stand on their contract rights and sacrifice

---

31 *See id.* at 538-39.

32 *See, e.g.*, Crystal, *supra* note 21, at 303 (most commercial cases not relational). *See also* Macaulay, *Empirical View, supra* note 6, at 473-74.

33 *See* Macaulay, *Preliminary Study, supra* note 4, at 60, 62 (conceding that "many business exchanges reflect a high degree of planning" and concluding that "detailed planning and legal sanctions play a significant role in some exchanges between business").

34 In short, parties plan when they perceive that the gains of doing so outweigh the losses. *See id.* at 65. *See also* Beale & Dugdale, *supra* note 14, at 47 (greater planning explained by higher risks); Macaulay, *Empirical View, supra* note 6, at 471; Hillman, *Long-Term Contracts, supra* note 9, at 4-6 (discussing the use of contract law by parties and courts to adjust terms).

35 Beale & Dugdale, *supra* note 14, at 50.

36 *Id.* at 51. "[W]e were told of and saw signs of a gradual change in attitude towards tightening up procedures and creating legally enforceable agreements. For instance, we came across several examples of purchasing departments who for years had bought from their main suppliers on 'back of order' conditions now negotiating standing supply contracts to govern future orders." *Id.*

their relationships rather than work out disputes.[37] In fact, this course appears to be gaining popularity[38] and many increasingly view legal sanctions for contract breach as "absolutely essential to business."[39] It is therefore inaccurate to conclude that contract law is irrelevant or marginal simply because many transactions are informal.

Contract law is important even where "business cultures" dominate, such as in Problem 10. Contract law provides an alternative approach should the parties determine that the costs of flexibility and cooperation outweigh the gains. Suppose MDM and XYZ Network determine that constant adjustment drains time and resources and creates bad feelings. They might decide that a more formal, sliding-scale licensing fee based on "Why Spy?'s" ratings would better serve their purposes.[40] Or they might include an express clause requiring renegotiation in the event of substantial increases in costs.[41] In short, the parties may determine that formal contracting is less expensive than custom. Although not always heeded, this is often the message of the planning lawyer.[42] Parties always have the option to change their approach even though they may initially ignore the benefits of a contractual model. Simply because informality is the norm in a given context does not mean that it is necessarily the least-costly approach or

---

37 Macaulay, *Preliminary Study*, *supra* note 4, at 60, 62. *See also* Robert B. Ferguson, *The Adjudication of Commercial Disputes and the Legal System in Modern England*, 7 BRIT. J.L. & SOC'Y 141, 151 (1980).

38 *See* William E. Nelson, *Contract Litigation and the Elite Bar in New York City*, 1960-1980, 39 EMORY L.J. 413, 415-17 (1990) (significant increase in contract filings in the United States District Court for the Southern District of New York).

39 Weintraub, *supra* note 7, at 25.

40 *See* Thompson, *The Prime Time Crime*, ENT. L.J. July 1982 at 1.

41 Weintraub, *supra* note 7, at 17. In Professor Weintraub's sample of general counsels of corporations of various sizes, 41.9% of the respondents included a renegotiation clause.

42 In-house counsel's "darkest fear" is that management will disregard their advice. *See* White, *supra* note 5, at 19.

that parties will view other potential strategies as irrelevant.[43]

Contract law may have an even greater role to play in Problem 10 than as an alternative planning tool. Suppose at the time of contracting the parties assume they will follow the practice of renegotiating the licensing fee based on changed circumstances. Under contract law's approach to "agreement," XYZ may have a legal duty to adjust the fee.[44] The modern meaning of "agreement" derives from Karl Llewellyn's view, now reflected in the Uniform Commercial Code (U.C.C.) and the *Restatement (Second) of Contracts,* that courts must focus on contextual realities.[45] Under this approach, a court investigating an agreement's content must consider not only its language, but also any course of dealing, trade custom, or other factor probative of the parties' intentions. XYZ therefore must renegotiate the fee if MDM reasonably believed that XYZ would do so in light of the trade practice.[46]

Even if the practice of renegotiating the licensing fee has not yet ripened into a distinct trade custom because of insufficient regularity of

---

43 *See* Thompson, *supra* note 40, at 20.

44 The U.C.C. defines "agreement" as "the bargain of the parties in fact as found in their language or by implication from other circumstances including course of dealing or usage of trade or course of performance." U.C.C. § l-201(3) (1978); *see also* RESTATEMENT (SECOND) OF CONTRACTS §§ 4 cmt. a, 5 cmt. a, 202 (1979). The UCC displaces the common law in a multitude of commercial transactions. In addition, courts often apply the UCC by analogy to cases that it does not cover as the best evidence of modern thinking about contract and other commercial problems. Moreover, the UCC had a dramatic influence on the drafting of the Restatement (Second) of Contracts.

45 *See generally* Eugene F. Mooney, *Old Kontract Principles and Karl's New Kode: An Essay on the Jurisprudence of Our New Commercial Law,* 11 VILL. L. REV. 213 (1966) (noting Karl Llewellyn's role in molding contract law through the U.C.C.). Of course, common law and equity fill significant Code gaps. *See generally* ROBERT A. HILLMAN ET AL., COMMON LAW AND EQUITY UNDER THE UNIFORM COMMERCIAL CODE (1985).

46 *See* Hillman, *Long-Term Contracts, supra* note 9, at 10-11. *But see* Richard E. Speidel, *Article 2 and Relational Sales Contracts*, 26 LOY. L.A. L. REV. 789, 794 (1993) (definition of "agreement" possibly limited). Some scholars would also criticize this focus on intentions as falsely preserving freedom of contract at the expense of a broader recognition of community. *See* Chapter 5.

observance or otherwise, XYZ may still have to renegotiate.[47] In problems of performance, we saw in Chapter 4 that good faith requires "cooperation on the part of one party to the contract so that another party will not be deprived of his reasonable expectations."[48] In Problem 10, performance by XYZ contrary to MDM's reasonable expectations is therefore in bad faith. MDM's argument would be that, at the time of contracting, each party reasonably expected the other to be flexible and cooperative in order to preserve the relationship if serious problems arose.[49] In addition, developments subsequent to the parties' agreement could also create a duty in XYZ to adjust MDM's fee. The parties could agree to renegotiate the fee, XYZ could waive the right to enforce the original fee, or the parties' flexibility during the course of their performance could establish a duty to adjust in the contract.[50]

Although silent on adjustment, then, an agreement such as in Problem 10 may impliedly require the parties to make reasonable modifications so that, if observance of business norms did not persuade XYZ to adjust, MDM could turn to the contract. In this way, contract law

---

47 Even if a practice of adjusting has not yet ripened into a trade custom, the parties nevertheless may expect the practice to be observed. Charles J. Goetz & Robert E. Scott, *The Limits of Expanded Choice: An Analysis of the Interactions Between Express and Implied Contract Terms*, 73 CAL. L. REV. 261, 277 n.47 (1985) ("[U]nofficial or other context-generated understandings might be legally enforceable, implied terms.").

48 E. Allan Farnsworth, *Good Faith Performance and Commercial Reasonableness Under the Uniform Commercial Code*, 30 U. CHI. L. REV. 666, 669 (1963). For a discussion, *see* Chapter 4.

49 One "informality" in many long-term agreements is the limited use of dispute resolution clauses. Business people are reluctant to haggle over an appropriate dispute resolution clause. They prefer to discount the possibility of future problems or to believe they will settle any future issues amicably. Most commercial contracts therefore fail to contain a dispute resolution clause, although some contain boilerplate arbitration provisions. *See* S. GOLDBERG ET AL., DISPUTE RESOLUTION 540-41 (1985). The lack of a dispute resolution clause therefore does not necessarily suggest that the parties expected a promisor to perform according to the letter of the contract under all circumstances.

50 *See* Hillman, *Long-Term Contracts, supra* note 9, at 9 n.50.

is a "club" held in reserve,[51] reinforcing the parties' business practices.[52] In fact, the "contract-as-club" theory turns the irrelevancy-of-contract argument on its head by suggesting that contract law internalizes parties' norms of flexibility and cooperation, the very characteristics that cause some theorists to discount contract law in the first place.

Of course, not every contract raises a duty to adjust when circumstances change. For example, a party may not reasonably expect her counterpart to renegotiate terms if the agreement is a one-time deal involving a standardized commodity.[53] Alternatively, parties may intend to be flexible simply as a matter of accommodation or comity, but hold in reserve the right to insist on the letter of the contract. For example, in Problem 10, MDM may have believed only that XYZ probably would not

---

51 The term is Professor Macaulay's. *See* Stewart Macaulay, *The Use and Non-Use of Contracts in the Manufacturing Industry*, PRAC. LAW., Nov. 1963, at 15-16.

52 *See* Beale & Dugdale, *supra* note 14, at 48:

> It would be a mistake . . . to assume that contract law has very little relevance. Firstly, it is always in the background: contract law may not be mentioned but the parties probably know in general what the legal position is and may adjust their attitudes accordingly. . . . But secondly . . . while non-legal factors and extra-contractual devices do commonly reduce the need to use contract law, there are certain problems which for one reason or another are not infrequently dealt with by contract planning and sometimes by the use of contractual remedies.

53 Professor Goldberg has suggested that a "thick market" commodity contract involving future delivery typically would not include price adjustment features. On the other hand, "[t]he more isolated the exchange is from the market, the more likely it is that the parties would find price adjustment efficacious." Goldberg, *supra* note 12, at 543. *See also* Thomas M. Palay, *Comparative Institutional Economics: The Governance of Rail Freight Contracting*, 13 J. LEGAL STUD. 265, 279-85 (1984) (statistical study shows specialized agreements much more open to adjustments than nonspecialized agreements); William M. Evan, Comment, 28 AM. SOC. REV. 67, 68 (1963) (the greater the difference in bargaining power, the less likely the parties intend to be flexible).

exercise its contract right to insist on performance.[54] Under that interpretation, XYZ could utilize the contract club and rightfully refuse to adjust the licensing fee.[55]

In either case, modern contract law establishes the boundaries of the parties' permissible conduct[56] and thus reinforces their expectations of performance.[57] If one party exceeds a boundary, the other can resort to the contract club. Although empirical work cannot resolve normative issues such as the appropriateness of this relationship between contract law and business practice, recent studies confirm the importance of the contract club.[58]

---

54 It will rarely serve a party's interests to drive her counterpart out of business or into bankruptcy. *See, e.g.*, Stewart Macaulay, *Elegant Models, Empirical Pictures, and the Complexities of Contract*, 11 LAW & SOC'Y REV. 507, 516 (1977) (buyers of uranium from Westinghouse Electric Corporation had a stake in Westinghouse's solvency, because Westinghouse provided parts and service for reactors). Professor Dawson observed that Westinghouse faced losses of greater than $2 billion in supplying uranium to 49 nuclear power plants, due to large increases in the market price of uranium. Although the trial judge believed Westinghouse was not entitled to relief, Westinghouse's creditors "motivated presumably by their own self-interest in preserving it as a fully functioning enterprise, agreed to settlements that were vastly more lenient than any that a court would have been bold enough to propose." John P. Dawson, *Judicial Revision of Frustrated Contracts: The United States*, 64 B.U. L. REV. 1, 25-26 (1984).

55 *See* Hillman, *Long Term Contracts, supra* note 9, at 8-10.

56 *See* Llewellyn, *supra* note 16, at 713.

57 Professor Llewellyn noted that: "[T]he real major effect of law . . . [is] strengthening . . . attitudes toward performance as what is to be expected and what `is done.'. . . This work of the law-machine at the margin, in helping keep the level of social practice and expectation up to where it is, as against slow canker, is probably the most vital single aspect of contract law. . . . " *Id.* at 725 n.47. *See also* Beal & Dugdale, *supra* note 14, at 48.

58 65.8% of the corporate counsel in Professor Weintraub's study thought that there would be a "substantial detrimental effect" in doing away with legal sanctions. Nobody thought that business would improve substantially by the move. Weintraub, *supra* note 7, at 24. Moreover, almost 70% of the sample supported the award of expectancy damages even when the injured party had not relied, *id.* at 30, apparently because of the belief that people should keep their commercial promises.

Although we need additional empirical work to substantiate each of the following arguments, contract law may be important in "business cultures" in several additional ways. First, contract expectations derive from more than the knowledge that an injured party can enforce its rights in a judicial proceeding.[59] A contract is an independent source of rights and duties because of the normative significance of contracting.[60] Parties make claims and justify their actions based on their contracts, believing that people should perform their agreements.[61]

Modern contract law also constitutes a basis for negotiation when disputes arise during performance and for dispute resolution upon contract breakdown. In such situations, contracts help shape the parties' negotiating strategies[62] and the ultimate terms of adjustment.[63] Contract

---

Id. at 31-32.

59 Llewellyn, *supra* note 16, at 712-13.

60 *See generally* H.L.A. HART, THE CONCEPT OF LAW, Chs. IV, V (1961) (stressing the normative character of private law duties).

61 *See* ROBERT S. SUMMERS & ROBERT A. HILLMAN, CONTRACT AND RELATED OBLIGATION 45-46 (2d ed. 1992); *see generally* CHARLES FRIED, CONTRACT AS PROMISE: A THEORY OF CONTRACTUAL OBLIGATION 17 (1981) (stating that the "moralist of duty ... posits a general obligation to keep promises"). Contract law is thus more than an "amoral . . . storehouse of bargaining chips." Gordon, *supra* note 23, at 573; *see also* Roscoe Pound, *Promise or Bargain?*, 33 TUL. L. REV. 455, 457-58 (1959) (discussing whether there should be a moral duty to keep a promise and suggesting that the common law increasingly enforces contracts based on moral obligation).

62 Some scholars assert that parties use lawsuits merely as a strategy to improve their bargaining positions. *See, e.g.*, Gordon, *supra* note 23, at 572. Parties with ample resources but poor legal positions also may use delay tactics to procure favorable settlements. *Id.* But we need additional empirical evidence before we can dismiss contract law on these grounds.

63 *See generally*, Robert H. Mnookin & Lewis Kornhauser, *Bargaining in the Shadow of the Law: The Case of Divorce*, 88 YALE L.J. 950 (1979) (outlining a model of how parties to a divorce can bargain over its terms).

law therefore supports private mechanisms for resolving problems.[64]

Contract law is also relevant to business parties when they specifically do not intend to bind themselves legally. Although not always effective, contract law establishes the rules for avoiding promissory liability.[65] For example, XYZ could have avoided a duty to adjust the licensing fee by making its intention clear prior to contracting.

B. Is Contract Law Unsuitable?

Problem 11: Assume that instead of facing the ax, as in Problem 9, Michele Green suddenly becomes very popular and substantially overshadows Tom Slack and the rest of the cast. In fact, Green's participation in the show actually increases its ratings. Green now seeks to renegotiate her contract, which provided for a salary of $2500 per episode, with a ten percent increase over three years, but MDM refuses to adjust.

In 1937, Karl Llewellyn observed that contract rules poorly reflect the reality that many business agreements constitute only small components of long-term relationships:

> Our contract-law has yet built no tools to really cope with this vexing and puzzling situation of fact. The standing relation is not only real in business fact, it is also vibrant with legal implication. The trouble is that the legal implication is still--legally--inarticulate. It is felt--no question about that. It is felt--but it is not felt with any clarity . . . .
>
> It is not a theorist's creation; it is a fact, at work in the courts, warping the older inadequate theory of the single deal.[66]

---

64 Macaulay, *Contract Law, supra* note 2, at 464. But Macaulay points out that "[t]he costs to one's reputation and business relationships of threatening to sue or using a loophole are extremely high." *Id.* Official recognition, not enforcement, is the most important "official aid on the contract side." Llewellyn, *supra* note 16, at 711.

65 *See* Chapter 1.

66 Karl Llewellyn, *On Warranty of Quality, And Society*, 37 COLUM. L. REV. 341, 375, 379 (1937). Professor Schlesinger has written that "[t]here seems to be no doubt in American law that a contract can be formed without an identifiable sequence of

Ian Macneil and others have taken up and expanded this theme. They argue that modern contract doctrine is unsuited to today's world of relational contracting.[67] Relational contracting occurs over time through long-term interaction between parties, such as the dealings between XYZ and MDM in Problem 10, or between MDM and Green in Problem 11.[68] Conversely, a discrete exchange, such as buying gasoline on a highway far from the motorist's home, involves relatively little interaction between the parties.[69]

The more relational an exchange, the less likely that the parties can plan and allocate risks effectively.[70] Instead, such parties rely on relational norms, including flexibility, reciprocity, and solidarity, to govern their agreements when the written contract gives out.[71] In

---

offer and acceptance." RUDOLPH B. SCHLESINGER, *Manifestation of Assent without Identifiable Sequence in Offer and Acceptance, in* FORMATION OF CONTRACTS 1583 (1968).

67 *See* Ian R. Macneil, *Contracts: Adjustment of Long-Term Economic Relations Under Classical, Neoclassical and Relational Contract Law*, 72 NW. U. L. REV. 854, 873-886 (1978) [hereinafter Macneil, *Adjustment*]; Whitford, *supra* note 11, at 549 n.9 (1985). Macneil refers to "classical" and "neoclassical" contract law. Classical contract law developed in the nineteenth century and reached its "pinnacle" in the early twentieth century with the *Restatement (First) of Contracts.* Neoclassical contract law, evidenced by the *Restatement (Second) of Contracts* and Article 2 of the Uniform Commercial Code, is founded on classical contract, but modifies it "considerably." Macneil, *Adjustment, supra*, at 855 n.2. According to Macneil, neither formulation is suited for today's world. *See id.* at 862-86.

68 *See* Ian R. Macneil, *Restatement (Second) of Contracts and Presentiation*, 60 VA. L. REV. 589, 595 (1974) [hereinafter Macneil, *Presentiation*].

69 *Id.* at 594. According to Macneil, discrete exchange plays a very limited role in our economy. Ian R. Macneil, *Relational Contract: What We Do and Do Not Know*, 1985 WIS. L. REV. 483, 485-491 [hereinafter Macneil, *Relational Contract*].

70 *See* Ian R. Macneil, *Values in Contract: Internal and External*, 78 NW. U.L. REV. 340 (1983).

71 *See, e.g.*, Gillian K. Hadfield, *Problematic Relations: Franchising and the Law of Incomplete Contracts*, 42 STAN. L. REV. 927, 930 (1990) ("courts should determine the likelihood that the contracting parties *themselves* implicitly or explicitly relied

franchise agreements, for example, Professor Hadfield points out that parties rely "on commonly understood features of that relationship which fill in the gaps of the written contract and create an understanding of the full range of commitments involved."[72] Supported by the empirical studies of Macaulay and others, Macneil asserts the centrality of relational contracting.[73] He therefore concludes, contrary to Charles Fried, that contract doctrines' "addiction to promise" is an "immense intellectual barrier" to our understanding of contract law.[74]

According to Macneil, one must investigate the social environment and the "great sea of custom"[75] that form the foundation of parties' bargains in order to comprehend relational norms and hence to understand contract law.[76] Mainstream contract doctrine, however,

---

on the relational norms to supply the commitments they could not reduce to written form."); Macneil, *Adjustment, supra* note 67, at 901 ("[A] relation [is] a mini-society with a vast array of norms beyond the norms centered on exchange and its immediate processes."). *See also* Gordon, *supra* note 23, at 570 (asserting that norms of "solidarity and reciprocity" create mutual trust that permits economic planning); Hadfield, *supra* (pointing out that "incomplete contracts often exist deeply embedded in an ongoing relationship"); SUMMERS & HILLMAN, *supra* note 61, at 31 (noting that relational agreements require cooperation and compromise); Whitford, *supra* note 11, at 555 (suggesting that the values and norms of relational contracting undermine theories based on wealth maximization).

72 Hadfield, *supra* note 71, at 957.

73 One recent study of commercial cases questions this view. *See* Crystal, *supra* note 21.

74 Macneil, *Relational Contract, supra* note 69, at 525. For a discussion of Fried, *see* Chapter 1.

75 Ian R. Macneil, *The Many Futures of Contract*, 47 S. CAL. L. REV. 691, 731 (1974) [hereinafter Macneil, *Many Futures*].

76 *See* Macneil, *Presentiation, supra* note 68, at 595. "[R]especting the parties' control over their relationship means that obligations must be understood to have arisen not only from the written document but also from the relation itself." Hadfield, *supra* note 71, at 930.

relegates these elements to the background.[77] For example, Macneil asserts that parties' minds do not meet at any single time with regard to important contract terms. The choice of contract terms is instead an "incremental process," with parties gradually agreeing to "more and more as they proceed."[78] Classical contract law fails to acknowledge this reality and, instead, searches for a single point in time when a contract springs into existence with all of the terms nailed down.[79] Such law, which may fail to enforce an obligation even when the parties' intend to be bound and which may impede freely made alterations of agreements, is unsuited to the realities of modern contracting.[80]

The relational point of view has been very helpful and influential because it focuses on the variety of relations that comprise modern

---

77 Gordon, *supra* note 23, at 574-75.

78 Ian R. Macneil, *Economic Analysis of Contractual Relations: Its Shortfalls and the Need for a "Rich Classificatory Apparatus,"* 75 NW. U.L. REV. 1018, 1041 (1981) [hereinafter Macneil, *Economic Analysis*]. *See also* Macneil, *Presentiation, supra* note 68, at 604 ([N]o commitment in ongoing relations is ever quite a 100% commitment . . . .").

79 Macneil, *Presentiation, supra* note 68, at 592-593.

80 *See* Whitford, *supra* note 11, at 547-48. Llewellyn observed the "difference...between the running, flexible obligation understood in fact by the parties and the rigid, stereotyped obligation which is all the law will recognize." Llewellyn, *supra* note 16, at 712-13. According to Llewellyn, the "[l]aw *must* grow fixed, in most of its parts, and relative to most of the ways of society apart from law." *Id.* at 713. Thus, society will inevitably develop new extra-legal theories of obligation.

Macneil also criticizes classical contract's objective theory of interpretation:

> [T]he limited extent to which it is possible for people to consent to all the terms of a transaction, even a relatively simple and very discrete one, soon forces the development of legal fictions expanding the scope of 'consent' far beyond anything remotely close to what the parties ever had in mind. The greatest of these in American law is the objective theory of contract.

Macneil, *Adjustment, supra* note 67, at 883-84. For further discussion of the objective theory of interpretation, *see* Chapter 1.

contracting, highlights the inadequacies of some contract rules,[81] and emphasizes the role of values in exchanges other than wealth-maximization.[82] The theory is not without critics, however. Some argue that relational theory concentrates on describing the behavior of contracting parties and fails to offer adequate guidance to parties and courts.[83] For example, relational theory lacks a "divining principle" to distinguish enforceable from unenforceable agreements.[84] In fact, it cannot "yield determinate legal principles" because it "entails a highly amorphous sociological inquiry that seems well beyond the competence of courts in case-by-case adjudication . . . ."[85] In addition, relational

---

81 *See* Gordon, *supra* note 23, at 565 (noting that the relational perspective has "alter[ed] the foundations of the subject.")

82 Feinman, *supra* note 5, at 1302.

> The core of Ian Macneil's lasting contribution to contract theory is his insistence that the values of 'discreteness' and 'presentiation' are not synonymous with all contracts, but comprise one pole of a continuum that ranges from highly discrete relations to those that are highly intertwined. Furthermore, even highly discrete contracts are embedded in a complex fabric of relations.

Randy E. Barnett, *Conflicting Visions: A Critique of Ian Macneil's Relational Theory of Contract*, 78 VA. L. REV. 1175, 1200 (1992).

83 *See, e.g.*, Steven J. Burton, *Default Principles, Legitimacy, and the Authority of a Contract*, 3 S. CAL. INTER. L. J. 115, 142 (1993) ("there is no easy conversion of empirical or analytical truths to normative status as guides to conduct.").

84 Barnett, *supra* note 82, at 1203, 1181. *See also* Whitford, *supra* note 11, at 548: "If the results of cases purporting to enforce [relational] contracts are not to appear unpredictable and ad hoc, some basis outside the framework of classical contract law must be established for determining when liability begins, defining the terms of relationship, and setting the remedy upon breach."

85 MICHAEL J. TREBILCOCK, THE LIMITS OF FREEDOM OF CONTRACT 141-142 (1994). *See also* Melvin A. Eisenberg, *Relational Contracts*, *in* GOOD FAITH AND FAULT IN CONTRACT LAW 291 (Jack Beatson and Daniel Friedmann, eds. 1995) (relational "literature has failed to show that there is a set of legal rules that should be applied to some contracts . . . but not others"); Richard Craswell, *The Relational Move: Some Questions from Law and Economics*, 3 S. CAL. INTER. L. J. 91, 103, 108, 111

theory depends on norms generated by the relation and establishes no criteria for policing these norms.[86]

These criticisms seem to underestimate the judicial capacity to engage in a highly contextual investigation and to evaluate the relevant relational norms, as we shall soon see. Nevertheless, one *can* overstate the conclusions suggested by relationalism. One writer interprets Macneil as suggesting that contract law and commentaries inhabit "academic museums of quaint curiosities . . . bearing but slight resemblance to the law-in-action known to contracting parties and their lawyers."[87] Modern contract law is much more than this.

Modern contract rules are not oblivious to the needs of a relational world. Consider the situation in Problem 11. Whether MDM can refuse to adjust Green's salary should depend on whether the parties reasonably expected the salary formula to apply rigidly or whether they reasonably expected to adjust the formula on account of changing circumstances, such as a minor cast member's unusual rise to stardom.[88] Some courts, influenced by traditional contract doctrine, refuse to look at the circumstances surrounding the written agreement in order to ascertain the

---

(1993). Professor Feinman concedes that "relational theory may raise more questions than it answers," but insists that the questions "tend to be different ones than are raised by neoclassical contract law." Feinman, *Significance, supra* note 5, at 1304.

86 TREBILCOCK, *supra* note 85, at 141-42. *See also id.* at 144 ("[T]he relevant values . . . mainly reflect whatever the relevant contracting community at any given point in time regards as appropriate normative bases for allocating unexpected burdens and benefits . . . ."); Craswell, *supra* note 85, at 99.

87 Gordon, *supra* note 23, at 575. Professor Gordon adds that Macneil recognizes that this "is not the whole story," *id.*, and that contract law is "a (relatively modest) platform for the expression of ideology," *id.* at 576. *See also* Llewellyn, *supra* note 16, at 750 ([D]octrinal synthesis is . . . the marginal . . . case which 'tests' the sweeping generalization."); Macneil, *Presentiation*, *supra* note 68, at 592-94 (discussing the unsuccessful attempts of traditional doctrine to incorporate relational agreements); Whitford, *supra* note 11, at 547 (arguing that traditional theory cannot explain the enforcement of relational contracts because such contracts involve no "grand meeting of the minds").

88 Hillman, *Long Term Contracts, supra* note 9, at 4-14.

parties' reasonable expectations.[89] But in recent years, more and more courts have declined to confine their inquiry to the written language of a contract, and instead have examined the full contractual context.[90]

The contextual approach of the Uniform Commercial Code and the *Restatement (Second) of Contracts*, reflected in their use of broad terms such as "agreement," is consistent with relational analysis.[91] Under the contextual approach, we have seen, a court investigating an agreement's content must consider not only express language but also any course of dealing, trade custom, or other background factor probative of the parties' reasonable expections.[92] Suppose in Problem 11 that producers and actors are generally flexible and cooperative in their contractual dealings. Green might reasonably expect MDM to increase her salary to a level commensurate with her ability to attract higher ratings. Modern contract law would enforce those expectations.[93] On the

---

[89] *See, e.g.*, Young v. Hornbrook, Inc., 153 Me. 412, 140 A. 2d 493 (1958). For example, courts may be too reticent to find relational norms in franchising cases. *See* Hadfield, *supra* note 71.

[90] *See, e.g.*, Nanakuli Paving & Rock Co. v. Shell Oil Co., 664 F.2d 772, 780 (9th cir. 1981) (looking beyond the written contract to determine the "true understanding of the parties"); Columbia Nitrogen Corp. v. Royster Co., 451 F.2d 3, 9 (4th Cir. 1971) (holding that the trial court wrongly excluded evidence of course of dealing and trade usage); American Mach. & Tool Co. v. Strite-Anderson Mfg., 353 N.W.2d 592, 597 (Minn. Ct. App. 1984) (holding that evidence of trade usage and course of dealing was admissible even if the contract at issue was not ambiguous).

"[A] court has no choice but to look beyond the document and identify a configuration of commitments patterned not in the words of the contract but in the underlying relation itself." Hadfield, *supra* note 71, at 980.

[91] *See supra* notes 44-46, and accompanying text.

[92] For the definition of "agreement" in the Uniform Commercial Code, *see supra* note 44.

[93] *See* U.C.C. § 1-201(3) (providing that an agreement may arise by implication); *id.* § 2-202 (providing that a writing "may be explained or supplanted...by course of dealing or usage of trade...or course of performance"); *id* § 2-204 (providing that conduct recognizing agreement may give rise to agreement); RESTATEMENT (SECOND) OF CONTRACTS § 19 (1979) (providing that words and conduct are interpreted in light of all circumstances). *But see* Speidel, *supra* note 46, at 794.

other hand, if the parties reasonably expected the salary formula to apply regardless of Green's flight to stardom, MDM's obstinance would be acceptable under the contextual approach.[94]

Examples abound of contract rules directing courts to investigate commercial reality.[95] For example, courts sensibly restrict application of the parol evidence rule to allow evidence of the business context.[96] The implied covenant of good faith and fair dealing curbs abuses of power,[97] such as wrongful terminations and coerced contract modifications. Doctrines such as waiver and estoppel take into account the parties' post-contractual dealings.[98] Modern contract also relaxes the formal rules of contract formation. For example, the Uniform Commercial Code abandons the "mirror-image" rule, thereby recognizing the formation of an agreement even when the acceptance includes additional or different

---

94 In late 1983 and early 1984 Pennzoil Company engaged in merger negotiations with Getty Oil Company. The parties reached a preliminary agreement before Texaco interfered by promising to purchase Getty's stock at a higher price. Pennzoil later brought a successful suit against Texaco for tortious interference with contract. *See* Texaco, Inc. v. Pennzoil Co., 729 S.W. 2d 768 (Tex. App.-Houston [1st Dist.] 1987, writ ref'd n.r.e.), *cert. denied* 108 S. Ct. 1305 (1988). Although the *Wall Street Journal* criticized the decision in favor of Pennzoil as portending the "end of law for contracts," *Texas Common Law Massacre*, WALL ST. J., Dec. 12, 1985, at 30 col. 1, the trial judge's jury charge was replete with instructions focusing on the issue of whether Pennzoil and Getty intended to be bound to a contract. *See* CHARLES L. KNAPP & CRYSTAL, PROBLEMS IN CONTRACT LAW 287-89 (2d ed. 1987) (reproducing Pennzoil trial court instructions). Far from signaling the death of contract, the decision shows the adaption of modern contract law to sophisticated relational intentions.

95 *See generally* James J. White, *Promise Fulfilled and Principle Betrayed*, 1988 ANN. SURV. AM. L. 7 (discussing *inter alia* U.C.C. §§ 2-706, 2-712, 2-204, and 2-302).

96 *See, e.g.*, Robert Industries, Inc. v. Spence, 291 N.E.2d 407 (Mass. 1972); Keating v. Stadium Management Corp., 508 N. E. 2d 121 (Mass. App. 1987).

97 Modern contract law's increasing resort to good faith and reasonableness accommodates relational needs. *See* Hadfield, *supra* note 71, at 984-85 (courts should use good faith to police franchise agreements). *See generally* Chapter 4.

98 *See, e.g.*, Mapco Inc. v. Pioneer Corp., 615 F.2d 297 (5th Cir. 1980); Clark v. West, 193 N.Y. 349, 86 N.E.1 (1908).

terms.[99] Parties' conduct, as well as oral or written communications, can form enforceable contracts.[100] Courts no longer need to isolate the precise moment of a contract's formation.[101] Courts enforce contracts "instinct with an obligation" even when the parties have technically failed to bind each other or their agreement contains gaps.[102] Courts also enforce agreements to agree and other preliminary agreements if the parties intended to be bound.[103] Indeed, there are few situations left in which courts prevent the trier of fact from examining the parties' entire relationship.

In his discussion of relational contracting, Professor Feinman criticizes the neoclassical focus on the parties' intentions gleaned through contextual analysis as a "fundamental error . . . lead[ing] down the wrong path."[104] He believes that "empirical norms" are indeterminate because "there simply does not exist an agreed set of principles and practices of commerce."[105] He also does not believe that appellate courts, far removed from the business world, can ascertain the true facts and circumstances of

---

99 U.C.C. § 2-207(1).

100 U.C.C. § 2-204(1).

101 U.C.C. § 2-204(2). *See generally*, Robert A. Hillman, *A Study of Uniform Commercial Code Methodology: Contract Modification Under Article Two*, 59 N.C.L. REV. 335, 344 (1981).

102 *See, e.g.*, U.C.C. § 2-204(3); Wood v. Lucy, Lady Duff-Gordon, 222 N.Y. 88, 118 N.E. 214 (1917) (Cardozo, J.). *See generally* Robert A. Hillman, *"Instinct With An Obligation" and the "Normative Ambiguity of Rhetorical Power,"* 56 OHIO STATE L.J. 775 (1995).

103 *See* E. Allan Farnsworth, *Precontractual Liability and Preliminary Agreements: Fair Dealing and Failed Negotiations*, 87 COLUM. L. REV. 217, 219-20, 250 (1987).

104 Feinman, *Significance, supra* note 5, at 1303.

105 Feinman, *Critical Approaches to Contract Law*, 30 UCLA L. REV. 829, 837 (1983); *see also* Jay M. Feinman, *Promissory Estoppel and Judicial Method*, 97 HARV. L. REV. 678, 703 (1984) [hereinafter Feinman, *Promissory Estoppel*] (factual contexts often are uncertain).

a contractual relationship.[106] Nevertheless, the plethora of decisions successfully relying on the application of trade custom and course of dealing seem to refute Professor Feinman's assertions.[107]

Moreover, alternative modes of decisionmaking are unappealing. According to Feinman, instead of focusing on trade practices and the like, a case such as Problem 11 should first be "associated" with a relational paradigm, thereby accentuating the importance of the norms of flexibility and contractual solidarity. A court would then determine to what extent these norms "are manifest in the parties' action, the community's actions and understanding, the broader society's values, and the legal system's principles."[108] It is difficult to apply this analysis to a situation like Problem 11. Perhaps Feinman means to say that the parties' reasonable expectations are less important than determining the "most desirable" relationship in the setting.[109] But what standards could courts apply to determine the latter?

By focusing on contextual analysis and, concomitantly, the importance of parties' intentions, I do not mean to contradict Chapter 1's thesis that individualist and interventionist principles coexist in modern contract law or to relegate the latter to the background.[110] After all, a fine line separates ascertaining parties' actual intentions and intervening to fill gaps based on predictions of what reasonable parties would have intended under the circumstances. Moreover, we have seen that courts often engage in gap filling of the latter kind even when engaged in a highly

---

[106] Feinman, *Promissory Estoppel, supra* note 105, at 703.

[107] *See, e.g.*, Nanakuli Paving & Rock Co., 664 F.2d R 804-05 (finding that parties history of dealing revealed agreement that asphalt seller would not raise prices on quantities that buyer had included in paving contract bids).

[108] Feinman, *Significance, supra* note 5, at 1303.

[109] *Id.*

[110] *See* Chapter 1. According to some, a focus on assent preserves private agreement as the dominant structure and relegates communal values to a "sporadic" and "anomolous" status. *See* ROBERT UNGER, THE CRITICAL LEGAL STUDIES MOVEMENT 74 (1983). *See generally* Chapter 5.

contextual investigation.[111] Nevertheless, the thrust of relationalism is its description of reality. For the relationist, the crucial question in Problem 11 should be: What are the facts? Should Green have expected MDM to be flexible and cooperative when circumstances changed or should she have expected MDM to adhere to the contract terms?[112] Put another way, the critical inquiry is whether the parties had "relational" intentions. Modern contract law invites such an inquiry.[113]

Despite modern contract law's adaptability to a relational analysis, we must not assume that the law should reflect all that occurs in our relational world. Amoral business conduct may call for sanctions, not the law's approbation.[114] The law should not allow one party to dominate a relation and take unfair advantage of another.[115] Moreover, to the extent that initial informality and flexibility necessitate costly subsequent negotiation and adjustment,[116] contract law that requires more precision in formation and modification may be superior to a structure of pure relationalism. Thus it is not always clear that the law should reflect the

---

111 *See* Chapters 1 and 6.

112 Professor Whitford points out that Macneil "rarely states his specific views about the desirable content of positive law." Whitford, *supra* note 11, at 551. Instead Macneil's theory "is a thesis about the preferences of parties to relational contracts as revealed by their behavior." *Id.* at 559.

113 This is not to deny the imperfections of our adjudicatory system in determining truth. "To ask `what really happened' of a reported case is something like trying to find the mood of a centerfielder by reading a box score." Arthur A. Leff, *Law and*, 87 YALE L.J. 989, 1008 n.46 (1978).

For an argument that the "conditions for judicial activism" are seldom satisfied in relational contracts, see Alan Schwartz, *Relational Contracts in the Courts: An Analysis of Incomplete Agreements and Judicial Strategies*, 21 J. LEGAL STUD. 271, 274, 314 (1992) ("courts act passively when parties observe process values and when courts cannot complete contracts with terms that knowledgeable parties would choose for themselves.").

114 *See* Richard Danzig, *A Comment on the Jurisprudence of the Uniform Commercial Code*, 27 STAN. L. REV. 621, 629 (1975).

115 *See* Gordon, *supra* note 23, at 570-571.

116 *See supra* notes 40-43, and accompanying text.

relational status quo.[117] Contract law may be suitable in some situations because it *resists* commercial reality.

Conclusion

Contract law facilitates private arrangements in many ways, even within informal bargaining cultures.[118] Parties turn to contract planning when informality fails to serve their purposes. Contract law also defines the limits of permissible conduct; parties can enforce their contract rights when business norms fail. Contract law thus fortifies parties' expectations of performance. Contract law also defines whether a legal obligation actually exists. Freedom of contract generally includes the right not to contract, and parties may choose flexibility over a binding agreement. Empirical studies do not belie these truths, they reinforce them.

Modern contract law is not only relevant but also reasonably well-suited for today's relational world. Numerous rules and standards invite courts to analyze the context of agreements. These principles reinforce relational norms. In fact, in many situations relational norms also constitute enforceable contract terms.[119] The empirical and relational inquiries thus help establish the richness and importance of contract law, they do not signal its demise.

---

[117] Llewellyn observed not only that the law reflects the values of society, but also that society is influenced by the law. Llewellyn, *supra* note 16, at 711.

[118] *See supra* notes 40-65, and accompanying text.

[119] *See supra* notes 44-46, and accompanying text.

CHAPTER 8

MODERN CONTRACT LAW AND THE LIMITS OF CONTRACT THEORY

This book has surveyed, analyzed, and critiqued various modern theories of contract law. My goal in each chapter was to compare the principal insights and perspectives of two largely contrasting theories in order to find possible areas of agreement and to construct a consensus or pluralist thesis. Ultimately, I argue that this synthesizing thesis constitutes the most persuasive account of contract law's nature and functions.

In this final chapter, I want to review many of the themes developed in the book and to conclude with a few final thoughts about contract law and contract theory. Two primary questions about contract law emerge from the discussion in this book. I shall organize this closing discussion around these questions: What is the nature of contract law? What role does it play?

A. What Is the Nature of Modern Contract Law?

Much recent contract theory constitutes a debate over whether contract law facilitates the exercise of private preferences or, instead, whether freedom of contract defers to principles legitimizing state control of the contracting process, ranging from fairness, equality, and morality to efficiency. However, neither vision adequately portrays contract law because each focuses on one perspective at the expense of the other. In reality, freedom of contract and interventionist principles share the contract law spotlight. The debate among theorists therefore diverts our focus from the reality that freedom of contract and outside principles are all important.[1] Expending resources in an attempt to determine which set of principles "wins" hardly seems worth the effort.

What is the effect of admitting that we do not have a dominant vision and that it is enough to know that contract law embraces multiple social norms? We would have to concede the bankruptcy of attempting to concoct a unified theory of the whole (other than that contract law is multidimensional) and to accept the disorder and contradiction of contract law. This, in turn, raises many questions. For example, does contract law of this nature succeed? Does it facilitate the exchange process? Does it do so better than other conceptions? What are its effects on third parties? Beyond intuitive assessments and rough comparisons with other methods of economic organization, these questions may not be answerable to anyone's satisfaction. They implicate fundamental issues involving the meaning of voluntariness and whether and how much the state should intervene not only to correct problems of assent but to achieve redistributive and paternalistic goals.

In my view, no one should minimize the chinks in contract law's armor. Nevertheless, for all of its failings, our system of "private" exchange seems to work better than alternatives precisely because it does seek to harmonize the value of private preferences and the need for social control. The various norms of contract law reflect the major social, economic, and institutional forces of a pluralistic society. Not only do these norms often clash, but they are themselves frequently internally inconsistent. Freedom of contract may ironically sometimes require intervention to ensure that each party exercises a free choice. Equality may be furthered by granting parties greater autonomy, such as in the marriage setting, or it may require intervention to correct market failures or existing inequitable wealth distributions. A promise creates a moral

---

1 "Is there perhaps, between individual sovereignty of the contract and collective sovereignty of the law, a difference only in degree and in application, and should we finally cease opposing them to each other as if one was destined to triumph over the other?" GEORGES DAVY, LA FOI JUREE--ETUDE SOCIOLOGIQUE DU PROBLEME DU CONTRAT 374 (1922), *quoted in* Lyman Johnson, *Individual and Collective Sovereignty in the Corporate Enterprise,* 92 COLUM. L. REV. 2215, 2249 (1992) (reviewing FRANK H. EASTERBROOK & DANIEL R. FISCHEL, THE ECONOMIC STRUCTURE OF CORPORATE LAW (1991) and ROBERT N. BELLAH, ET. AL., THE GOOD SOCIETY (1991)).

obligation unless the promise was coerced, but the meaning of coercion is itself inherently controversial. In short, contract law flourishes largely because it is the fruit of the legal system's reasonable and practical compromises over conflicting values and interests in a diverse society.

These observations may trouble some readers. Some may assert that the analysis is atheoretical or unrigorous because it fails to take a stand on whether freedom of contract or moral or social considerations should or do dominate contract law.[2] However, the time is ripe for an analysis that stresses the multiplicity of principles, goals, and methods of contract law. For example, instead of battling over which principle should and does provide the "key" to contract law, theorists should address how to utilize each principle in particular contexts: "A good society depends on both autonomy and heteronomy, each present in large measure. Theorists ought to face up to this point and then see what headway, if any, can be made in devising principles for setting the optimal mix."[3] An example of such an effort can be found in Chapter 3 of this book, dealing with marriage and corporations.

These observations may also trouble some analysts because of the insights' implications concerning the rule of law. We would have to concede that judges possess some discretion to decide "hard" cases in conformity with either the principle of contractual freedom or of some nonconsensual principle (or a combination of both). Contract law therefore does not offer complete certainty. Some scholars find this portrayal unappealing or even unsettling. Nevertheless, "to be certain of uncertainty . . . is to be certain of at least one thing."[4] Moreover, acknowledging the reality of limited determinacy in contract law would not threaten the institution's legitimacy or mean that judges have unbridled discretion. Many, if not most, cases fall within one principle or

---

2 For a discussion of the pitfalls of conventional views in another context, *see* Daniel A. Farber & Suzanna Sherry, *Telling Stories Out of School: An Essay on Legal Narratives,* 45 STAN. L. REV. 807, 854-55 (1993).

3 Robert C. Clark, *Contracts, Elites and Traditions in the Making of Corporate Law,* 89 COLUM. L. REV. 1703, 1726 (1989).

4 Milton Y. Dawes, *Multiordinality: A Point of View,* ET CETERA, Summer 1986, at 128, 131.

another. Judges simply enjoy room in hard cases to attempt to harmonize the principles to fit the context. Far from undermining contract law, this flexibility helps ensure fair results and enables contract law to adapt and grow.

Some theorists may also find this pragmatism crippling in its implicit acceptance of the status quo.[5] Acknowledging the law's inevitable struggle to accommodate both the "individualist" and "collective" visions, however, does not necessarily support present social structures. Recognizing this reality actually may release judges from the shackles of the status quo, because they could then directly confront the need to decide in favor of one view or the other in particular cases.

Consider again *Local 1330, United Steel Workers v. United States Steel Corp.*,[6] discussed in Chapter 5. Recall that the steelworkers contested the steel company's plan to close two large steel mills operated for over seventy years in Youngstown, Ohio. The company had stated that it would keep the plants open if, through the steelworkers' extra efforts, the plants became profitable. The Sixth Circuit affirmed the district court's holding that the plants did not become profitable according to the "normal corporate profit accounting" measure of profitability despite the steelworkers' efforts and therefore denied the workers' promissory estoppel claims.[7]

We are all sympathetic with the plight of the workers and the people of Youngstown, whose livelihoods immediately depended on the operations of the steel plants.[8] Nevertheless, we should also appreciate the immense challenge of determining the best solution for the workers, for Youngstown, and indeed, for society. Even if we are convinced of the merit of the workers' claims, we should acknowledge contract law's

---

[5] *See* Chapter 5.

[6] 631 F. 2d 1264 (6th. Cir. 1980).

[7] *Id.* at 1278-79.

[8] Forty-seven percent of the former steelworkers in Youngstown were unemployed in 1987. Sharon Cohen, *Steel Town is Struggling Back from Depression,* Ithaca Journal, August 22, 1987 at 11A, col. 2. For a description of the devastation of Youngstown brought about by the closing of the steel mills, *see id.*

potential to protect the workers instead of talking about "utopian visions"[9] and the indeterminacy of law. A court could have realized this potential by finding that the plants became profitable according to an alternative definition of profitability used by the company to induce the steelworkers' extra efforts.[10] On the other hand, the court could have found that good faith required the steel company to provide some fair warning and additional time before withdrawing in order to give the community an opportunity to save itself. If there were no factual support for such a theory (suppose, for example, the steel company expressly reserved the right to withdraw without notice), a court might utilize unjust enrichment theory to find that a business such as the steel company can withdraw from a community from which it has drawn a "benefit" for so many years only on some reasonable basis. A court might also find a "reliance interest in property" to protect the workers' reliance on the continuation of their jobs.[11] The need for such theories demonstrates not that existing contract law is indeterminate or unsuited to govern the world of private arrangements, but that the law is capable of change, growth, and evolution. In short, if our goal is legal reform, we may achieve better results from working within the system, albeit an imperfect one, than from scrapping it.

B. What Is the Role of Contract Law in Modern Society?

Contract law serves an important role facilitating private arrangements and supporting freedom of exchange. Parties continue to plan and draft agreements in large numbers. Lawyers trained in the art of competent contract planning and drafting often help them achieve their

---

9 Jay M. Feinman, *Critical Approaches to Contract Law,* 30 UCLA L. REV. 829, 857 (1983).

10 The court held that the company should not have reasonably expected the steelworkers to rely on the alternative definition.

11 Joseph W. Singer, *The Reliance Interest in Property,* 40 STAN. L. REV. 611, 699 (1988).

goals.[12] These lawyers often view their chief purposes as effective planning and concise drafting to establish the ground rules of a relation and to avoid costly litigation.[13] One should remember that many theories intimating the demise or sickliness of contract law present an incomplete view, because they focus on judicial opinions depicting atypical disputes and breakdowns of contractual arrangements.[14]

We have seen that modern contract law serves three primary roles in facilitating private-exchange transactions even within bargaining cultures that exhibit a good deal of informality. First, contract law is a safety-valve held in reserve. Parties can turn to contract planning should informality fail to serve their purposes. Second, contract law defines the outer boundaries of permissible conduct even within existing informal arrangements. Parties may look to their contract when business norms fail. Contract law thus reinforces parties' expectations of performance. Third, contract law defines whether parties created any legal obligation. Freedom of contract generally includes the right not to contract, and parties may choose not to bind themselves by adhering to the rules of contract law.

Facilitating private exchange is not contract law's only role, however. Contract law can contribute to equality and justice, as we saw in the context of intimate agreements. Moreover, enforcing promises also coincides with the moral precept that people should keep their promises.

---

12 *See, e.g.*, David F. Cavers, *Legal Education and Lawyer Made Law*, 54 W. VA. L. REV. 177, 180 (1952); Ian R. Macneil, *A Primer of Contract Planning*, 48 S. CAL. L. REV. 627, *and especially* 650, 691, 693 (1975); David W. Maxey, *Fundamentals of Draftmanship -- A Guide for the Apprentice in Preparing Agreements*, 51 PA. B. ASS'N. Q. 47 (1980).

13 *See, e.g.*, David Crump, *The Five Elements of a Contract: Avoiding Ambiguity in Them*, 43 TEX. B. J. 370 (1980); Joseph C. Benage, *Planning Opportunities With Contracts to Make a Will*, 39 J. OF MO. B. 395 (1983).

14 Most analysts choose to study judicial opinions instead of collecting data about the operation of contract in the real world. *See, e.g.*, Robert W. Gordon, *Macaulay, Macneil, and the Discovery of Solidarity and Power in Contract Law*, 1985 WIS. L. REV. 565, 568 (moral and economic theorists rely on appellate cases and ignore empirical data). Case law reveals little of the importance of contract law outside of litigation. *See* Cavers, *supra* note 12, at 179.

In addition, although theorists debate the extent to which this is true, contract law contributes to distributive justice through its program of mandatory terms and policing standards.

Modern contract law is not only relevant but also reasonably well-suited for today's highly relational world. Modern contract law's broad view of "agreement" and numerous other doctrines that invite an analysis of the context reinforce relational norms such as cooperation and compromise. In fact, these norms also constitute enforceable contract terms in many instances. Moreover, contract standards such as unconscionability and good faith authorize courts to police agreements for the effects of market failures and to evaluate the adequacy of an exchange. Through the use of standards, contract law ensures some degree of voluntariness and fairness in exchange transactions.

* * *

In the end, the most compelling theory of contract law extracts from each of the theories discussed in this book what is best and most helpful. For example, Fried and Gilmore taught us the importance of both promissory and nonconsensual principles in contract law. The mainstream's market orientation and CLS's focus on the shortcomings of markets and the need for legal intervention substantiate this conclusion. The failure of strict contractarian models to resolve the issues presented by either intimate or remote specialized relations, such as marriages and corporations, also underscores contract law's duality.

In addition, mainstream and CLS theorists show that, at minimum, judges are not rule-bound in "hard" cases. Moreover, contextualists and neo-formalists diminish the barrier separating contract rules and standards by acknowledging the judicial process of generating criteria for the application of standards on the one hand and of exercising discretion in selecting and applying rules on the other. Economic analysts and their critics teach us the contributions and shortcomings of efficiency analysis of contract law. Finally, empiricists and relationalists demonstrate the many roles of contract law while also highlighting the importance of alternative norms.

Contract law and theory include contradictions and distinctions. Subject to competing norms and distinct theories of obligation and to various exceptions within the main body of doctrine,[15] and divided by special rules applying to distinct kinds of contracts, contract law does not fit neatly into any slot.[16] A highly abstract core theory simply cannot account for the entire subject.[17] Instead, contract law is a plausible, if not perfect, reflection of various normative choices of the surrounding society.

Viewed collectively, the passionate but diverse approaches of the contract theorists surveyed herein emphasize the pluralist conception and, for that matter, the continued relevance and importance of modern contract law. After all, contract law would command less attention if it were simple and insignificant. Contract theory therefore benefits us by illuminating the subject's true nature. The reader's challenge is to attain perspective from studying the theories without losing sight of contract law's overall richness and vitality.

---

15 *See* Roberto M. Unger, THE CRITICAL LEGAL STUDIES MOVEMENT 58, 83 (1983).

16 *See id.* at 58; Melvin A. Eisenberg, *The Principles of Consideration,* 67 CORNELL L. REV. 640, 642-43 (1982). A "general theory of contract must almost certainly come ultimately to assert a less absolute dominion over the `entire field' than has been the case in this heyday of its hope." Karl N. Llewellyn, *What Price Contract?--An Essay in Perspective,* 40 YALE L.J. 704, 749 (1931).

17 Llewellyn, *supra* note 16, at 749-50.

INDEX

Law and Philosophy Library

1. E. Bulygin, J.-L. Gardies and I. Niiniluoto (eds.): *Man, Law and Modern Forms of Life.* With an Introduction by M.D. Bayles. 1985 ISBN 90-277-1869-5
2. W. Sadurski: *Giving Desert Its Due.* Social Justice and Legal Theory. 1985 ISBN 90-277-1941-1
3. N. MacCormick and O. Weinberger: *An Institutional Theory of Law.* New Approaches to Legal Positivism. 1986 ISBN 90-277-2079-7
4. A. Aarnio: *The Rational as Reasonable.* A Treatise on Legal Justification. 1987 ISBN 90-277-2276-5
5. M.D. Bayles: *Principles of Law.* A Normative Analysis. 1987 ISBN 90-277-2412-1; Pb: 90-277-2413-X
6. A. Soeteman: *Logic in Law.* Remarks on Logic and Rationality in Normative Reasoning, Especially in Law. 1989 ISBN 0-7923-0042-4
7. C.T. Sistare: *Responsibility and Criminal Liability.* 1989 ISBN 0-7923-0396-2
8. A. Peczenik: *On Law and Reason.* 1989 ISBN 0-7923-0444-6
9. W. Sadurski: *Moral Pluralism and Legal Neutrality.* 1990 ISBN 0-7923-0565-5
10. M.D. Bayles: *Procedural Justice.* Allocating to Individuals. 1990 ISBN 0-7923-0567-1
11. P. Nerhot (ed.): *Law, Interpretation and Reality.* Essays in Epistemology, Hermeneutics and Jurisprudence. 1990 ISBN 0-7923-0593-0
12. A.W. Norrie: *Law, Ideology and Punishment.* Retrieval and Critique of the Liberal Ideal of Criminal Justice. 1991 ISBN 0-7923-1013-6
13. P. Nerhot (ed.): *Legal Knowledge and Analogy.* Fragments of Legal Epistemology, Hermeneutics and Linguistics. 1991 ISBN 0-7923-1065-9
14. O. Weinberger: *Law, Institution and Legal Politics.* Fundamental Problems of Legal Theory and Social Philosophy. 1991 ISBN 0-7923-1143-4
15. J. Wróblewski: *The Judicial Application of Law.* Edited by Z. Bańkowski and N. MacCormick. 1992 ISBN 0-7923-1569-3
16. T. Wilhelmsson: *Critical Studies in Private Law.* A Treatise on Need-Rational Principles in Modern Law. 1992 ISBN 0-7923-1659-2
17. M.D. Bayles: *Hart's Legal Philosophy.* An Examination. 1992 ISBN 0-7923-1981-8
18. D.W.P. Ruiter: *Institutional Legal Facts.* Legal Powers and their Effects. 1993 ISBN 0-7923-2441-2
19. J. Schonsheck: *On Criminalization.* An Essay in the Philosophy of the Criminal Law. 1994 ISBN 0-7923-2663-6
20. R.P. Malloy and J. Evensky (eds.): *Adam Smith and the Philosophy of Law and Economics.* 1994 ISBN 0-7923-2796-9
21. Z. Bankowski, I. White and U. Hahn (eds.): *Informatics and the Foundations of Legal Reasoning.* 1995 ISBN 0-7923-3455-8
22. E. Lagerspetz: *The Opposite Mirrors.* An Essay on the Conventionalist Theory of Institutions. 1995 ISBN 0-7923-3325-X
23. M. van Hees: *Rights and Decisions.* Formal Models of Law and Liberalism. 1995 ISBN 0-7923-3754-9
24. B. Anderson: *"Discovery" in Legal Decision-Making.* 1996 ISBN 0-7923-3981-9

25. S. Urbina: *Reason, Democracy, Society.* A Study on the Basis of Legal Thinking. 1996 ISBN 0-7923-4262-3
26. E. Attwooll: *The Tapestry of the Law.* Scotland, Legal Culture and Legal Theory. 1997 ISBN 0-7923-4310-7
27. J.C. Hage: *Reasoning with Rules.* An Essay on Legal Reasoning and Its Underlying Logic. 1997 ISBN 0-7923-4325-5
28. R.A. Hillman: *The Richness of Contract Law.* An Analysis and Critique of Contemporary Theories of Contract Law. 1997 ISBN 0-7923-4336-0

KLUWER ACADEMIC PUBLISHERS – DORDRECHT / BOSTON / LONDON